THE
Antiques
HANDBOOK

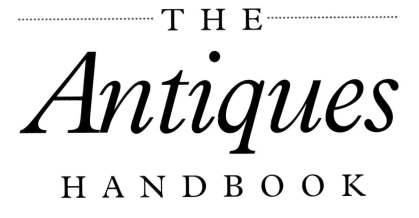

THE
Antiques
HANDBOOK

Abbeydale Press

This edition published in 1998 by
Abbeydale Press
An imprint of Bookmart Ltd
Desford Road, Enderby,
Leicestershire LE9 5AD
England

© Bookmart 1991, 1998

Originally published in 1991 by Bookmart Ltd
as *The Encyclopedia of Antiques*

ISBN 1-86147-016-9

Printed in Italy

CONTENTS

INTRODUCTION

BY DAVID BATTIE

There are fashions in antiques as there are in any other aspect of life. For example, in the mid 18th century, excavations of Roman objects changed taste from the wild extravagance of the rococo to restrained Neoclassicism. Disinterred vases, bronzes and sculpture changed hands for considerable sums. Changes of style meant that those members of the aristocracy who wanted to remain in fashion had to remodel their houses, inside and out. Then, as now, second-hand furniture and works of art were unsaleable, and many of the objects in the previous fashion were stored away in the attics and outhouses or relegated to servants' quarters. These rejects are today's masterpieces.

The idea of collecting yesterday's cast-offs simply because they are old is, in fact, of recent origin. It was not until the middle of the 19th century that a gentleman would consider collecting much but books and manuscripts. Admittedly antiquities were acceptable, as were prints and maps and coins, but even paintings attracted very few dedicated collectors. There were almost no books on antiques (as opposed to antiquities) until the second half of the 19th century when research began to be conducted into objects made in previous centuries. Then the Victorians, enthusiastic recyclers of early styles as they were, set in motion the modern drive to know the last tiny fact about one's prized antique.

There is, in fact, nothing wrong with wanting to know everything about the history of a piece, unless the collector becomes blinded by background and stops looking with an unbiased eye at what it is he is collecting. This can often upset the market. Once a group of objects comes into vogue – the crazes for Clarice Cliff in 1988 and minor Impressionist paintings in 1989/90 are two recent examples – too many unknowledgeable collectors and investors jump on the bandwagon, which rolls for a year or two and then grinds to a halt. The market collapses and for a matter of months, or occasionally years, the outlook seems bleak. But the market always recovers, as collecting works of art will never go out of fashion for long. From this follows the first and only real rule of collecting: buy what you like. Regardless of the market conditions, you will own something that you love.

The hobby of collecting has spread from a very few dedicated amateurs at the beginning of this century to millions today. As every year passes, it seems, a new area is discovered, usually one previously despised and ever closer to the present day. The term antique has come to mean almost anything second-hand and collectable. While this may exclude the kitchen sink it certainly does include refrigerators, typewriters and old Coca Cola bottles.

Antiques programmes on television have had two important effects on the market. One, they have stopped families throwing out everything onto the local tip, and two, they have made the chance of finding a bargain in a shop that bit more unlikely. However, the drive to strike it rich should not be the overriding drive for anyone interested in works of art. Certainly the possibility is there, but it is very small. Many antique dealers spend their lives, all day every day, buying and selling, and never finding the one-off bargain on which to retire. It has to be faced, however, that one way for a collector to support buying for his collection is to undertake a little trading on his own behalf, weeding out poor or damaged examples and replacing them with better pieces. This constant upgrading of a collection is one of the greatest satisfactions of antique ownership.

Right
MAHOGANY LONGCASE CLOCK ENGLISH c.1780

Works of art can give hours of pleasure in the search, buying, research and ownership. Against this they do cost money to own – but they do, it must be admitted, have the marvellous advantage of increasing in price year by year (well, most years).

There is little doubt that there is such a thing as an 'eye'. This is the term used by those in the antiques profession to describe the natural ability that some people have of recognizing the only promising piece from a sea of junk. Undoubtedly, that 'eye' can be improved by looking long, hard and frequently at objects in one's chosen field. Museums have their place, but touching is forbidden in them. Flogging round car boot sales, yard sales, junk shops, flea markets, fairs, antiques shops and auctions is the only real way to learn. Much is absorbed through the eyes and the finger tips, and nothing can replace this continual contact with objects. The ear is the other receptor well worth cultivating, for a willing teacher is a most valuable asset. The smallest scrap of information from a friendly dealer, auctioneer or fellow collector can make a whole set of previously confusing facts suddenly fall into place. Nevertheless, however much time one dedicates something will be lacking from one's knowledge – background. To be able to sit in comfort and browse through a book at one's leisure will be time well repaid.

The tyro collector will need a general book which will guide him through the thousands of terms, definitions, periods, techniques and so on, which seem to bedevil the antiques business. At some later date, once settled on a particular group of objects on which to lavish his love, time and money he will need a book, or books, with more detail and depth. Even so, few collectors are completely single-minded, and the eye to the bargain in a different field will always be there. For that reason no collector's library should be without its general handbook.

In fact, thumbing through a handbook can have hidden benefits. By constantly coming across objects which the reader had never previously considered, a change of direction may take place. The collector who only has eyes for, say, first-period Worcester porcelain, is going to have his understanding of that factory widened by looking at porcelain from contemporary English factories. Still more will he benefit from looking at Chinese and Continental porcelain, from which Worcester drew much of its inspiration. Ceramic shapes usually imitate those of silver, and the silver follows in its turn the decoration of the furnituremakers and architects. All these interwoven themes and movements will only be appreciated in a comprehensive volume such as this.

FURNITURE

Above
COMMODE, LOUIS XIV COPY
FRENCH c.1860

ENGLISH FURNITURE

JOHN TAYLOR

From the Tudors to the Commonwealth

LITTLE FURNITURE FROM before about 1500 can be seen outside museums or medieval buildings preserved as historic monuments. Most antiques that might come on the market probably date from the Tudor period and later.

From 1500 to about 1650 oak was the timber most commonly used for furniture as a whole. Although often painted, few pieces bear traces of original decoration. Grander pieces of furniture were inlaid with arabesque patterns, occasionally in bone or mother-of-pearl. However carving is the most common form of decoration during this period and is usually a corruption of continental renaissance or mannerist motifs, such as grotesque figures or architectural details. The techniques of construction were comparatively simple. Furniture was usually panelled and joints were secured by pegs.

The most commonly found pieces dating from this period are the simple oak chests used to contain linen. These have a hinged lid, a panelled front and sides within a simple pegged framework. Sometimes the panels were carved with patterns although often a mechanical

feel to the carving betrays the 19th or 20th century improver's hand.

As the 17th century wore on case furniture increasingly began to include drawers and gradually the modern chest-of-drawers evolved. Drawer fronts were usually heavily panelled often with geometric designs. Often chests were carried on stands incorporating further drawers or supported on turned legs.

The simple turned forms of seat furniture used in the earlier 17th century began to be superseded in fashionable circles towards 1670, and gradually arms and backs, together with legs and stretchers became the subject of the carver's lavish attention. On the grandest examples the frames resembled

a continuous deeply carved pattern of scrollwork. Panels of cane were introduced to fill seats and backs at about this time, although the upholstery of the grandest chairs became ever more extravagant. In general backs became higher towards the end of the century while seats were a little lower.

By this period the practice of veneering case furniture was beginning to become increasingly prevalent. This technique consisted of glueing thin layers of a decoratively figured or unusually coloured wood to the solid structural members or carcase of a piece. Initially small areas were treated in this way but gradually the whole piece was covered in veneer.

Below
WALNUT SIDE TABLE
ENGLISH c . 1690

The expansion in trade with the East during this period was paralleled by a fashion for all things Oriental. Lacquer cabinets, usually with two doors enclosing an arrangement of small drawers, were imported from China and Japan and mounted on domestically produced stands. English cabinet-makers took advantage of this trend by mimicking eastern lacquer cabinets 'japanning' and mounting them on elaborate gilded stands.

The golden age

THE LATER PART of the 17th century saw a revolution in the construction and types of furniture produced in England. This revolution was largely instigated by the influx of foreign craftsmen following the expulsion of Huguenots from France in

1685 and the arrival of the Dutch Prince of Orange, William, on the English throne in 1688. These changes were to see the establishment of basic types of furniture which were to remain in favour through the 18th century and beyond.

Among the new types to evolve were the bureau, a writing table with a hinged flap enclosing an arrangement of drawers and folding out to form a horizontal writing surface. Initially these were supported on turned legs but gradually were supported on a solid carcase with an arrangement of long and short drawers. By the early 1700s bureaux of this type were often to be seen with a cabinet with one or two doors above the writing flap. Doors were often mirrored to reflect light onto the writing surface and took on a quasi-architectural form, often pedimented, domed or double-domed.

It was towards the end of the first decade of the 18th century that a new type of chair began to evolve. The back had a gently moulded frame which contained a single shaped splat. The seat was upholstered, contained within a frame and supported on gently curved or cabriole legs. In about 1730 walnut began to be superseded as the most fashionable timber by mahogany imported from

Left
WALNUT BUREAU-BOOKCASE
ENGLISH c. 1720

the Spanish colony of San Domingo.

The middle of the century saw the influence of the French rococo style on English decorative arts and furniture produced in this style introduced a golden age of furniture-making. The style drew its inspiration from the organic forms of nature: flowers, foliage, rocks and shells, even waterfalls, freeing them from the rigidly architectural forms of early styles. The most common decorative motif was the scroll in the form of a 'c'.

Other influences were also at work on furniture designers. A resurgence of interest in the arts of the East produced a range of decorative motifs culled from Chinese ceramics and wallpaper. These included geometric fretwork patterns, pagoda-like canopies, and ho-ho birds.

One of the most innovative furniture types to appear at this time was the tripod table. Originally designed for the taking of tea, these have circular tops carried on a pillar and then supported on three cabriole legs. The tops normally fold down when not in use, and some tops revolve, as well. On this essentially simple form designers were able to make the most elaborate decorative pieces of furniture using rococo, gothic and chinoiserie motifs. Tops were very often shaped and dished, as well as which they were carved with elaborate borders or given fretted or spindle galleries.

short deep drawers. Dining tables were made of various sections which could be placed together in different combinations. There were two main types. The pedestal table was the more prized; the top of each section was carried on a pillar and supported on splayed legs. The tops of the end sections had rounded corners on one side, and could be placed against the wall when not in use. The table could be extended by the use of separate leaves.

Left
ROSE WOOD CYLINDER BUREAU
ENGLISH c.1780

Below
MAHOGANY WINE TABLE
ENGLISH c. 1750

Neoclassical forms

THE FLOWERING OF the rococo style in England was comparatively brief and by 1770 the neoclassical style championed by Robert Adam (1728-92), William Chambers and James Stewart, had established itself, although residual rococo forms continued to linger until about 1780. Drawing on classical antiquity, the new style saw a gradual return to more simple architectural forms. The style of the cabriole leg also slowly disappeared to be replaced by square tapering legs or tapering, fluted legs.

Carved decoration ceased to be as important as it had been during the height of the rococo fashion, but attention was lavished on the surface of furniture. Mahogany continued to be the favoured timber but much more richly figured veneers had begun to be imported from Cuba and great pains were taken to match grains to create perfect decorative effects.

Among new forms to appear during this period were the sideboard and the dining table. Typically the sideboard had a long top often of serpentine or bowed outline, and a single long drawer flanked by a pair of

Above
MAHOGANY DINING TABLE
ENGLISH c. 1790

The growing pace of change in fashion is testified to by the French-influenced designs that appeared in Thomas Sheraton's *The Cabinet-Maker's and Upholsterer's Drawing Book* of the early 1790s. Satinwood was the most highly prized timber during this period and was very frequently embellished with painted decoration.

The 19th century

THE TURN of the century saw a change in direction in the design of furniture. Design became archaeological in character. Chairs were modelled on the Klismos chair of ancient Greece, while tables were supported on lion monopodia. Rosewood began to replace satinwood as the most fashionable timber although mahogany continued to be generally used. Cut-brass inlay inspired by the work of the 17th century cabinet-maker Andre-Charles Boulle (1642-1732) was popular.

Heavy neo-classical forms were used throughout the first quarter of the 19th century but increasingly the style was rivalled by historicist styles. Jacobean and Gothic revival furniture became increasingly popular in the 1820s. The so-called 'Louis Quatorze' style adapted various French 18th century styles to create a hybrid.

Among the more popular pieces was the credenza, a side cabinet, often of serpentine outline with mirrored or glass panels. These could be in walnut, sometimes with inlaid decoration, although boulle-work was also popular.

Certain designers reacted against these eclectic styles. Among the first was A. W. Pugin (1812-1852), who was responsible for much of the decoration of the new Houses of Parliament and who wanted to return to authentic Gothic forms. Later in the century, the designer William Morris produced simply constructed furniture which broke away from the mechanization which had taken over so much of the furniture industry.

CONTINENTAL FURNITURE

JOHN TAYLOR

The Italian Renaissance and its influence

DURING THE 14th and 15th centuries the innovations of its painters, sculptors and architects gave Italy a pre-eminent position in the development of the decorative arts. The influence of the Italian Renaissance was felt in France in the early part of the 16th century. Designers such as Jacques Androuet DuCerceau, who published a series of influential designs for furniture in 1550, applied Italian mannerist ornaments, such as swags and caryatids, to a whole variety of beds, tables and wardrobes or armoires.

The most important piece of furniture during this period was the dresser with an upper stage, usually of architectural form, enclosed by cupboard doors, and supported on columnar supports. Gradually a new form of cabinet appeared with upper and lower sections each with two doors and often with a pediment cresting.

In Germany too, Italian influence was paramount. Hans Holbein the younger and Albrecht Dürer had both visited

Left
PARQUETRY AND PORCELAIN DISPLAY CABINET
ENGLISH c. 1840

Italy in the first decade of the century and Italian applied arts had clearly made a deep impression on them. However it was not until the middle of the century that designers such as Peter Flottner of Nuremburg began to evolve a mature approach to the new decorative trends from the south. Decoration culled from Italian sources and grafted on to simple German forms was typified by dense floral arabesque carving in low relief, often

centred by classical portrait medallions. Carving of this type was incorporated into low chests and large cupboards. Different regions interpreted the new style in varying ways. In the south, soft woods were favoured and these were usually applied with painted decoration or inlaid with classical-type motifs. The city of Augsburg produced high quality panels of

Below
CARVED WALNUT CABINET
FRENCH c.1580

pictorial marquetry, set into cabinets. In the north of Germany, oak was the favoured timber and although cabinets and chests were carved with decoration in the new style they retained a sober outline.

From 1650 to 1720

THE MIDDLE OF the 17th century saw the introduction of the cabinet-on-stand throughout Europe. Although of much the same form, they were developed in different ways. In Italy they were frequently set with *pietra dura* panels, a form of marquetry executed in marble and semi-precious stones. In the Low Countries they were embellished with panels of red tortoiseshell. The unrivalled splendour of Louis XIV's court demanded furniture of the utmost luxury. Highly sophisticated floral marquetry in wood was developed by Pierre Gole and by André-Charles Boulle.

Boulle also developed a type of marquetry which juxtaposed veneers of ebony, cut-brass and tortoiseshell, a technique to which he gave his name. Boulle seems to have been responsible for the development of the commode – a chest with drawers and usually with a marble top. It was to be among the most important of 18th century furniture types.

The mid-18th century

TOWARD THE THE end of Louis XIV's reign a new informality was discernible in French decorative arts. Ornamentalists such as Berain, Audran and Gillot reworked the grotesque work of the Renaissance into a new, much lighter style based around sinuous curved lines. The first fruition of this style was fostered under the patronage of the Regent, the Duc d'Orléans, the young Louis XV's guardian.

Above
WALNUT ARMOIRE
GERMAN c.1750

Below left
EBONY TABLE CABINET
FLEMISH c.1650

He employed the architect and decorator Oppenord and the cabinet-maker Cressent on the interiors of the Palais Royal, his Paris residence, and there they created the style which has become known as *Régence*.

Commodes gradually became more sophisticated in shape. They were normally serpentine in plan and bombe in profile. Early *Régence* commodes are quite bulky but they became increasingly graceful; the initial three drawers were reduced to two drawers and were raised on slender cabriole legs. Commodes were veneered *sans traverse* so that the two drawer-

fronts were treated as a single uninterrupted decorative surface rather than as two surfaces, and the division between them was ignored or obscured.

The arrangement of mounts reinforced the illusion. Case furniture was usually veneered in kingwood or tulipwood and arranged in quartered panels whereby the veneers of any section were cut into quarters and positioned with the grain converging on the central join. Often floral marquetry was inlaid into quartered panels. An increasing informality in domestic life necessitated the creation of new forms such as ladies' writing desks (*bureaux-en-pente*), usually with a hinged sloping flap. Small, easily portable tables (*tables-a-milieu*) were another innovation of this period.

Above
CARVED WALNUT ARMCHAIR
FRENCH c. 1730

....

Below
VENEERED COMMODE
FLEMISH c.1750

The same influences affected the design of seat furniture. The simple contours of Louis XIV chairs were replaced by undulating lines. The wooden frame of the chair was exposed and contained the upholstery within a border of moulded curves. The arms of chairs were brought back from the front of the seat rail to accommodate new dress fashions. In some cases (known as *fauteuil-en-cabriolet*) the back itself was curved while the seat was usually bowed at the front. Chairs were still made largely from beech or walnut and frequently painted or gilded. Carved decoration took the form of scrolls, *cartouches* and small sprays of flowers.

The early part of the 18th century found German cabinet-makers producing cabinets of complex serpentine and canted form. Usually veneered with walnut, they were decorated with inlaid strapwork borders and much play was made of contrasting figured veneers. The armoire continued to develop in various centres. Those made in Frankfurt had doors carved as a series of concentric rectangular concave mouldings. Others had doors divided by Corinthian pilasters.

The influence of the French *Régence* and Louis XV styles became influential and was soon to be felt in Germany through the work of designers who had trained and worked in Paris.

Commodes gradually lost their cabriole legs and were supported on short fluted legs or feet, while their general proportions became more bulky. Commodes with three drawers returned to fashion. Once again furniture mounts were used to define the form of furniture. Although marquetry continued to be popular, advanced taste increasingly favoured simple, unadorned mahogany veneers after the English fashion.

The period immediately after the French Revolution, known as the *Directoire*, saw a continuation of many of the themes of this simpler late Louis XVI furniture. Among the most popular forms in the late 1780s were the so-called Etruscan chairs. In the late 1790s the architects Percier and Fontaine

However the forms of the German rococo style tended to be more robust and vigorous than their French counterparts. The asymmetry which was a natural part of the style was exaggerated to extraordinary lengths.

Italian designers began to be influenced by the new French styles during the 1730s and it was in Italy that the style was to find its most vigorous expression. In the North, Venetian craftsmen in particular used exaggeratedly bombe forms. Walnut veneers were widely used although furniture was also frequently painted.

The revolutionary period

A REACTION TO the curved lines of the Louis XV style began to set in after about 1750. Designers looked back to the more architectural furniture of the Louis XIV period and

searched for a more authentically classical style. Towards the middle of the 1760s there was a noticeable change in the form and decoration of furniture. The relaxed curves of the Louis XV style began to stiffen. Commodes retained their cabriole legs but lost their bombe profiles and serpentine outlines. Mounts ceased to be moulded as abstract *rocaille* and took the form of classical architectural features.

By 1770 the new style was beginning to influence the design of seat furniture. Gradually chair backs lost their sinuous curves and became rectangular or oval, and the style of cabriole legs were replaced by turned, fluted legs. The elaborate scroll work and naturalistically carved flowers disappeared to be replaced by formal architecturally derived motifs such as *guilloche* and wreaths.

produced a series of lavish interiors culminating in the refurbishment of the Château de Malmaison for the wife of the First Consul, Napoleon Bonaparte. The style derived directly from late Louis XVI and Directoire taste, but the architects' interest in particular in the splendour of Imperial Rome led them to develop a new style, which reached fruition with Napoleon's coronation as Emperor in 1805.

Typically, Empire Furniture is sombre and architectural in character. Decoration was usually confined to a few mounts in shallow relief. Seat furniture became stiffer even than Directoire forms. Towards the end of the Empire, armchairs acquired scrolled arms and simple scrolled front legs. Pier tables and circular centre tables, or gueridons, were often carried on monopodiae, or simple columns.

Above
EMPIRE STYLE SIDE TABLE
FRENCH c. 1805

In Germany the Louis XVI style was quickly adopted. Typically, northern German furniture of this period is of simple geometric form, executed in mahogany and applied sparingly with gilt-metal or brass mounts. This type of furniture was taken to its pinnacle by the Neuwied cabinet-maker David Roentgen (1743-1807). Roentgen furniture of this period is distinguished by the quality of its construction and by unusual mechanical devices such as complex locking systems and spring-operated drawers and compartments. Although it owed much to French fashions, neoclassicism in Italy acquired its own distinctive flavour. In Milan, cabinet-makers produced commodes of simple rectangular form raised on tapering legs lavishly inlaid with marquetry based on neo-

classical motifs. In Turin the virtuoso wood carver Giuseppe Maria Bonzanigo produced elaborate neoclassical cabinets, commodes and a whole range of other pieces, profusely carved with swags and foliage.

Napoleon's conquests meant the diffusion of the Empire style throughout Europe.

Below
DEMAY MAHOGANY CHAIR
FRENCH c.1785

Below
NAPOLEONIC MAHOGANY DAY BED
FRENCH c. 1800

After Napoleon's demise neo-classicism continued to be favoured by the aristocracy throughout Italy. The highly sculptural gilded furniture designed by Pelagio Pelagi for the Palazzo Reale in Turin typifies this heavy style.

Empire influences were also strong in Germany and Austria in the early part of the century. At the same time a distinctive style of furniture, known as *Biedermeier*, began to appear. Using the same austere architectural forms as the Empire style, *Biedermeier* furniture was shorn of ornament and executed in local timbers such as yew and maple.

The 19th century

AT A TIME when cabinet-makers were at last able to exploit new industrialized techniques, the character of French 19th century furniture was determined, ironically, more and more by a fascination with the past. A renewed interest in the Middle Ages led to the increasing appearance of gothic decorative details on furniture. Throughout the 1830s cabinet-makers were taking as their inspiration the decorative arts of the 18th century. Initially this revived style was an eclectic melange of 18th century styles. Thus Boulle marquetry was often applied to Louis XV forms. However, by the middle of the century, cabinetmakers such as Henri Dasson were producing

accurate copies of royal 18th century furniture. Other periods also found favour. The rococo style was a particular favourite, while from around 1860 onwards Renaissance forms were popular.

From the early 19th century the use of mechanical tools inevitably affected the quality and individuality of pieces, however, early 20th century

Above
PARTRIDGEWOOD WORK TABLE BIEDERMEIER STYLE
S.GERMAN/AUSTRIAN c. 1810

Chippendale style suites are now in heavy demand and it seems that, whatever the method of production, good quality furniture will always eventually acquire value.

AMERICAN CHIPPENDALE FURNITURE

LEIGH KENO

Among the most popular items of antique furniture in the United States are those made in Colonial America in the Chippendale style. American Chippendale pieces date from a time, after 1750, of unprecedented peace and prosperity. Although thousands of pieces of furniture were imported from England throughout the 18th century, a vital domestic cabinet-making industry developed. Cabinet-makers could choose from an abundance of native woods, such as cherry, walnut, white pine, poplar and chestnut, as well as West Indian or Honduran mahogany.

The 'Queen Anne style' (which came into fashion in America some ten years after her death in 1714), was characterized by a use of the S-shaped line and a consideration of the scale of the human body. In America this style has come to mean graceful walnut pieces with cabriole legs ending in pad, trifid, or in some cases, claw-and-ball feet.

The Chippendale style, which would integrate these Queen Anne design elements with a new decorative repertoire, takes its name from Thomas Chippendale whose pattern book called *The Gentleman and Cabinetmaker's Director* discussed three basic styles: Gothick, Chinese and French, stressing imaginative and fanciful variations of each one. American furniture made in the Chippendale style did not differ drastically at first from Queen Anne furniture. For example, in some cases the only difference lay in ornamentation. Noticeable decorative changes in the Chippendale period include flared ears on chairs and balloon seats giving way to more a right-angled format. In contrast to the subdued walnut prominent in the Queen Anne period, richly figured imported mahogany was the wood of choice.

Regional variations in style

COLONIAL CENTRES OF cabinet-making were separate entities. While substantial interaction existed, each region answered to England in its own way. While the primary wood used in urban areas was mahogany, each region relied on available native woods for secondary structuring.

Left

PAIR OF WALNUT SIDE CHAIRS IN THE QUEEN ANNE STYLE
RHODE ISLAND c.1760

Each area interpreted the Chippendale style in its own way. Boston, the first great American cabinet-making centre, was not directly affected by Chippendale's design book. Instead, imported pieces in the Chippendale style seemed to be the primary inspiration for local artisans. In case-pieces, the bombe and blockfront forms reached their zenith in this city.

Claw-and-ball feet with raked-back talons and cabriole legs with flat, stylized leaf-carving characterized the best work of this city.

From 1750–76, Newport, Rhode Island, become famous for the monumental and work-intensive block-and-shell case pieces of Honduran mahogany made by the Townsend and Goddard families. The originality, design and quality of materials and workmanship found in furniture produced by these two clans is unmatched in other Colonial urban areas.

Below
MAHOGANY, CHEST OF DRAWERS
BOSTON, MASS. c.1770

Above
CARVED MAHOGANY CARD TABLE
NEWPORT, RHODE ISLAND
c.1770

Cabriole leg furniture from these shops – including high-boys, lowboys, card tables, chairs and tea tables – is greatly cherished by collectors today. The knees, embellished with graceful stylized scrolls, lobes and leafage, have no precedent: they are uniquely American designs.

Furniture from Connecticut does not have a single style.

Fashioned primarily of native cherrywood, the often whimsical and charming pieces made there seem to have been influenced more by neighbouring colonies than England. New York, however, produced pieces which closely followed English practices, and, with the exception of the famous serpentine-side card table, its craftsmen did not create any uniquely American forms.

Philadelphia would become the centre of American cabinet-making by the 1770s, at a time when the rococo style reached its zenith in the colonies. The furniture from this period comprises some of the most elegant and elaborate interpretations of Chippendale design found on this side of the Atlantic. Typical motifs include claw-and-ball feet and acanthus carved knees.

Upper-class Philadelphians looked to England as a barometer of taste, and many citizens ordered directly from London. General John Cadwalader, a widely travelled merchant, furnished his home in the grand manner. In 1771, he commissioned Thomas Affleck (1740-1795), an immigrant cabinetmaker, strongly influenced by Chippendale's *Director,* to make one of the most ambitious suites of 18th century American furniture on record. Decorative details included elaborately carved C-scrolls, cabochons, acanthus leaves and hairy paw feet.

Value and authenticity

CHIPPENDALE FURNITURE FROM Newport and Philadelphia has always brought record prices.

....

Right
MAHOGANY SIDE CHAIR AND LEG DETAIL.
PHILADELPHIA, PA
c.1765

A mahogany Chippendale tea table made for Jabez Bowen by John Goddard of Newport brought the record-breaking sum of $29,000 (see top picture opposite). In a subsequent sale, this figure was surpassed when a Philadelphia Chippendale highboy sold for US$33,000. In 1986, an easy chair from the famous Cadwalader suite broke all records for furniture, fetching US$2,750,000 (see lower picture opposite). This held until 1989, when a mahogany six-shell Newport secretary-desk brought US$ 12,100,000

The condition of a piece of American furniture affects its value more than any other factor. Collectors who are interested in purchasing an American Chippendale piece should consult an expert whom they can trust. Many fakes abound in the current market, and examples that are seemingly intact may have parts replaced or recarved within the last hundred years. Knowledgeable buyers use four criteria for authenticity: quality, rarity, condition and provenance.

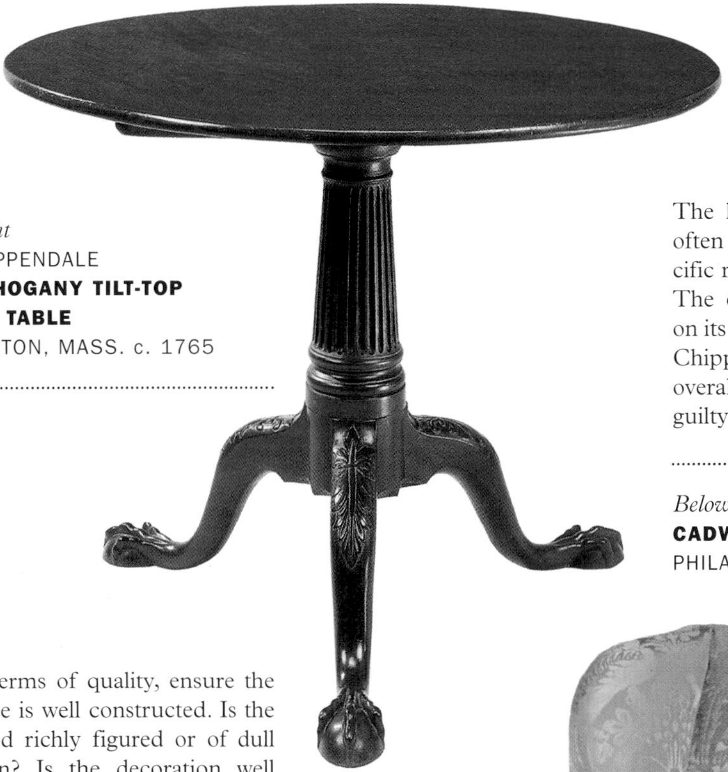

Right
CHIPPENDALE
**MAHOGANY TILT-TOP
TEA TABLE**
BOSTON, MASS. c. 1765

The history of ownership can often give a clue as to the specific region of its manufacture. The object must always stand on its own. In judging a piece of Chippendale furniture, the best overall advice is to consider it guilty until proved innocent!

Below
CADWALADER EASY CHAIR
PHILADELPHIA, PA. 1770

In terms of quality, ensure the piece is well constructed. Is the wood richly figured or of dull grain? Is the decoration well done, and does it relate to other known pieces? In terms of rarity, find out if the form is unique. Does it have a precedent? Too rare a form suggests that the piece is possibly a fake, made up from old parts or altered from a genuine item.

To judge condition, look for an old surface. Has it been completely stripped and refinished? Fakers today can simulate antique finishes with uncanny accuracy.

Finally, in terms of provenance, where has an alleged antique been from the time it was made until the present day?

SHAKER FURNITURE

The Shakers were a group formed in England in the 1760s and 1770s by a splinter faction of the Quaker movement, led by the visionary Mother Ann Lee.Naming themselves 'The Society of Believers', they left England for America in 1774 to avoid persecution, and founded a settlement at Watervliet, New York. Shaker communities spread as widely as New York, Ohio, Kentucky, and New England, consisting of nearly 6,000 members in total. Since this heyday, the population has dwindled until there are only a handful of true Shakers alive.

The craft ethic of the Shakers was shaped by their beliefs: everything fashioned was made for God, and therefore had to be as perfect as possible. All Shaker objects are as finely finished underneath, behind and inside as they are on the surface.

Below *left*
SHAKER TILTER SIDE CHAIR
MASSACHUSETTS c. 1830

Right
SHAKER MAPLE TILTER SIDE CHAIR
NEW YORK c.1840

Below
SHAKER MINISTRY TABLE
MASSACHUSETTS c. 1830

In addition, their work rate was phenomenal: in effect, outside of their worship, their craft was their lives, and they devoted themselves to it with incredible energy.

In terms of design, the Shakers were extraordinarily inventive. Their inspiration mainly came from the English country styles in which they had been raised, but was further driven by their immediate responses to their difficult lifestyle. Their inventions are wide-ranging and eccentric. The Shakers can lay claim to having invented the modern square-headed broom, forms of threshing machinery, a washing machine, the circular saw, and the clothes peg, as well as innumerable domestic labour-saving and storage devices.

The principal stylistic concern was simplicity: frippery and embellishment was scorned, as was the making of anything that did not have a specific and valuable function within the community. The result was a range of beautifully crafted but very plain objects which celebrated the intrinsic shape and line of the piece.

Above right
SHAKER REVOLVING CHAIR
NEW ENGLAND c.1860.

Right
SHAKER CHEST
NEW YORK c.1837

CHINA AND CERAMICS

Above

DERBY PORCELAIN LEOPARDS

ENGLISH c.1765–70

The wares of China's Han-Song dynasties

FROM AS EARLY as 4000–3000 BC the Chinese potter was making useful wares of great beauty. Before the introduction of the potters' wheel, these were made by handforming or coiling and were sometimes painted with exciting and vigorous patterns using coloured earth pigments.

It is due to the Chinese practice of tomb burials, including the interment of 'wares for the usage of the dead', that we have so many fine examples of ceramics available for study today.

During the Tang dynasty (618–906 AD) many tomb figures of this kind were still produced, but decorated from about the 8th century with lead-glazes stained with high temperature oxides to produce greens, blues, yellows and rich browns. It was at this time also, that refined stonewares replaced the coarser earthenwares. This led to the production of a white-bodied porcellaneous ware, referred to

as 'Samarra' which evolved into the white porcelain that we know today.

New kiln firing techniques resulted in many new and beautiful monochrome glazes, individual kilns producing their own particular type in different areas. It was nevertheless in the northern area in the province of Hebei that the first Ding porcelains were produced.

Equally beautiful are the late Southern Song porcelains named Qingbai (bluish white), which often have delicately incised or moulded decoration. During this period also, a form of ware was produced known to us as 'Celadon'. This term refers to the grey-green glaze applied to a stoneware, the colour resembling jade, the mineral so highly regarded by the Chinese.

It was during the short-lived Yuan dynasty (1279–1368 AD) of Khubilai Khan, that the use of the metallic oxide of cobalt (underglaze-blue) and the rarer copper (underglaze-red) was first used as a common means of decoration.

....

Above left
HAN DYNASTY
EARTHENWARE WATCH-DOG
CHINESE 206BC–220AD

Right
TANG DYNASTY
EARTHENWARE FIGURE
CHINESE 618–906AD

The Ming dynasty

DURING THE MING dynasty (1368–1644 AD) the kilns at Jingdezhen in Jiangxi Province were further developed and became the main centre of production. The tradition of underglaze-blue decoration was continued and improved. Under the Emperor Chenghua (1465–87) a particularly fine

delicate porcelain was made. It was then decorated with an underglaze-blue outline with a fired glaze to which colourful enamel colours were added.

Another fine white porcelain was produced at this time, known as *blanc de chine*. It was made at the kilns of Dehua in the Fujian Province. These wares are mainly in the form of sculptural figures of deities, libation cups and items for the scholar's table.

During this period also, a reddish brown stoneware was made at Lake Tai in the Jiangsu Province at potteries in Yixing Sian. Many teapots of this material were later exported to Europe. It was during the later reigns of the Ming dynasty that direct foreign trading began, and by 1557 the Portuguese had been granted concessions to trade from off-shore Macao.

It was from the commencement of the Ming dynasty that the Chinese potter began to mark his wares in underglaze blue with the reign-name of the incumbent Emperor. However these marks are sometimes an unreliable guide, for they were at times back-dated as a form of reverence to outstanding periods of production.

The Qing dynasty

ALTHOUGH THE QING dynasty started in 1644 it is the Emperor Kangxi to whom we most frequently refer. He reigned from 1662–1722, dur-

ing which time many excellent porcelains were made. The blue and white of this period show a rich royal blue on a pure white ground, often favouring wrap-around landscapes. During the reign of Kangxi the use of underglaze-red, which had virtually ceased by about 1425, was re-introduced. A new range of enamel colours was introduced, taking their name from the predominant colour used. They are referred to in French terms, such as *famille noire*, when black dominated, *famille verte* or *famille jaune* where greens or yellow were the main colours. Other wares were introduced during this reign such as 'enamel on the biscuit', which is simply enamels painted onto a ware fired without a glaze. Many fine monochromes were also made, from the pale blue *Clair de Lune* to the 'mirror-blacks' which were often further decorated with gilt.

The porcelains produced during the short reign of the succeeding Emperor Yongzheng (1723–35) were usually more delicate, and the fashion for blue and white was giving way to colourful copies of Ming times. At the same time a new enamel was introduced, the *famille rose*, composed of varying shades of pinks to a deep ruby.

During the long reign of the Emperor Qianlong (1736–95) heavy bronze forms, and a tendency to overdecorate, heralded a decline in the manufacture of Chinese porcelain.

Chinese export porcelain

AS EARLY AS the Tang dynasty wares were being exported to the Near East, but today we are familiar with those made for Europe and dating from the 17th century. The first English East India Company was formed in 1600, soon followed by the Dutch *Vereenigde Oestindische Compagnie* (V.O.C.) in 1602, who were to monopolize the China trade during the 17th century, when the English were more involved with India. It was from 1699, when Canton was opened to foreign traders, that the English Company began to dominate the trade, despite newly established competition from the French, Danes and Swedes. One must remember, however, that the major trade was in tea, silks and spices. Trading with the Chinese was not easy, and from 1757 merchants were confined to a small area in Canton where European 'Hongs' or warehouses were built outside the walls. It was in 1784 that the first American ship, *The Empress of China*, sailed from New York, and although no American East India Company was formed, the 'New People' as they were called had sent 28 trading ships to Canton by 1790.

Right
KAKIEMON GOURD-SHAPED VASE
JAPANESE 1660s or 1670s

polychrome-decorated porcelains were produced from the later decades of the 17th century, known as Kakiemon, the name of the family attributed with the introduction of these colourful wares which were to prove so popular in Europe. They are to be seen among the Far Eastern wares purchased by Augustus II of Saxony, and which were later copied at Meissen, Chantilly, Bow, Chelsea and other English factories.

The wares made during the 17th century at Kutani in central Honshu are in complete contrast to those at Kakiemon and are decorated with thickly applied strong greens, yellows, purple and blue, usually with foliage and flowers. Other Japanese regions are known for their exclusive styles of decoration, such as Nabeshima wares. The ceramic wares of Hirado are distinctive with their sparse decorative scenes painted in a bright blue.

Although much of the highly decorated cream-coloured earthenware known as Satsuma is enjoying a period of popularity today, many of these wares are of a very poor quality, as are some of the so-called Imari wares. Most of these pieces were produced in Japan after it was forced to open to European trade by the American Commodore Perry in 1854. Regrettably there is very little reliable material written on the wares produced during the successive Meiji period.

Japan

It is known that various areas of Japan had been producing earthenware for over three thousand years. The earliest wares were shaped by hand, resulting in a ruggedness which is still much admired and emulated today. The production of porcelain does not appear to have started in Japan until the early 17th century. Much appreciated and much copied

Islamic pottery

THERE SEEMS LITTLE doubt that it was the awareness of the pottery made in China during the Tang dynasty (618–906 AD) that provided the Islamic potter with the initial impetus to produce similarly decorated wares with green, yellow and purple glazes, as seen for example on Tang pottery horses and camels. Very few of these wares, dating from about 800 AD, have survived intact, the majority having been restored from fragments found on rubbish tips.

It was during the 9th and 10th centuries that the influence of Tang wares was most obvious, and the Islamic potter began to produce pieces which not only served a useful purpose, but also were pleasing to the eye. At Samarra and Nishapur (in present-day Iraq and Iran) excavations unearthed important evidence of the early Chinese porcellaneous white wares being imported during the 9th century.

It was probably due to the fact that Islamic potters were unable to locate the necessary ingredients to make a Chinese type of porcelain that led them to apply a white, opaque tin-glaze to their earthenware. This was often decorated prior to firing with simple floral designs of Kufic inscriptions in cobalt-blue, copper-green and antimony-yellow. A further important decorating technique was that of lustre decoration, probably first discovered by the early Egyptians when decorating glass. These metallic lustres vary from a deep red, or copper-tone, to a pale yellow, and were applied on to a previously fired glaze, and then subjected to a further firing in a reduction kiln, where the intake of air was restricted in order to create the necessary atmosphere. This technique became very popular on decorative tiles, but declined in Mesopotamia from about 950 AD.

The main pottery centres producing these wares during the 9th and 10th centuries, were Baghdad and Basra in Iraq. During the 9th to the 11th centuries, Iran and Afghanistan also became important centres of pottery production, and excavations during this century have revealed a wide variety of slip-decorated bowls and dishes in the regions of Samarqand and Nishapur.

During the reign of the Fatamid dynasty in Egypt (969–1171 AD) X lustre continued to be a favourite method of decoration for their buff or reddish clays. These were often signed by the potter, who painted subjects as diverse as the figure of Christ or a cock-fight.

Left
BROWNISH-GOLD LUSTRE EARTHENWARE BOWL
EGYPTIAN, 12th C.

Left
ISNIK EARTHENWARE DISH
TURKISH, 1550–1660

mid-13th century Moorish potters were at work in Malaga producing tin-glazed earthenware decorated with blue and lustre, which we today term Hispano-Moresque ware. This production continued in the following century in Granada, Manises, and Valencia.

The most common shapes produced in these centres were dishes and tall, waisted jars, called *albarellos*. Made for the apothecary, they were often decorated with mock-Arabic script. The high quality continued well into the 16th century, and the manufacture of lustre wares has continued until today at Manises, near Valencia.

By the 12th century migrating Egyptian potters had brought the technique of lustre decoration to many Mesopotamian and Iranian centres, including Rayy, Hashan, Sava, Gurgan and Sultanabad. The known Turkish wares, which were for many years wrongly termed 'Rhodian', are now recognized as having been made in Isnik, in Western Anatolia, dating from between 1555 and 1700. These wares are remarkable for their use of rich 'sealing-wax' red, together with greens and blues painted onto a white slip under a clear glaze.

Some interesting pottery was also made during the 18th and 19th century at Kutahya, which had become the centre of, the Turkish pottery industry by this time. The decoration on these wares reminds us that the kilns were in the midst of the Armenian and Christian communities of the Ottoman Empire of that day.

Spanish pottery and porcelain

TWELFTH CENTURY SPAIN may well be considered the converging point of Eastern and Western pottery styles. The Arabs had invaded the Iberian Peninsula in 711 AD and by the

It was the influence of the Arabic potter which was doubtless responsible for the large production of Spanish tiles (*azulejos*) starting during the second half of the 15th century, with a form of decoration called *cuerda seca* (dry-cord). The later alternative method, used at Toledo and Seville, resulted in raised ridges, so forming compartments into which the liquid glaze was applied, suggested by early Chinese *cloisonné* enamels. This technique was called *cuenca*.

During the mid-18th century more fashionable forms were introduced at Alcora, in the Province of Valencia. This factory, was established in 1726 by Count Aranda and owed its success to a French potter, Joseph Olery. During the second half of the 18th century, Alcora was one of the many European factories where the potters were forced to produce a form of cream-coloured earthenware in an attempt to survive against the extensive importation of Josiah Wedgwood's Queen's Ware.

When the production of Capodimonte porcelain was transferred to the grounds of the Buen Retiro Palace, near Madrid, in 1759, a certain amount of Italian clays were transported to the new premises. In consequence, the earliest wares produced at Buen Retiro were better than those which followed, which were made from Spanish clays and often have the appearance of a cream-coloured earthenware.

Buen Retiro porcelain is seen at its best in the porcelain room of the Aranjuez Palace, south of Madrid.

Portuguese earthenware

DUE TO THEIR early association with China during the 16th century, Portuguese potters were familiar with the blue and white porcelain of the Ming dynasty. In consequence the tin-glazed earthenwares made in Lisbon resembled the Oriental wares made for export to Europe. Portugal was one of the many European countries which produced tile-pictures

during the 16th century. These were made from painting continuously over a number of square tin-glazed tiles, which was also a favourite art form in Spain.

The average collector is more likely to be familiar with the lead-glazed wares made by Mafra & Son at Caldas da Rainha from 1853, imitating Bernard Palissy's 16th century creations. These are very poor quality and should not be mistaken for the original light, brightly glazed pieces.

Italian earthenware

THE ITALIAN TERM for tin-glazed earthenware is *maiolica*. It is thought that the name derives from the fact that Hispano-Moresque wares from Spain were imported to Italy via the trading-ships from the Balearic island of Majorca. The earliest Italian productions date from 1400, but most examples have been excavated, are usually discoloured and not seen at their best.

Finer mid-15th century pieces came from Florence, such as the so-called 'oak-leaf' jars. These were large drug-pot painted in a blackish-blue often with heraldic beasts set against a background of stylized oak-leaves. Another popular Florentine type of ware was the large pan-shaped dishes, painted in purple, green and yellow high temperature colours with human heads or animals.

Fine Italian *maiolica* is not seen at its best until the first half of the 16th century. Colours included blue from cobalt, yellow from antimony, orange and shades of violet and purple from manganese, with an occasional use of red derived from an earth known as Armenian bole, which was a very difficult colour to fire successfully.

The city of Faenza became the centre of influence for these wares, and it has remained an important area to this day. There are very few collectors of this colourful pottery, the finest having been acquired by major museums. They were frequently referred to as 'Raphael Fayence', a term almost certainly due to

the similarity of the painting to the style of Raphael's painting in the *loggie* of the Vatican. This style of painting particularly appealed to Ulysse Cantagalli, whose work is well known and can often be identified by a broadly painted cockerel in blue on the reverse. Cantagalli worked in Florence from 1878 until his death in 1901.

Above
TIN-GLAZED EARTHENWARE
MAIOLICA PLATE
FLORENCE, ITALY c.1510

....

Facing page
ALBARELLO (DRUG JAR)
SPANISH c.1435

Italian porcelain

THE FIRST ATTEMPT to produce porcelain in Europe was made in Florence, between 1575 and 1587, when an early soft-paste, or artificial porcelain, was made from white-firing clays, with about 20% of frit (glass). This was made for the family of the Grand Duke Francesco I d'Medici. Being a soft-paste porcelain, the body was first fired to a biscuit, then painted with cobalt-blue and occasionally with manganese-purple, after which it was covered with a transparent lead-glaze and again fired.

The first hard-paste porcelain to be produced in Italy was made between 1720 and 1727 by Francesco Vezzi, aided by C. H. Hunger, the arcanist previously employed at Meissen. He is considered responsible for the closure of the factory, when in 1727 he returned to Saxony and stopped the export of the necessary clays to Vezzi. During this seven year period some very good table-wares were made in silver baroque forms, decorated in enamel colours, which favoured a distinctive iron-red.

There were few serious attempts to produce porcelain again in Italy until 1764, when Geminiano Cozzi founded a production of hard-paste porcelain, which survived until 1812. In consequence it is one of the few Italian porcelains frequently seen outside of museums.

Above

DOCCIA PORCELAIN FIGURE
ITALIAN c.1770

Cozzi's porcelain was not of a high quality; it had a rather thickly potted grey body, with an ill-fitting glaze, but was often decorated with fine gilding.

The important factory at Doccia, near Florence, was founded by the Marchese Carlo Ginori, who started marketing a coarse, greyish, hard-paste porcelain in 1746, which between 1770 and 1790 was made to look more attractive by the addition of a white, opaque tin-glaze, which was sometimes painted with enamel colours in a Japanese porcelain manner.

From 1745 to 1755, large vases, plaques and table-wares were often moulded with high relief mythological subjects, painted in colours. The figures produced at Doccia are lively and pleasing in typically exaggerated theatrical poses, usually on simple square bases, painted to resemble marble.

The really beautiful soft-paste Italian porcelain was made in the factory of Charles of Bourbon, at Capodimonte, from 1743–59. These wares are extremely rare and are very expensive, especially the figures, all of which are invariably marked with the *fleur-de-lis*, impressed or in blue. Their table-wares, which were mostly in the baroque style, were very much under the influence of the Meissen factory in Saxony. At this same time they produced some beautifully designed and painted snuff-boxes, cane-handles and other small pieces.

It was at the Royal Factory of Naples, established by Ferdinand IV in 1771, that we first find wares marked with a '*N*' under a crown in blue. This mark was never used at Capodimonte, to which it is often attributed, but was frequently copied on later Doccia wares and the porcelains of Ernst Bohne, who operated at Rudolstadt in Germany from 1854.

The majority of porcelain made at Naples came under the influence of the early finds that had been made during the excavations on the sites of Herculaneum and Pompeii, which were to bring about the fashion for neoclassical art.

German, Austrian and Central European earthenware

THE POTTERS OF Germany, Austria and other Central European countries, did produce tin-glazed earthenware, but not on the scale of the Italians. Probably the most important contribution of German potters to the history of ceramics was salt-glaze stoneware. The manufacture of salt-glazed stoneware began in Siegburg, in the Rhineland in the 14th century. The majority of these stonewares were jugs or drinking vessels, in a variety of different shapes.

....

Below
SALT-GLAZED STONEWARE JUG
GRENHAUSEN GERMANY c. 1691

The other important centre was Cologne. It was in these two major centres that the majority of the bearded bottles, or Bellarmines, were produced. Drinking vessels in grey salt-glaze with blue decoration have remained a popular form of tourist souvenirs which are sold in that region to this day.

From the 17th century Hamburg, Hanau, Nuremberg and Frankfurt-am-Main were among the major cities where tin-glazed earthenwares were made, often decorated in imitation of Chinese styles of the late Ming dynasty, or in some of the popular styles being applied at the same period to Delftware. Prior to making porcelain several other German factories, including Höchst, Ansbach and Fulda, also produced some colourful, well painted tin-glaze wares.

Meissen porcelain

THE PRODUCTION OF a Chinese type of hard-paste porcelain was established in Saxony at the Meissen factory, situated 25 kilometres from Dresden and the Court of its patron, Augustus the Strong, in 1710.

Under the direction of Johann Friedrich Boettger, a young alchemist, experiments resulted in the production of a hard, red stoneware, which could be engraved and polished to make it resemble a semi-precious stone. The production of this material continued until about 1730 and the later pieces are frequently marked with the incised crossed swords.

The first Meissen porcelain was not a good colour. Their earliest wares were mostly tea or coffee-services, tankards or vases, most of which were moulded or decorated with applied reliefs, whilst their earliest figures were left in the white or with touches of gilding.

Following the arrival from Vienna in 1720 of J. G. Höroldt, a skilled painter and designer, Meissen wares were decorated with stylized flowers, chinoiserie and harbour-scenes, all in bright enamel colours. Some of the larger pieces of this early period were marked with an underglaze-blue monogram of 'A.R.' (Augustus Rex). This indicated that they were made for the Elector to help decorate the *Japanisches Palais* he had purchased in 1717 to house his collection of porcelain, which included large quantities of Japanese and Chinese wares.

In 1727 the sculptor, J. G. Kirchner, was appointed to produce the original models from which moulds were made to make the porcelain figures, including large fantastic models of animals and birds. Kirchner was soon to be replaced by a more skilful modeller, J. J. Kaendler. Kaendler's best figures must be those of Harlequin, Columbine and other asorted well-known characters from the *Commedia dell'Arte*, which were modelled and produced from about 1738.

but others extended into the 19th century.

Although established in 1717, Du Paquier's factory at Vienna had little success until aided by S. Stözel and C. H. Hunger, whom he had lured away from Meissen with a promise of rich living (which did not materialize). After their departure the factory continued until 1744, when Du Paquier was forced to sell to the Austrian Empress Maria Theresa, under whose patronage the factory ran until 1784. It was from the start of this State Period that the much-copied two-bar shield of Austria was adopted as a factory mark. From 1784 until its final closure in 1866, some highly decorated wares were produced.

Left
MEISSEN PORCELAIN HARLEQUIN
GERMANY c. 1750

Below
NYMPHEMBURG PORCELAIN FIGURES
GERMANY c. 1760

During the Seven Years War the Meissen factory was occupied by the troops of Frederick the Great of Prussia and by the end of the war in 1763, the new French factory at Sèvres had become the new trend-setter. Meissen were never again to regain its lead, and could only endeavour to reproduce, in hard-paste, the beautiful soft-paste wares of the new French factory.

By the middle years of the 18th century, many workmen from Meissen, were prepared to sell their skills. Within a short time, porcelain factories, some of which had previously only made tin-glazed earthenwares (*faience*), were in production at Höchst, Fürstenberg, Berlin, Nymphenburg, Frankenthal, Ludwigsburg. All made porcelain from the original Meissen formula. Some were shortlived

The unmarked wares of the Du Paquier period were usually decorated in enamel colours and gilding with extreme baroque ornament, scrollwork, shell-like palmettes, lattice-like gilding, *chinoiserie*, or Meissen-type flower painting; only very few figures were made.

The wares in the early years of the 19th century attracted many other later European porcelain makers, who produced copied wares often termed old Vienna, complete with bogus marks.

French earthenware

THE MAIN PRODUCTION of French potters was of tin-glazed earthenware, known in France from the early part of the 17th century as *faience* after Faenza, the large distribution centre of Italian *maiolica*. Before considering these wares it is worth noting that two other outstanding and rare types of lead-glazed earthenwares were produced. The name of the potter who made the particularly fine ivory-coloured pottery sometimes known as Henri II ware, is not known, but 16th century references leave little doubt that it was made in St Porchaire, in the department of Deux-Sèvres. It was at one time thought that the very precise decoration in contrasting coloured clays was inlaid, but it is now accepted, that the under-glaze coloured clays were applied to the surface with the

'possible collaboration of a printer'. There are only about 64 genuine examples of this work recorded. During the 1860s some very good reproductions of these wares were made by the Staffordshire firm of Minton and that of Charles Avisseau at Tours, in France.

The other much reproduced earthenware was of the type attributed to Bernard Palissy, at Saintes from about 1542. Palissy's best known wares are decorated with snakes, lobsters, lizards, fish and shells etc.

There is little doubt that the production of French tin-glazed earthenwares was started in the early decades of the 16th century by immigrant potters from Spain and Italy, which at times make it difficult to be certain of the country of origin. This is the case with those of Lyons, Nimes and Rouen. From the early 17th century,

Above

FAIENCE POT-POURRI AND ENAMEL-PAINTED DISH
STRASBOURG, FRANCE c.1755

Nevers produced pieces made in imitation of Chinese blue and white, and wrongly termed *blue-persan*, in which tin-glaze was stained to a dark royal blue and then decorated in white and sometimes yellow, with flowers or a Chinese landscape. From the late years of the 17th century Rouen potters produced a wide range of wares, painted in dark blue on a white ground, with so-called *lambrequin* designs.

At Strasbourg and Marseilles we find the well-painted and original styles of decoration. Early pieces resemble Italian maiolica, but by mid century, enamels were used to paint beautiful flower groups in the manner of Meissen porcelain.

Marseilles, in the south, had several factories during this period, but the best known is certainly that of *Veuve Perrin* (Widow Perrin) who continued to run the pottery after the death of her husband in 1748, until she died in 1793. Here the painting depicted fish, vegetables and insects all painted in a delightful free manner.

French porcelain

PRIOR TO THE establishment of the Vincennes factory in 1738, there were only a few concerns making porcelain in France. The limited wares that are attributed to Louis Poterat, who was working at Rouen from 1673, were made from a very glassy soft-paste body, decorated with dark inky-blue , marked with an inexplicable 'A.P.'

From about 1690, a porcelain production of soft-paste was started at St-Cloud, near Paris, by the family of a maker of *faience*, Pierre Chicaneau. Chicaneau had passed the secret to his widow, who later married Henry Trou, under whose name the factory continued until 1766. Many of their small wares were painted in Japanese Kakiemon styles with bright enamel colours.

From 1725 the factory of Chantilly, under the patronage of the Prince de Condé, produced a range of wares almost solely fashioned after the large collection of Japanese porcelain already owned by the Prince.

The other important French factory was at Mennecy, established in 1734 and closing in 1806. Early Mennecy porcelain is milky-white with the glaze 'wet' and brilliant, absorbing the well-known rose-pink enamel until it almost appears to run. Due to the harsh monopolies granted to the Vincennes and Sèvres factories, Mennecy were prohibited from applying gilding to their wares.

Above
**CHANTILLY PORCELAIN
TEAPOT IN THE KAKIEMON
JAPANESE STYLE**
FRENCH c. 1730–40

Below
**MENNECY PORCELAIN
SAUCE TUREEN IN THE
MEISSEN STYLE**
FRENCH c. 1750–60

Vincennes and Sèvres

THE IMPORTANT FRENCH production centre at Vincennes was established in about 1738, but very little porcelain was produced, with the exception of flowers, until after 1745. Few profits were being made and to avoid closure, King Louis XV bought the centre, making Sèvres a Royal Factory. This royal interest was continued by Louis XVI and Marie Antoinette from 1774. In 1793, the factory was taken over by the Republic, and production has continued to this day.

Many talented designers, sculptors and painters were called upon to apply their skills resulting in the graceful shapes of the period. These included ice-pails, jugs and slender vases, sometimes decorated only with underglaze-blue or outstanding quality gilding.

Other popular colours were added in quick succession, *bleu celeste* or turquoise in 1752, *jaune jonquille*, yellow, 1753, green in 1756 and *rose* 1757. It was not until 1763 that use was made of a dark-blue enamel, *blue de roi*, a colour much copied by such English factories as Minton and Coalport.

The very informative marks used at the factory are a great aid to the collector. The interlaced 'L's' of the French crown were used as a mark from about 1750, into which from 1753 a series of date-letters were introduced. In addition many of the

Above
SÈVRES PORCELAIN BASIN AND EWER
FRENCH c. 1761

....

385 painters and gilders applied their initials or a distinctive symbol, to help identify their work. For example any piece with *rose* as a ground colour, should not bear a date-letter prior to E, 1757, when the colour was first used.

From 1793, into the early 19th century many pieces of soft-paste Sèvres, which had been sold by the factory either blank or slightly faulty, were frequently redecorated in a popular style. Production has continued to the present day, however, the quality of their early wares has never been equalled.

Scandinavian earthenware

THE COUNTRIES OF Scandinavia made very few original wares, and apart from those on show in museum collections, they are rarely seen. The major styles followed those of Holland and Germany.

One of the most interesting potteries was founded by Johann Christoph Ludwig von Lucke, at Schleswig in 1755. The wares produced were mostly painted in a manganese-purple.

The well-known Rorstrand factory in Sweden was founded in about 1726, they produced fine tin-glazed wares, decorated with so-called *bianco-sopra-bianco* which involved painting a tinted glaze with white enamel.

Dutch Delftware

TIN-GLAZED WARES were being made in the Low Countries at Antwerp, Haarlem, Rotterdam, Amsterdam and Middelburg for many years before 1600. These 16th century wares are difficult to attribute, but it is the later Dutch wares which are most frequently seen, made from the middle of the 17th century in the town of Delft. Many potters had moved there, occupying buildings previously housing breweries whose trade had declined, hence the names of many of the potteries, such as *The Hatchet*, *The Golden Flowerpot* and *The Two Little Ships*.

Some of the best Delftware, made between 1650 and 1710, was decorated in the fashion of the Chinese blue-and-white porcelain of late Ming times, and is sometimes difficult to separate from the Chinese porcelain. In the 18th century, Delft potters copied the Oriental *famille-verte* colours of the Kangxi period and the Japanese porcelains of Arita.

Scandinavian porcelain

The production of fine hard-paste porcelain was established in Copenhagen in 1775; in 1779 this concern was taken over by the King and became The Royal Danish Porcelain Factory. Early wares were based on Meissen, often decorated in underglaze-blue. In 1789 they produce the famous 2,000 piece *Flora Danica* service, painted in enamel colours by Johann Christoph Bayer. It can be seen today in the Rosenborg Castle, Copenhagen. True hard-paste porcelain was eventually made by Jacob Dortu, who had gained his knowledge from Berlin, but the production of hard-paste porcelain only continued until 1782.

Above
FAIENCE PLATE
MARIEBERG, SWEDEN 1768

Facing page
DELFT EARTHENWARE DISH
DUTCH 1650

Below
ROYAL DANISH GILT AND ENAMEL PORCELAIN BOWL
DANISH Late 18th C.

English pottery

THE AREA OF Stoke-on-Trent in North Staffordshire has remained the centre of the English ceramic industry since the early 17th century, when the early form of bottle-kilns were being fired with local coal and all the necessary clays were available nearby. The majority of the decorative wares made there are slipwares, usually thrown or moulded from a warm-red clay. The best of these slipwares were produced to order, to commemorate a coronation, birth, marriage or some special event. Wares signed 'Thomas Toft' date from the reign of Charles II.

John Dwight took out a patent in 1672 to make salt-glazed stoneware, or 'Cologne Ware'. Despite the patent, by the end of the century, other potters were making similar wares in Nottingham, Derby and Staffordshire. Among the potters accused of infringing the patent were John and David Elers of Staffordshire. During the last years of the 17th century they made some fine red-stoneware mugs and tea-wares, all unglazed. This type of ware was continued well into the 18th century by other Staffordshire potters.

From the beginning of the 18th century, salt-glazed stoneware and lead-glazed earthenware developed. The former was soon improved upon to become a fine white body, with a glaze often likened to orange-peel, and used in a wide range of table-wares and simple but pleasing figures, such as 'pew groups'. By the middle of the century some salt-glaze was decorated with enamel colours. When fired to a lower temperature, this material remained earthenware, upon which a lead-glaze was applied at a second firing. This resulted in the first English cream-coloured earthenwares, a type which was to be perfected by Josiah Wedgwood.

From about 1740, Staffordshire potteries began to make many delightful human and animal forms, using the natural colour clays under a rich lead-glaze. This is known as Astburyware, or, when further decorated with metallic oxides, Astbury Whieldon, although other potters made similar wares. The most famous English potter was Josiah Wedgwood (1730–95), who after serving his apprenticeship with his elder brother went into a partnership with Thomas Whieldon from 1754–59, after which he became an independent master-potter in Burslem, Staffordshire. Among his first productions were useful wares covered with a fine green glaze, soon to be followed by a refined creamware, which he was permitted to name 'Queen's Ware'. In 1767, he produced black

Left
WEDGEWOOD
EARTHENWARE VASE IN BLACK BASALT
ENGLISH c.1775.

....

Below
JOHN OR RALPH WOOD.
EARTHENWARE GROUP
ENGLISH c.1775.

Returning to Staffordshire, it was from about 1770 that the Wood family of Burslem produced a wide variety of well-modelled figures, decorated with glazes which had previously been coloured green, yellow, blue or purple. This let them apply the colours where required, rather than the earlier Whieldon method. It is at this time that so many Toby Jugs are credited to John Wood.

basalt stoneware, from which the famous vases were made to commemorate the start of his partnership in 1769 with Thomas Bentley, who died in 1780. It was during this period that the now famous blue-jasperware was first introduced, decorated with white moulded reliefs. One of Wedgwood's outstanding achievements was his 1790 copy in black jasperware of the early Roman glass vase, the Portland Vase.

During these years the British potter had also been producing English delftware, (small 'd'). Unlike later European potters engaged in this manufacture, the British potters only rarely used enamel colours. Because British potters did not try to make wares look like Chinese porcelain, they have become much sought after collectors' items, especially if dated.

During the second half of the 19th century the Lambeth firm of Doulton produced some interesting art-pottery, which was decorated from 1871 by artists from the Lambeth School of Art.

A further range of late salt-glazed stonewares which attract today's collectors are those made by the three Martin brothers. Their decorations were confined to natural clay colours, with the occasional use of a high temperature colour. Usually they took on a distinctive Japanese style. They also produced some rather grotesque drinking vessels in the form of human faces or birds, which are highly regarded today. Their pottery in London was at its height between 1873 and 1910, but by 1915, three of the brothers had died and the firm had virtually ceased trading.

Another interesting figure was William De Morgan (1839–1917), more concerned with design and decoration than production, he is known to have purchased 'blanks' on which he applied many of his Persian and Near-Eastern lustre decorations. From 1872 to 1905, De Morgan was very influenced by William Morris, as can be seen by some of his beautifully decorated large dishes and tiles.

Among the many earthenwares made during the last century, there is little doubt that those decorated with underglaze-blue prints, taken from an engraved copper-plate, formed the bulk of the output of Staffordshire until well into the 19th century. The most common design used was one of the various versions of the popular Willow pattern. In addition to the numerous *chinoiserie* designs, plates and other table-wares show typical British scenes, stately homes, views of Italy and India, and views of excavations taking place in Asia Minor, many of the latter taken from contemporary topographical prints.

Among many highly collectable Victorian wares are the so-called '*majolicas*', which include a wide range of useful, decorative forms, painted with highly coloured lead-glazes. Wares of this type were first exhibited by the Staffordshire firm of Minton, at the Great Exhibition in Hyde Park, London in 1851.

Top
SPODE UNDERGLAZE-BLUE
EARTHENWARE COMPORT
STOKE, ENGLAND c.1815

Left
MARTIN BROTHERS
STONEWARE BIRD
LONDON c.1895

English & Welsh porcelain

ALTHOUGH SINCE ABOUT 1745 British porcelain manufacturers have produced an enormous number of wares, they only rarely showed any great originality in the shapes or forms of decoration.

Above

CHELSEA PORCELAIN JAR

ENGLISH c.1750–54

The Chelsea factory started up in 1745 by a Huguenot silversmith, Nicholas Sprimont, who made a wide range of useful, ornamental wares and figures until 1769. Then, William Duesbury, the proprietor of the Derby factory, bought Chelsea and ran both productions until 1784, in the period known as the Chelsea/Derby period.

Over recent years, details have come to light about a second Chelsea concern, which seemingly only ran from about 1749 to 1754, producing a few

useful wares and figures, making them into very expensive collectors' items. It appeared to specialize in small scent-bottles, mostly of human form. This factory, of which we still have much to learn, is called 'The Girl-in-a-Swing' group on account of one rare model. No factory-marks are recorded.

Chelsea frequently used a factory-mark. First, an incised triangle, c. 1745-49, then a raised-anchor on an applied oval medallion, c.1747–52, followed by a small red painted anchor, c.1752–58, and finally the much copied gold anchor. This was used until the takeover, after which the anchor was used with a 'D' for Derby until nearer 1784, usually in monogram form.

The Bow factory, in Essex, east London, was also producing a soft-paste porcelain which contained calcined animal-bone from about 1747, continuing

Above

CHELSEA PORCELAIN ASPARAGUS DISH

ENGLISH c.1755

until 1776. They produced a large quantity of table-wares and figures and at the peak of their prosperity were employing three hundred hands in their 'New Canton' factory. Unlike Chelsea, their main production

Below

CHELSEA PORCELAIN BASKET FIGURES

ENGLISH c.1760–65

was of useful wares decorated in a Chinese manner with underglaze-blue, although they did in addition produce a great variety of poorly modelled figures, some of which were sold 'in the white' and decorated by independent painters such as William Duesbury.

The Derby factory continued with an unbroken history until 1876, when the present-day Royal Crown Derby was established. The best wares made at Derby are those in neoclassical style, which were produced during the partnership of the two factories between 1770 and 1784.

The only English factory that has survived until today with an unbroken history is Worcester established by Dr Wall and his partners in 1751.

Until about 1755, most of the Worcester wares were decorated in underglaze-blue painting, but from about that time they also produced many very attractive pieces painted in enamel colours in a variety of styles. Some very high quality decoration was added to Worcester 'blanks' or those only decorated with underglaze-blue grounds, by James Giles, an independent decorator working in London from about 1765 into the early 1770s.

The potters of Staffordshire produced a very glassy type of soft-paste porcelain at Longton Hall from c.1749 to 1760, but the undertaking was far from a success, although these some-

times very poorly produced wares are much sought after by today's collectors.

Some small, useful wares were made from bone porcelain at a factory in Lowestoft on the east coast of Suffolk, where they operated from 1757 until c.1799. Prior to 1768 all their porcelains were decorated in only underglaze-blue, but from that time they also decorated a wide range of wares in Chinese styles. The most interesting pieces made at Lowestoft are those named and dated for the recipients and those which are painted with the words 'A Trifle from Lowestoft', an early

Above
**LONGTON HALL
PORCELAIN FIGURE**
ENGLISH c.1756–7

form of a 'Present from the Seaside'.

Thomas Turner ran a successful factory at Caughley, in Shropshire, from about 1772 until 1799, when it was taken over by John Rose, the owner of the Coalport factory. Many Caughley wares decorated with underglaze-blue prints have a lot in common with the contemporary wares of Worcester, but the Caughley wares are superior to their rival.

Above
ROCKINGHAM BONE-CHINA VASE
ENGLISH c.1830

It was 1768 before William Cookworthy put to use the materials he had discovered in Cornwall for the production of a hard-paste porcelain. His first factory at Plymouth was moved to Bristol in 1770, where it continued under the charge of Richard Champion until 1781. During this period many well-decorated table-wares were made, together with some rather large figures of the Seasons and the Continents.

In 1781, a group of Staffordshire potters purchased the unexpired years of Champion's patent for the production of hard-paste porcelain and established the New Hall factory, where they continued to make hard-paste teawares and other small table-wares until about 1812, when in common with many other English factories, they made bone-china, until closing in 1835.

There are numerous other British factories which produced hybrid porcelains and bone-china from the early 19th century, including Coalport, Minton, Spode (which was later called Copeland), Davenport, Rockingham and Daniel, to name but a few.

Among the many porcelains sought by today's collectors are those made in South Wales at Nantgarw and Swansea from 1813–20. 'Blanks' of these wares were much in demand by independent decorators in London and elsewhere, working mostly for retailers.

American pottery & porcelain

MOST OF OUR knowledge of the manufacture of earthenware and stoneware among the early American colonies centres around New England, where prior to the 17th century all their needs were imported from Europe. From the mid-17th century and well into the 1800s the settlers were producing their own basic ceramics from a red earthenware,

Right **HARD-PASTE PORCELAIN HARE FROM PLYMOUTH**
ENGLISH c.1768–70

covered with a honey-coloured lead-glaze. It was sometimes decorated in a simple fashion with manganese, which fired to a dark-brown or black.

Although salt-glazed stone-wares were imported from both Germany and England prior to the Revolution at a low rate of tax, the higher duties later imposed saw a growing production of stoneware in New York, New Jersey and New England, which in turn gradually replaced the softer and more vulnerable earthenwares. One well-known major supplier was Edmands Pottery, in Charlestown, Massachusetts.

Left
**UNDERGLAZE BLUE
SOFT-PASTE PORCELAIN
BASKET**
PHILADELPHIA, AMERICA
c.1770

Collecting ceramics

Ceramics are highly sought after by collectors and prices can be very high. For instance an 11th century Chinese celadon dish was sold at auction for £7,500 ($12,400) in 1987, an Isnik piece of 1580 reached £10,500 (US$17,500) a 19th century fake even achieved £2,200 (US$3,650), and a pair of Meissen *Commedia dell'arte* figures went for £4,800 (US$8,000). Fashions do often change however; in 1990 some of the highest prices were paid for English wares: a Minton maiolica fountain went for £6,100 (US$10,000), whilst a Wedgwood fairyland lustre vase went for £8,500 (US$14,000), and a pair of Whieldon figures reached £32,000 (US$53,000).

A variety of red earthenware and salt-glaze continued to be produced in New York and Bennington, Vermont, to serve the local communities well into the mid-19th century, including jugs, pans and storage jars, often decorated with cream-coloured slip and so similar to the 17th and 18th century English wares that sure attribution is often difficult. One major pottery was that of Hervey Brooks, a farmer-potter of Connecticut, who worked from 1802 until firing his last kiln in 1864 at the age of 84.

William Ellis Tucker, produced a hard-paste porcelain in Philadelphia from 1826, after which various partners were involved. In 1831, Alexander Hemphill became a partner and the concern continued to produce porcelain under members of the two families until 1838.

Many other later 19th century potteries, including the United States Pottery Company at Bennington, Vermont and Christopher W. Fenton, also from Bennington, and the Trenton Pottery Company, New Jersey, all made large quantities of Parian ware figures and decorative tablewares.

Production of art pottery was not popular in the USA. until the 1870s, when at least six major concerns started up in Cincinnati alone, but by 1890 only that of Rookwood was still active. Rookwood was started by Mrs Maria Longworth Nichols, in 1880 and survived until 1941. The pottery flourished, aided by the production of commercial and utility wares. Some of the finest of the art pottery wares are widely sought today.

In 1889, Rookwood was transferred to the ownership of WilliamWatts Taylor who by 1899 was employing thirty-six artists in the art department.

Although it could be said that there are no 'cheap' antique ceramics, there is scope for the more modest collector to buy good pieces for between £300 and £500 (US$500–900) or less. Excellent pieces of New Hall porcelain, made in Staffordshire between 1781 and 1835, can be obtained for quite modest prices. Look at the work of modern studio potters to find the antiques of the future.

G L A S S

SIMON COTTLE

Above
RUBINGLAS
GERMAN LATE 17th C.

Glass is one of the most under-valued of collectable antiques. From stained glass windows to paperweights, from decanters to scent flasks, glass has been used through history in many different ways, sometimes as a substitute for ceramics, wood or metalwork, but very often as a wonderfully adaptable material in its own right. The recent development of the wine glass and goblet especially in the last 300 years now provides much interest for collectors and historians. This common crystal clear product, so often over-looked in its colourless state, may embody skills which in the present machine age can hardly be rivalled.

The manufacture of glass has its origins in the Eastern Mediterranean where it was developed by the Egyptians in the 3rd century BC. Most glass at this date was made by casting methods. Glass was considered as a substitute for precious and semi-precious gemstones and was made into beads for bracelets and necklaces and as insets in furniture.

Early glass

THE EARLIEST TYPE of glass known, soda glass, was used by the Egyptians, Romans and, from the 15th century AD, by the Venetians who called it 'cristallo'. From the 1st century BC entire glass vessels were made by a very simple, yet revolutionary new method which

involved the aid of a long pipe. The technique of freeblowing glass is still today the chief method used for producing high quality table-wares and studio glass.

Much early glass is incomplete and bears an iridescence which is largely due to a degrading ageing process or from burial in the ground. This unintentional decoration has inspired artists, such as Emile Gallé and L. C. Tiffany at the turn of the 20th century. Together with bowls and drinking vessels, large numbers of mould-blown flasks for holding ointments and oils were made.

The rarer and more intricate

examples command very high prices and faithful 20th century reproductions can fool the unwitting collector.

Cameo glass was known to the ancient Egyptians but was perfected by the Romans in the 1st century BC and the 1st century AD. The Portland Vase at the British Museum is one of the best known examples of an art form which required the casing of a glass vessel within a second or even third layer which was then carved to

Below

CLASSICAL GLASS
ROMAN 200BC–200AD

expose the different layers. The technique was revived by the Chinese in the 18th century on Peking Glass, especially for snuffbottles, and used highly creatively at the end of the 19th century by artist-glassmakers in the West Midlands most notably John Northwood and George Woodall. It was popular during the Art Nouveau period in France and in the United States where Gallé and Tiffany were the leading exponents.

Glass-making in Venice

VENICE WAS, BY 1292, a well-established and very influential glassmaking centre. Its early glassware consisted of beads, jewellery, mirrors and window glass. Enamelled ceremonial cups and winged goblets were popular in the 15th century and by the 16th and 17th centuries glassmaking in Venice had reached its height of popularity and its products were copied throughout Europe – especially in Spain and the Low Countries (known as *façon de Venise*), where immigrant Italian glass-makers practised their skills.

A more complicated glass was also made from soda which is very light in weight and conse-quently extremely brittle. Elegant bowls and goblets with white enamelled threads form-ing gauzes and intricate lace-like networks, are typical. Efforts to reproduce this glass in the 19th century in Venice and elsewhere were only partially successful.

Early Northern European glass

A SEPARATE PROVINCIAL tradi-tion of glassmaking occurred in Northern medieval Europe, especially in the areas that we now know as Germany, and in the South of England. *Waldglas* or forest glass was made in the woodland regions of central Europe, and generally stained green in colour by the wood ash

from the timber furnaces. The best-known vessels are *roemers*. Later, in the 16th and 17th cen-tury, German glassmakers based in towns and small settle-ments rather than in forests or woodland, produced some of the finest communal drinking vessels – *humpen* – of a straw-tinted glass decorated with brightly enamelled coats of arms, many of which were dated.

Right
WINE GLASSES
ENGLISH Early 18th C.

Left
HUMPEN, DRINKING VESSEL
GERMAN 1652

The emergence of the English style

THE DEVELOPMENT OF lead crystal meant that not only was the glass a great deal more robust and less liable to the 'crizzling' which affects much soda glass causing it to disintegrate internally, but it was also more brilliant in colour and softer so that it could be deeply engraved. English glassmakers at first continued to produce glass in the style that they were used to – namely Venetian. However, a more idiosyncratic approach was adopted, influenced by architectural forms, and a definite English style began to emerge.

Trailed decoration, whereby threads of glass were laid onto the surface of the vessel, is a continuation of the earlier Venetian tradition, whilst the moulded 'gadroons' found on posset pots and sweetmeat glasses closely resemble silverware at this date. However, it is drinking glasses which are amongst the most collectable items of the 18th century. Traditionally made in either two or three sections – the bowl,

stem and foot – the variety of shapes and forms provides a rich range of wares from which one may form a collection. Although the rarer items can fetch several thousand pounds it is still possible for collectors to purchase early 18th century glasses at reasonable prices.

With changing fashions, each section of a wine glass was adapted, too. Economics have also had an important part to play in these developments. The changing shapes provide a guide to date glasses more accurately. From the heavy balusters of the first quarter of the 18th century, their stems based on the architectural baluster, such as one finds on a staircase, and combining a variety of 'knops' such as mushroom, acorn or simple ball shapes, to the light balusters of the mid-18th century with their slender multi-knopped stems, one can see the evolution of the English wine glass.

The shape of the bowl has evolved generally from the Anglo-Venetian styles of the 17th century, but by the mid-

18th century recognizable types appeared which were peculiar to England alone. The capacity of bowls continued to decrease throughout the century and with the introduction of the glass excise tax in 1745 with its emphasis on the weight of the glass, the style of drinking glass-generally became much lighter. The size of the bowl may also be an indication of its intended use. Deep and rounded funnel bowls were most probably designed for drinking short ale. Smaller capacity bowls on tall stems were for cordial, whilst the average-sized bowl can correctly be referred to as a wine glass.

Single bubbles, or tears, of air found in the stems and knops of the earlier heavy balusters were incorporated as concentric beading in ball knops on light balusters and used more elaborately from the 1740s to produce airtwist-stemmed wine glasses and goblets. The domed and folded foot, a typical feature of pre-1745 glass, wass replaced by a conical foot which uses less glass in its design.

A further development from about the 1760s is the introduction of opaque-white enamel canes into the stems to form intricate spirals and gauzes of a similar nature to the earlier airtwist variety. Closely resembling Venetian glass *latticinio* and *lattimo* techniques of the 15th and 16th centuries, these were made by initially juxtapositioning the required number of short thick canes of enamel and encasing them in a gather of clear glass. The glass was then drawn out, sometimes to a length of thirty feet – the canes being twisted at the same time. On completion, the rod of twisted glass was cut into three-inch lengths, each length applied to a previously-blown wine-glass bowl. A disc foot, shaped from a gather of glass held by the glassmaker's assistant on the tip of a pontil rod, is added to the other end to make a three-piece wine glass. Coloured canes of various shades of red, blue, yellow and green were popular in the 1770s but this fashion was short-lived. This makes colour-twists, as they are generally known, quite rare, consequently highly desirable and expensive for the average collector.

The advent of glass-cutting in the mid-century saw by the 1770s the introduction of facet-cut stems. Bowls and feet were usually left plain, though the pontil – the rough mark often found on the underside of the foot where it was broken away from the pontil rod – was often ground away. The existence of a pontil mark is not a guarantee of age as this method of attaching feet to stems is still used by glassmakers today.

Glass decoration and engraving

THE WORK OF glass decorators – engravers, enamellers, gilders and cutters – adds greater value to the product. Engraving techniques were perfected in the 18th century both in England and on the Continent. The use of a diamond-point on Venetian and Dutch glass either to incise or stipple-engrave – i.e. building-up feint pictures from a series of dots leaving one with the impression that the image has been breathed on to the glass surface – was popular in the 17th and 18th centuries. By 1720, wheel-engraving, using a spinning copper wheel, had been developed which allowed the engraver literally to slice away at the surface of the glass. Some of the leading exponents of this technique were Dutch, Jacob Sang (1725–69) being one of the best known. Sang decorated light baluster wine glasses with ship portraits in particular. This type of glass has until recently been called a 'Newcastle light baluster' since it was thought for almost a century that the Dutch engravers imported their wine glass blanks from the long-established glass-making centre at Newcastle-upon-Tyne. We now know, however, that lead crystal was also manufactured in the Low Countries in styles similar to those which have long been considered to be typically English, so much of this Dutch engraved glass is probably of local origin. It is now known, too, that the Dutch also made opaque-twist and colour-twist glasses, and experts are still endeavouring to differentiate between English and Continental lead crystal examples.

English 18th century glass engravers were also responsible for some fine work. Engraved decoration can add a substantial amount to the value of a glass, especially if the engraving commemorates a significant datable event. Toasting or commemorative glass associated with the Protestant William III, bearing equestrian portraits of the king as a celebration of the Battle of the Boyne of 1690, and Jacobite glass in support of the Old and Young Pretenders, James Edward Stuart and his son Charles, fetch very high prices at auction. As a result this type of glass has been forged especially in the 1920s and 1930s after in-depth research on English glass, drew attention to the special clandestine nature of such glasses. As much 18th century engraving was of poor quality it is not difficult for a 20th century engraver to acquire a plain 18th century glass and copy the engraved subject of an original example from either a photograph, book illustration or a drawing. Collectors beware!

In the 1930s, several Midlands glassmakers produced airtwist glass, Jacobite glass and other popular 18th century styles which were widely advertised as legitimate reproductions. Today, some unscrupulous antique dealers have taken these later examples and aged them by adding wear to the feet.

Enamelling of English glass is generally quite rare, with the exception of that produced in Newcastle-upon-Tyne between 1760 and 1775 by William Beilby. His goblets and decanters painted with highly elaborate armorials, a few of which are signed, fetch very high prices. Traditionally a Continental art form, Beilby enamelled glass is amongst the most desirable and the most expensive of 18th century English glass.

Gilding of coloured glass towards the end of the 18th century was a speciality of Bristol glasshouses. Coloured glass – especially blue, green and amethyst – produced in Bristol and in other parts of the country, often bears gilt decoration. Decanters, cruets, wine glasses and other table wares of coloured glass were generally made between 1790 and 1820. The rarest and most collectable of coloured glasses are generally earlier in date, circa 1750–60, and possess composite stems such as a green-tinted ribbed mead or champagne glass with an opaque-twist stem encased in colourless glass and a green-tinted foot – or have unusual bowl and stem forms – honeycomb-moulded bowls, for example, and incised or airtwist stems.

Below

TWO GILDED GLASS FINGER BOWLS
BRISTOL, ENGLAND c.1810

Bowls, vases, candlesticks and tea cannisters in opaque white glass, enamelled in the manner of porcelain, or gilded, was the main speciality of the South Staffordshire area in the 1760s, and although often highly attractive, disappointingly their value is considerably less than their porcelain counterparts.

Cut glass

CUT GLASS WAS produced in both Ireland and England in response to the heavy penalties imposed by the glass excise tax on the weight of glass. This style reached the peak of perfection in the period 1800 to 1820. There were several factories operating in Ireland, and a distinct Irish style emerged. However, unless clearly marked with the name of an Irish glasshouse this glass is not as popular as the earlier plainer English forms. Surprisingly, it is still possible to buy intricate Irish jugs, boat-shaped bowls and covered jars for half the price of a plain English 18th century decanter. A marked Irish decanter, on the other hand, usually exceeds all expectation at auction.

Above
GLASS VASE ENAMELLED IN CHINESE STYLE
SOUTH STAFFORDSHIRE
ENGLAND c.1760

Right
CUT GLASS
ENGLISH AND IRISH
Early 19th C.

European glass

FROM THE LATE 17th century separate traditions evolved from the various glassmaking areas based especially in Central Europe.

The engravers of the Low Countries were responsible for some of the finest copperwheel engraved wine glasses, many of which portray elaborate ships or bacchanalian scenes and are inscribed with sentiments of goodwill and friendship.

Stipple engraving – the image desired is produced by many tiny shallow dots indented in the surface – is amongst the finest of the work of Dutch engravers such as Frans Greenwood and, later, David Wolff. They employed images which include attractive coats of arms - particularly those of the House of Orange.

Above
GOBLETS ENGRAVED WITH ROYAL MOTIFS
ENGLISH AND GERMAN
c.1750

Below
'ZWISCHEN-GOLDGLAS' HUNTING BEAKERS
BOHEMIAN c.1730

Right
COPPER WHEEL ENGRAVED WINE GLASS
DUTCH c.1750

Engravers in Germany from the late 17th century onwards decorated characteristically tall goblets and covers using relief and intaglio cutting methods. From 1700, polished highlights enhanced the engraving's sculptural effects. Engravers of German glass were often itinerant, peddling their wares around the Continent and undertaking commissions when called upon to do so.

The products of Saxony, Silesia and Thuringia can often be distinguished by their characteristic bowl shapes, stem forms and foot types. The many glassmakers of Bohemia, however, copied some of these forms but in a less elaborate manner. Coloured glass, especially ruby, emerged in the last quarter of the 17th century when Joseph Kunckel developed *rubinglas* by adding gold to the clear molten glass. Such items often have silver or silver-gilt mounted feet and covers. This glass is highly prized and, like the precious metal mounts adorning it, an example can be quite costly. The silversmiths of Augsburg and Nuremburg were closely associated with the glassmakers and supplied much of the metal mountings.

Scandinavia was much less influenced by Venice than other countries, producing by around c.1780 German-style cut and engraved glass and chandeliers and wine glasses which closely resemble typical English products. This may have something to do with a small number of immigrant English craftsmen from Newcastle-upon-Tyne. Some Norwegian glass bears engraved decoration which is highlighted with gilding, the glass being of a slightly cloudy nature. Although closely resembling English and Dutch glass, 18th century Scandinavian glass is inexpensive and not highly regarded by collectors.

Some of the coarsest glass was produced for the Russian market by Saxon and Bohemian glasshouses. Whilst a limited number of glasshouses operated in St Petersburg in Russia, imported glass often bears Russian crests and sentiments in cyrillic characters or is decorated with the imperial arms of the Czars and Czarinas.

American glass

AMERICAN 18TH CENTURY glass, like that of Scandinavia, was largely based on English imports or on small pockets of immigrant German makers working in Pennsylvania in the glasshouses of the Cologne-born Henry William Stiegel (1729-85). It was in the 19th century with the development of press-moulded glass, in the 1820s, that most American glassware developed an independent style which was later to be partly copied by the Europeans

Below
GLASSES WITH COLOURED ENAMEL THREADS
FRENCH Mid 19th C.

The 19th century

DURING THE FIRST half of the 19th century, cut glass was the dominant style in Europe, affecting most of the popular glass shapes. By 1850 elaborate cut glass, especially from Bohemia and France, highlighted the innovation and skills which characterized the century. Developments in design in the decorative arts throughout the 18th and 19th centuries were mirrored in glass products.

Clear cut glass was superseded by vividly coloured glass made by flashing or staining the glass. The new forms became massive, were intricately cut, and generally quite coarse in appearance. New techniques of glass staining were developed, the most popular colours adopted being ruby and amber. The surfaces were cut through or engraved to reveal the colourless glass below. This style was particularly popular between 1815 and 1848 where new shades of yellow were developed from uranium. Engraved decoration often features scenes of deer – especially stags – in continuous woodland landscapes wrapped around the bowls of covered goblets, vases and jars.

Towards the end of the 19th century cranberry glass, pinkish ruby, was fashionable, some of which was turned into unusual decorative items for Indian palaces.

Popular Bohemian products were overlaid decanters and vases made by coating transparent coloured or colourless glass with a layer of opaque coloured glass, particularly white. They were often picked out with gilding and enamelled flowers, occasionally depicting portraits of young girls or embellished with paste gemstones. There were many glasshouses in North and South Bohemia Some years ago their products were often considered tasteless and were dismissed by serious collectors of glass. Today they are amongst the most sought after.

Above
GROUP OF TALL FLASHED AND ENGRAVED GOBLETS AND COVERS
BOHEMIAN c.1850–60

Left
**PAIR OF GREEN GLASS
OVERLAY LUSTRES**
BOHEMIAN Late 19th C.

Below
SALVIATI & CO
FACON DE VENISE EWER
VENETIAN c.1870

Right
**LATE VICTORIAN PRESS-
MOULDED GLASS FROM
MIDLANDS AND NORTHERN
GLASSMAKERS**
ENGLISH Late 19th C.

After about 1860, historical revival glass was a speciality of Bohemian, Venetian and Austrian glasshouses. Direct reproductions were made in these countries as well as inspired copies of earlier glass examples. It was not produced with the intention of deceiving and is today greatly undervalued and sadly ignored. On the other hand, the similar *façon de Venise* revival wares of some English manufacturers, such as James Powell and Sons' Whitefriars Glass at the turn of the 20th century, is highly desirable because it is considered to have artistic merit.

Press-moulded glass

THE TECHNIQUE OF making press-moulded glass was first patented in the United States in the 1820s and introduced to Europe at some point in the 1830s. It was made in the English Midlands and in France

and Belgium, particularly, and was to revolutionize the glass industry by providing cheap mass-produced copies of luxury glasswares. Today, pressed glass is widely collected because unlike so much antique glass it can be identified. The attaching of a label to a product is always significant for the collector which is why this market has grown so convincingly. T h e fancier ornamental wares of Midlands and Northern glass-makers are highly sought after, with collectors eager to find unusually coloured or limited production examples. The manufacture of pressed glass has continued into this century and is perhaps now the standard method by which most cheap glass is made.

19th century engraved and cameo glass

COLOURLESS ENGRAVED GLASS continued to be produced in most glass making countries during the 19th century, often accompanied by cut decoration such as strawberry diamond or hobnail cutting and facets. Subjects found engraved on English glass include commemorative themes, masonic devices, racehorses, inscriptions for marriages or christenings, views of buildings and popular sentiments amongst many others. By the 1860s, tableglass was manufactured in large quantities in the Stourbridge area, much of it decorated by acid-etching.

By 1900 the Stourbridge firm of Thomas Webb were producing designs of overlapping flowers, delicately drawn marine life or intricate scrollwork, carved out of semi-translucent white glass which had been laid over a coloured glass ground.

Above
COIN GOBLETS AND RUMMER
ENGLISH
Early and Mid 19th C.

Below
THOMAS WEBB
CAMEO GLASS VASES
ENGLISH c.1880–90

Encased glass

ENCASED GLASS SUCH as paper-weights and *crystallo ceramie* (or sulphides) was popular from the start of the 19th century. The technique of encasing white porcellaneous cameos and medallions of prominent people in colourless glass was first developed in Bohemia and then patented in France and England. Paperweights were manufactured in large quantities in France, Germany and in Bohemia from the 1830s, the classic period being 1845–55.

Paperweights were the cornerstone of the glass industry for which France is remembered now. These paperweights came in three different sizes: miniature (under 5cm), average (between 5 and 10cm) and the magnum weights, which were over 10cm in diameter. The factory at Baccarat dated several of their weights from 1846 to 1849 and sometimes put a small 'b' beside the date. They are the easiest of the French paperweights to identify, having many small distinguishing 'trade marks'. Baccarat produced mushrooms, snakes, butterflies and flower weights in profuse variety.

The St Louis factory weights are also quite distinctive. Their colours are far softer than those of Baccarat and for some years they were also dated, sometimes with the initials 'S.L.' preceding the date. St Louis is most famous for its fruit weights set on latticinio baskets and hollow-blown crown weights.

Clichy weights were very different. Their colours were bright and attractive. The most famous of their 'trade marks' was a very small stylized rose, which came in several colours and varieties, the most common being a distinctive pink.

Paperweights were also made in Italy at Murano by Pietro Bigaglia, by English firms such as Whitefriars and in the United States the most notable were made by the New England Glass Co. The French weights are the most collectable with some examples attracting many thousands of pounds.

Above
BACCARAT PAPERWEIGHT PANSY ENCASED IN GLASS
FRENCH c.1850

The use of the artist designer

TOWARDS THE END of the 19th century the role of the artist designer was developed and glass vessels and ornaments incorporated the designs and styles of leading craftsmen of the period. During the 1890s the Art Nouveau style was adapted to glassware – especially vases – using *pâte de verre* (glass paste made from ground glass, fused together in a mould) and cameo techniques. Émile Gallé's oriental-inspired carved cameo glass and *pâte de verre*, with its fluidity, subtle colour tones and its emphasis on natural forms, has in recent years become amongst the most sought after glass. His enamelled work, which like his cameo, was generally signed, was also inspired by oriental forms. It reveals, too, his interest in nature, an idea which is central to the Art Nouveau movement of which he is one of the leading lights.

In the United States, the style was promoted by Louis Comfort Tiffany, who produced some of the most glorious coloured glass of the 20th century. From iridescent stained glass windows to vases and tablelamp shades, Tiffany's products now attract huge sums at auction.

Contemporary European glass firms such as Loetz in Austria were influenced by Tiffany and they even exported their Tiffany-like products to the United States. Today, as this glass increases steadily in value, the similar but poorer quality unmarked wares of rival Bohemian firms are frequently passed off as Loetz.

By the early 20th century glassmaking had reached a very significant point in the development of style. Even despite the conservatism of much industrially produced glass of this time, experimentation in the 1920s and 1930s led to a broadening of the distinction between glass as a luxury ornament and the work of art in glass. New mass-produced ranges which came from European and American glassmakers included a limitless variety of vases, tableware, dressing-table items and jewellery. It is through the artist-designer René Lalique, who was both versatile in glassmaking and jewellery manufacture, that the gap between Art Nouveau and the later Art Deco style is bridged. Initially manufacturing perfume bottles for Coty, he established a glass factory near Paris around 1908 making large quantities of moulded, pressed and engraved glass. He was interested in surface treatment by acid or sand-blasting, resulting in a frosty opalescence. As a follower of Émile Gallé, Lalique made pieces in Art Nouveau fashion until he developed his own original style. His best-known glass was produced after 1925 which, although colourless, has a pale blue opalescent matt surface.

After 1900 many artist designers became involved in the mass-production of glass. In England, the United States and in Continental Europe ranges of glassware produced by cheap factory methods such as press-moulding were created by some of the leading designers of the day. Important Austrian and German architects designed glass tablewares, as well as other domestic items in wood, ceramics and metal. This is particularly true of the Vienna Secession movement prior to the First World War, where Josef Hoffman and Kolo Moser were chief among those involved in a unique design production. This helped to produce a comprehensive personal style into which all the decorative arts could fit.

Whilst individual pieces by leading designers command high prices today and may be in many cases outside the pocket of the average collector, it is glass of a more popular mass-produced nature which is attracting the attention of many glass devotees. In Europe, the press-moulded wares made for table and sideboard are actively pursued. Prices can be quite low for the more common pieces. In America, the most popular type of glass is known as 'Depression' glass. This is a term applied to a wide range of cheap ornamental and useful wares, often coloured pink, green and yellow and made in the 1920s and 1930s.

Depression glass is often confused with 'Carnival' glass, a similar cheap mass-produced ware which was given away as prizes at fairgrounds and bought as trinkets at inexpensive stores. Such wares – plates, jugs, bowls – are iridized in either rich peacock-feather hues or an orange marigold colour and were made both in Europe and in the United States around the time of and just after the First World War.

Apart from Lalique, high quality glass of the 1920s and 30s in the Art Deco style is still comparatively inexpensive. Individual French and Swedish designer wares are naturally keenly sought after and their productions in part heralded what is now termed 'studio-glass' – a movement which emerged more strongly in the early 1960s. However, the wares of British manufacturers of the 1930s, like Thomas Webb and Stuart and Sons and others working in the Stourbridge region of the West Midlands, are by comparison relatively undervalued. Some of these firms employed leading designers of ceramics such as Keith Murray. Collectors may be richly rewarded if they find examples today, as such glasses, together with those products of the current studio glass movement, are likely to be amongst the leading glass antiques of the future.

Below
GLASS VASES MADE BY LEADING DESIGNERS
ENGLISH MIDLANDS 1930s

SILVER

CHARLES TRUMAN

Above

QUENN ANNE SILVER EWER

ENGLISH 1705

Because of its comparative scarcity, its weight, solidity and immediate appeal through its brilliant reflective surface, silver is classed amongst the precious metals. Indeed until the dawn of the 19th century it shared this status with gold alone. After gold, silver is the most malleable and ductile of metals which makes it an ideal vehicle for design and decoration. From about 4000 BC, silver was used as ornamentation, but wrought silver vessels have only survived from between 2500 and 2000 BC. From about 800 BC until the early years of the 20th century, silver was also used as money.

Silver is found only rarely as a native metal, but it is alloyed naturally with gold in Electrum and in ores, the principal of which is galena or lead sulphide. This ore was smelted and the silver was separated from the lead by the process of 'cupellation'. This technique, which was used throughout the Middle East and Greece as early as about 2000 BC, involves the lead/silver alloy being heated over bone ash, causing the lead to oxidize and run off through the ash leaving a deposit of pure silver. The resulting metal was considered too soft to work satisfactorily and was frequently alloyed with another metal, usually copper in varying proportions. In England the sterling standard used is 92.5% pure silver but 80% and 96% are not uncommon in Europe.

At one time, the main silver-producing countries of the world were Germany, Spain and Austro-Hungary. However following the discovery of silver in Peru in 1533 and the uncovering during the 19th century of huge deposits in the United States, Canada and Australia and quantities in India, Burma, Siberia and Japan, by the start of the 20th century Europe only provided one tenth of the world's output.

Making and working silver

THERE ARE TWO principal methods of making silver artefacts, which remain virtually unchanged through time until toda. These techniques are casting and raising.

In the first, silver is melted and poured in liquid form into a prepared mould. On cooling it solidifies, shrinks a little and may be removed from the mould. Whole vessels may be made in this fashion, or parts of vessels such as decorative details may be made and applied by solder to a larger piece.

In the second method known as raising, a flat sheet of metal is hammered over various 'stakes' or anvils literally to raise the metal into vessel form.

There are a variety of decorative techniques available to the silversmith. The most usual methods are embossing, with the metal being struck from the back, and chasing, which is the reciprocal technique with the metal being worked from the front. In neither technique is any metal removed. Silver may also be engraved in which case the surface of the metal is cut away with a burin or sharp steel tool.

Right
SILVER-GILT BALUSTER VASES
CHARLES II
ENGLISH 1660s

Silver may also be decorated by the addition of other metals or metallic compounds. Filigree, strands of wire twisted into decorative patterns, or granulation, tiny pellets of metal, may be soldered to the surface. But the most common metal to be added to the surface of silver is gold, in the form of gilding. Until comparatively recently this was achieved by 'mercury' or 'fire' gilding. This requires an amalgam of gold and mercury being painted on to the surface of the silver and heated until the mercury evaporates, leaving the gold adhering to the silver. The process is exceedingly dangerous, as the mercury vapour is lethal, and was replaced in the 1840s by electroplating.

From antiquity to the Renaissance

BECAUSE OF ITS unique link between taste and wealth, silver was always intended for display as well as use. Homer describes the wealth of silver (and gold), used for display by the ancient Greek heroes and much survives from the Bronze Age cities of Greece and the Eastern Mediterranean, such as Mycenae and Knossos. This tradition of the conspicuous display of silver runs until at least the mid-19th century. A rich man was expected to show off his wealth and the principal way in which he did it was with silver.

Above

WILLIAM IV SILVER TANKARD

Trophy for the King's Cup Yachting race at Cowes.

ENGLISH 1830

There were two prime areas in a household where such displays were customary. The main one was in the dining room where silver was displayed not only on the sideboard, or buffet, where many pieces had an ornamental rather than a functional purpose, but on the table where the functional aspect was, of course, much more important. Certainly from the Renaissance, and probably even from Classical times, the most significant pieces of plate on the sideboard were large dishes, ewers and basins, whose functional use in the ritual of hand-washing was made obsolete by the introduction of the fork in the 17th century. Vases were also important, together

with a 'fountain', a vase-shaped vessel with a tap for water, and, at the base of the buffet, a cistern which served the dual purpose of chilling bottles and receiving the water from the fountain which stood above it.

The second setting for a display of plate was in the state bedroom, or its antechamber, where plate associated with the toilet was shown. It is perhaps not without significance that in both these rooms a rich man was at his most vulnerable, either eating or sleeping, and such displays of wealth, and in consequence power, were contrived as an antidote to these periods of weakness.

The habit of burying plate in tombs or to avoid discovery during the period of the barbarian invasions has resulted in the survival of a disproportionate amount of silver dating from the period between the time of Alexander the Great and the late Roman Empire (roughly from the 4th century BC to the 4th century AD). However most of what has survived is in the great museum collections of Europe and North America.

Whilst accounts survive to give a mouthwatering idea of the riches of court life from the 4th to the 14th century, very little secular silver survives, although there is a certain amount of extant church metalwork, by no means all of it in precious metal. Two types of silver objects dominated in the so-called Dark Ages:

the cup, of beaker form, and the *Hanap,* which was a shallow bowl. The custom of mounting classical vessels in precious metals is preserved in the treasury of St Maurice d'Agaunne, Switzerland. Of early church plate to have survived the most remarkable are the altar frontal by the goldsmith Wolvinus in the mid-9th century in the church of San Ambrogio, Milan, and the cross of Lothair, in gold set with gems, in the cathedral at Aachen which dates from about the year 1,000 AD. Of surviving chalices the most famous is probably that from Ardagh in Ireland and now in the National Museum of Antiquities, Dublin.

From the mid-13th century the influence of the Gothic style is found in metalwork, but still the majority of extant pieces are for ecclesiastical use. One can only guess at the magnificence of court life from manuscripts and the handful of extant pieces.

The Gothic style was replaced by classicizing motifs during the Renaissance. Originating in Italy, the style rapidly spread throughout Europe, although it had been virtually abandoned in the purest form in its birthplace almost as soon as it had crossed the Alps. Once again the amount of surviving plate is very small, but it is apparent that so far as silver is concerned Classical ornament was soon imbued with another decorative

style, the Mauresque, introduced from the East through Venice. As Italian craftsmen travelled north and as Italian engraved sources circulated in Germany, France and even England, or as Northern designers and craftsmen visited Italy, there emerged a curious compression of styles in Northern Europe where the Gothic style lingered into the 16th century, but was replaced by Mannerist ornament from the 1540s, giving very little scope for the absorption of pure Renaissance ideas.

During the 16th and 17th centuries national distinctions become blurred. Craftsmen and designers did not adhere to national boundaries, and in consequence one finds that the court goldsmith to the Medici in Florence was a Fleming Jacques Bylivelt; Hans Holbein moved from Switzerland to paint and design silver and jewellery for Henry VIII in London; and Benvenuto Cellini left Italy for the court of François I at Fontainebleau. Indeed Cellini is the most informative of all goldsmiths since he left an autobiography and a treatise on goldsmithing. For example, he tells of the salt now in the Kunsthistorisches Museum, Vienna, made for François I of France in 1543, which represents the 'Sea and the Earth seated' and a 'little temple of Ionic architecture . . . to contain the pepper'.

Northern European silverwork

THE PRINCIPAL CENTRES of innovation were Nuremberg and Augsburg in Southern Germany and Antwerp in Flanders. Nuremberg was the home of arguably the greatest of all goldsmiths of the 16th century, Wenzel Jamnitzer (1535–85). Jamnitzer was not only technically superior to virtually all his contemporaries, he possessed a skill in design and inventiveness unparalleled in the history of the craft. Much of his work has been lost but amongst his greatest triumphs are the Merckel centrepiece in the Rijksmuseum, Amsterdam, bought by the Nuremberg City Corporation in 1549, the silver-gilt mounted trochus shell ewer of 1570 in the Residenz-museum, Munich, and a jewel casket now in the Green Vaults, Dresden, made in 1562. In Antwerp, the designers of silver, were Hans Vriedman de Vries, Adriacn Collaert and Erasmus Hornick, although the latter in fact lived in Nuremberg for the later part of his life.

With so very many itinerant designers and workers, the Goldsmiths' Company of London decided to regulate the standard of silver used by devising and introducing a series of identifying marks which were intended to be a symbol of quality control. Since they were struck at Goldsmiths' Hall, they became known as hall-marks.

English silver in the 16th and 17th centuries

ENGLAND'S MOST SIGNIFICANT contribution at this date to the history of silver is the development of the great salt. From its late Gothic form, the so-called 'hourglass', composed of one conical section inverted upon another, the standing salt became, in the 16th century, a Mannerist column of relatively broad section, with a depression at the top for the salt, and frequently with a cover supported on scrolled brackets. These salts were set on the right hand of the most important person at the table, and lesser salts of comparable but simpler form were placed amongst the cups and trenchers. This is the origin of the phrase 'below the salt', meaning someone of distinctly lowly origin.

Silversmiths in the Low Countries

DURING THE EARLY years of the 17th century, artistic impetus in silver moved to the Low Countries, and specifically to Utrecht where the brothers Adam (1569–1626) and Paul (1570–1613) van Vianen pioneered the transition from the Mannerist to the Auricular style. The style developed the scroll into complex relief forms reminiscent of the shape of the human ear and appeared soon after 1610 when Paul returned to Flanders to work with his brother. The fluid contours of the plate that they produced were made possible by their extraordinary skill in the techniques of raising, embossing and chasing. Such was the fame of the family that Adam's son Christian (1600–37) who continued to work in his father's style, became court goldsmith to Charles I of England. Sadly all has been lost apart from three pieces, a basin in the Victoria and Albert Museum, and a salver and a covered bowl both in the collection of the Duke of Northumberland.

17th Century French style

BY THE MIDDLE of the 17th century a new style had begun to emerge in France. This was the use of lush scrolling foliage, frequently embossed in high relief, to decorate broad surfaces of silver. A silver-gilt coffer of about 1645, commissioned by Cardinal Mazarin, and now in the Louvre, is the earliest example but the style finds full range in the magnificent vases, tables and toilet services of the reign of Charles II in England. In fact surviving French silver from the late 17th century is very rare, having been the subject of a great melt down ordered by Louis XIV to help pay for the War of the Spanish Succession. The best evidence for the glories of French silver at this time is provided by illustrations in paintings and tapestries, and

Above

CHARLES II TOILET SERVICE
ENGLISH 1675–6

from English silver, much of which was made by Huguenot craftsmen who fled France after the removal of religious tolerance in 1685.

The great watershed in the history of English silver is the Restoration of the Monarchy in 1660. The court of Charles II moved from France to London bringing with it all the ideas which were current at Versailles. It was there that the taste for silver furniture developed, before spreading through Europe. In England, three suites survive, two comprising a table, a mirror, and a pair of candlestands, one at Knole in Kent, the other in the Royal Collection; the third, without candlestands, is also at Windsor Castle.

Electroplating

DURING THE SECOND quarter of the 19th century there were many experiments with electrolysis and electroplating. Several patents were bought up by the firm of Elkington & Co of Birmingham until by about 1846 they held a virtual monopoly. Unlike Old Sheffield Plate, where pieces were made from the plated sheet metal, items to be electroplated were first produced complete in base metal before plating. This means that certain elements could be cast, and there were no signs of the base metal showing through at the edges. In addition, instead of the base metal being copper, nickel alloys were also used and this yellow coloured metal can frequently be found showing through rubbed areas of silver plating.

English silverplate

THE FRENCH TASTE dominated table and sideboard plate at this period. Silver fountains, cisterns, dishes, ewers and basins, decorated with cast applied strapwork in the Régence taste after Jean Berain (1640-1711), abound in England but side by side this French style two other particularly English fashions in silver developed. In the 1680s the taste grew for silver flat-chased with chinoiserie figures, birds and foliage. Also found at the turn of the century is a taste for plain silver, devoid of all ornament but whose effect is enhanced by the play of light on the flat reflecting surfaces.

Another more common form introduced at the end of the century was the single bottle wine cooler or ice pail, which could be set on the table for an individual to serve himself rather than summoning a servant. The earliest English examples (1698) are at Chatsworth in Derbyshire, and a gold pair presented by Queen Anne to the first Duke of Marlborough is in the British Museum. However their use was still rare enough to cause comment at Versailles in the 1730s.

Glasses were frequently cooled and rinsed at the sideboard, or more informally at the table in a vessel with a notched rim called a 'Monteith', after a fantastical Scot of the same name who wore a scallop-edged cloak. The form is first recorded in 1683, and frequently the rim detaches to allow the bowl to be used for punch. In addition the newly acquired habit of drinking tea and coffee led to the development of plate associated with them. The principals were of course the tea and coffee pots, but tea caddies, kettles, milk jugs and even cups and saucers in silver appear. However beer and wine cups which had been so popular earlier in the century completely disappear with the introduction of good glassware.

The great revival in the use of silver led to a shortage of coin which had been melted to form wrought plate. To inhibit this trend, Parliament raised the standard of the silver used for plate to 95.8% in 1697. With the new standard, called New Sterling, came a rise in the cost of plate leading the goldsmiths to petition for the return of the old standard and from 1720 a choice of standards became available.

Below
QUEEN ANNE WINE COOLERS
ENGLISH c.1710

Rococo silver

IN FRANCE AGAIN, a new spirit of restlessness emerged to bring about the new style we now know as Rococo. Its greatest protagonist was a goldsmith born in Turin of French extraction, Juste Aurele Meissonnier (1695–1750). Principally a chaser and designer, he was admitted to the Paris Guild of Goldsmiths by Royal command but he preferred to style himself *Architecte*. He only appears to have marked one piece, a gold box made in Paris in 1728, but a pair of tureens bears his signature and a candelabrum closely follows his designs. All three were made between 1734 and 1738 for the Duke of Kingston. Much more prolific was Thomas Germain (1720–48), the French Royal goldsmith who espoused the rococo style and imbued it with an elegance unrivalled. His son, François-Thomas, continued in his father's style working also for the Portuguese and Russian monarchs.

However in England the most famous of the goldsmiths working in the rococo style was Paul de Lamerie (1688–1751). Of the French *petit noblesse*, de Lamerie arrived in London from Holland at the age of three. In 1703, he was apprenticed to another Huguenot, Pierre Platel, becoming free of the Goldsmiths' Company in 1713. He apparently had a considerable trade with Russia for he supplied two silver chandeliers,

probably for the Empress Anna, which hang in the treasury of the Kremlin. In 1726 de Lamerie was also involved in the trial of a Mr Dingley who was accused of exporting unhallmarked silver to Russia, over 2,000 ounces of which was by de Lamerie. However, his best-known commission is the extraordinary ewer and basin made in 1741 for the Goldsmiths' Company. De Lamerie was not alone in his adoption of the rococo style in silver. Nicholas Sprimont, a native of Liege, and better known as the founder of the Chelsea Porcelain Factory, worked as a silversmith in England from 1743 until 1749. His salts formed as shells and crayfish on a rock-work ground, derived from designs by Meissonnier and made in 1743 for Frederick, Prince of Wales, are still in the Royal Collection. Another goldsmith of distinction was George Wickes (1722–59) whose work is made especially interesting by the survival of his firm's ledgers which detail his commissions for the Prince of Wales and for Judge John Scrope in 1735 by the City of Bristol.

Silver and the Industrial Revolution

TECHNICAL DEVELOPMENTS IN metalwork enabled silver plate to be produced much more cheaply. In the mid-18th century, Thomas Boulsover developed Old Sheffield Plate, a process whereby sheets of silver are fused onto an ingot of copper and passed through rolling mills until it reaches a thickness suitable for raising. It enabled craftsmen to produce pieces at a fraction of the cost of silver. Various new techniques were introduced in the Industrial Revolution which made the process increasingly attractive commercially. Many of the techniques were also adopted by the goldsmiths of Sheffield and Birmingham.

In England the early 19th century was dominated by the Royal goldsmiths, Rundell, Bridge and Rundell, who had two workshops for their vast output, one at Lime Kiln Lane, Greenwich, run by Benjamin Smith, and the other at Dean Street, Soho, run by Paul Storr. With a design studio under the control of William Theed and employing John Flaxman, Thomas Stothard and Edward Hodges Baily, the firm adapted classical forms to contemporary use.

In almost total contrast to Rundells, the silver of the French Empire, designed by Charles Percier, achieves a lightness and elegance quite different to the solid 'Roman' English silver.

The Gothic revival

THE SECOND QUARTER of the 19th century was a period of reflection. The most dominant style in silver was the revived Rococo, championed by Paul Storr, free from the reins of Rundells, and by the firm of Robert Garrard. However, by 1830 the influence of the Gothic Revival was felt, with A. W. N. Pugin, who had worked for Rundells, designing silver, especially church plate in the Gothic style. Pugin's collaboration with the Birmingham firm of John Hardman & Co. led to some of the most spirited examples of Neo-Gothic plate.

The middle of the century is epitomized by the Great Exhibition of 1851 where plate of mediaeval, gothic, Renaissance and rococo taste were all on show. The major goldsmiths at this date were Elington and Co. in Birmingham, Hunt and Roskell (successor to Paul Storr), Garrards and Hancocks. The antiquarian taste survived throughout the century, to such an extent that at the Paris Exhibition of 1900, the Goldsmiths and Silversmiths Company were exhibiting replicas of pieces in the Victoria and Albert Museum.

There was an inevitable move away from this somewhat sterile attitude and the increased use of mechanical aids in the production of silver. The influence of John Ruskin and William Morris led to the establishment of the Art Workers' Guild in 1884 and whihc bred a number of Arts and Crafts goldsmiths at the close of the century. Without doubt the most famous of these is C. R. Ashbee (1863–1942) who began the School of Handicraft in London in 1888. A comparable body, the Birmingham Guild, was established two years later. The goldsmiths in these guilds and the commercial firms which copied them, such as Liberty and Co, were joined by a small body of artist-craftsmen who should be mentioned here; Alexander Fisher, Nelson Dawson, John Paul Cooper, Gilbert Marks and Omar Ramsden. This last had the habit of signing his work 'Omar Ramsden me fecit' to suggest a personal involvement in the manufacture. In fact he ran a relatively large workshop and is reputed to have given a hand-beaten finish to commercially manufactured plate that he bought in.

However, the Arts and Crafts movement fell to the onslaught of Modernism. Heralded by Dr Christopher Dresser's designs for silver and electron plate for Hukin and Heath in Sheffield in the 1870s, and by the Weine Werkstatte in Austria and Puiforcat in France, the movement in England is represented by the goldsmiths H. G. Murphy, Harold Stabler and the designer R. M. Y. Gleadowe. The emphasis was on plain polished surfaces, sometimes engraved, and clean crisp lines.

JEWELLERY
AND FANS

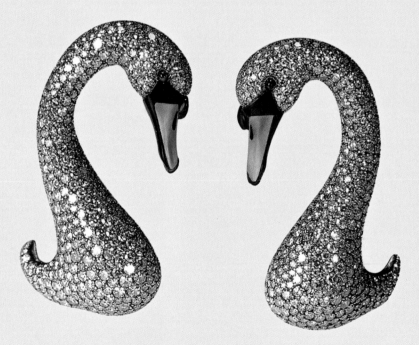

Above
JAR SWAN EARRINGS
FRENCH 1990

JEWELLERY

BY DAVID WARREN

Jewellery is by its very nature both expensive and ephemeral. Jewellery made from precious stones is often reset in new styles depending on fashion and it is therefore very unusual to find really old jewellery (that is pre-19th century) outside museums. 19th or 20th century jewellery however is accessible to today's collectors.

Women's rights, haute couture, travel, theatre, death and love are but a few of the forces to have influenced design and fashion in jewellery during the past two centuries. The opening of trade routes, advancements in technology, and the Industrial Revolution that began in the middle of the 18th century, were jointly responsible for expanding the jewellery market in which Britain and France were at the forefront. The dawning of 19th century Europe had arrived.

Mourning jewellery

ONE VOGUE, REVIVED from a 16th century tradition and activated by the Napoleonic wars at the turn of the 18th century, was mourning jewellery. Rings enamelled in black mourned those who had been married while white enamelling was reserved for the unmarried. Names, dates, compartments with plaited hair and inscrip-

Above
MOURNING BROOCH
ENGLISH
c.1810

Above
HEART-SHAPED LOCKET
ENGLISH
c.1830

tions such as *'in memoriam'* all served to preserve the memory of a loved one. Romantic love jewels of the first half of the 19th century counterbalanced the darker trends. Entwined hearts encrusted with diamonds and padlocks and keys were popular symbols. So too were forget-me-not brooches, and cryptic messages spelling such words as *'dearest'* or *'amor'* in gemstones such as diamonds, emeralds, amethysts or rubies.

Italian style

MEANWHILE, ITALIANS were manufacturing micromosaic suites with images of classical architecture, mythology and horticulture. Naples was the centre of production for coral jewellery between 1830 and 1860 and the coral craze swept throughout Europe, assisted by Napoleon's Italian campaign. Carved into bacchanalian scenes, winged cherubs, delicate flower sprays or simply left in its natural twig form, coral jewellery was at the height of popularity by 1850.

Above
CORAL AND TURQUOISE BRACELET
ITALIAN c.1840

Below
MICROMOSAIC BRACELET
ITALIAN c.1840

Two Italian craftsmen worthy of note are Pio Fortunato Castellani and Carlo Guiliano. Castellani (1793–1865) based in London, specialized in fine quality reproductions of the Roman and Etruscan styles. Guiliano (1831–95) who also worked in London, was inspired by the Renaissance style, producing jewels in polychrome enamels of intricate designs.

Top
CASTELLANI SHELL CAMEO
ENGLISH c.1850

Above
GUILIANO BROOCH
ENGLISH c.1840

Popular designs

Two of the most regularly employed designs over the past 300 years have been sprays and ribbon bow brooches which over the same period of time have recurred frequently in haute couture. The spray was becoming more naturalistic by early 19th century and as jewellers' skills improved, designs became more complicated. The invention of the *en tremblant* mechanism, where sections of the spray were mounted on springs allowing flowerheads and buds to quiver gently, proved to be highly popular.

Topical subjects were often portrayed in jewellery and in 1834 the discovery of Halley's Comet caused great excitement. Lunar jewels abounded, in the form of crescents, stars, sunbursts and comets.

While Europe had a centuries' old tradition of jewellery design, 19th century America was still a comparatively new country with little demand for sophisticated jewels. It was in fact silverware that was accepted as the premier status symbol in America until the Civil War of 1861–65. Jewellery then took over, compounded by Tiffany's purchase in 1888 of one third of the sumptuous French Crown jewels.

Top
ENTREMBLANT BROOCH
ENGLISH c.1840

Above
STAR BROOCH
ENGLISH c.1840

The influx of gemstones

SIGNIFICANT DISCOVERIES of gems and minerals worldwide in the 19th century reduced manufacturers' prices to a more widely affordable level. They included sapphires from Kashmir, Australian opals, gold from California, green demantoid garnets from Russia and South African diamonds to name but a few. The Kimberley mine founded in 1871 was enormous, yielding unimaginable supplies of gem quality diamond.

This influx of raw materials undoubtedly hastened jewellery manufacturers to feed the 19th century's demand for personal adornment. As a consequence jewellery production became more mechanized. William Morris (1834–96), founded the Arts and Crafts movement in 1856 in reaction to the increase in mass manufacturing. The movement's return to traditional labour intensive skills was more in keeping with their simple aims. Images of the Holy Grail, maidens with flowing hair, peacock feathers, Viking long boats and Celtic designs were trademarks of William Morris's guild of handicrafts. It was the beginning of a truly inspirational period that would eventually break the dominant Victorian styles of bows, sprays, hearts, crescents and stars.

Art Nouveau jewellery

THE LAST QUARTER of the 19th century gave rise to a new art style with its origins firmly in the Arts and Crafts movement: Art Nouveau. The basis of Art Nouveau consisted of delicate flowing, bending lines that seemed not to conform, beginning in parallel, converging and

Right
ART NOUVEAU BROOCH
FRENCH c.1880

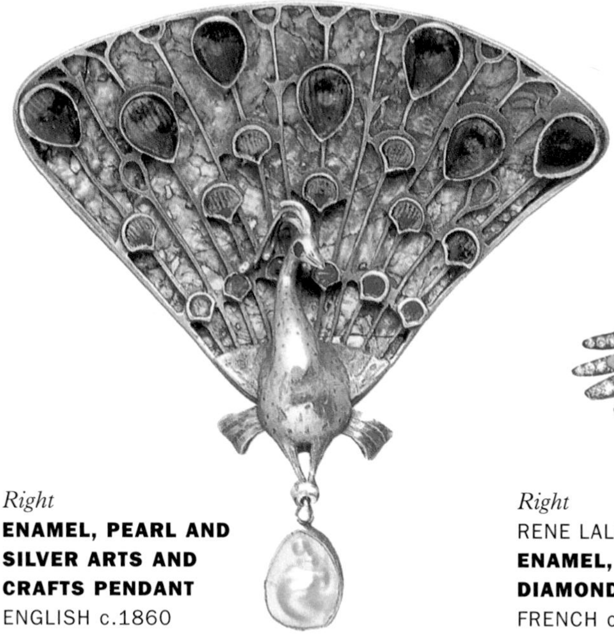

Right
ENAMEL, PEARL AND SILVER ARTS AND CRAFTS PENDANT
ENGLISH c.1860

Right
RENE LALIQUE
ENAMEL, PEARL AND DIAMOND PENDANT
FRENCH c.1890

contradicting each other and uniting. Horticulture and the female form lent themselves ideally to this new style and it was applied to most mediums including jewellery. Traditionalists regarded Art Nouveau as brash and vulgar, but despite this its popularity spread quickly throughout Europe and America finding particular favour in Paris, Vienna and Barcelona.

The French jeweller and craftsman, René Lalique (1860–1945), was undoubtedly the master goldsmith of this period. He created stunning and imaginative works of art using mixtures of precious and semi-precious stones, enamel and moulded glass, which was his favourite medium. One of his most significant works is housed at the Gulbenkian Museum in Lisbon, a huge predatory winged insect in the form of a stomacher. At first sight the insect resembles a dragonfly, but closer inspection reveals fearsome claws and from its hideous jaws extends the torso of a woman. In total contrast to the nightmare beast, the woman is beautiful and supremely calm in what appears to be a state of metamorphosis. Lalique, repulsed by 19th century industrial developments, created this symbolic work as the 20th century was about to begin. He may well have been expressing his future hopes for a more caring human society.

Top
BELLE EPOCH BOW BROOCH
FRENCH c.1905

Above
GARLAND STYLE EARRINGS
FRENCH c.1900

'The Garland Style'

FRENCH JEWELLERS, particularly Cartier, introduced 'The Garland Style' that so befitted the turn-of-the-century 'Belle Epoque' years. They based their ideas on the grand tradition of Versailles and the Court of Louis XVI. Acanthus leaf scrolls, wreaths and quatrefoils on lattice-work structures, bound with ribbon bows and cupola tassels epitomized this fashion.

A further reason for its success was the introduction of platinum which allowed jewellers to create lace-like settings with the minimum of metal and maximum delicacy. Cartier's great success with the Garland Style marked the beginning of the firm's position as world leaders of design that lasted for almost half a century.

The Cartier influence

THE NEXT 50 YEARS would transform Cartier's name into a legend. A contributing factor to its success was the company's close links with haute couture and in particular the Englishman, Charles Frederick Worth (1825–95). Worth was one of the most dominant designers of the late 19th century, commissioned by European Royal families and rich American hostesses. Cartier provided a range of items under the title of *Boutique 'S'*, that included evening bags, compacts, belts and buckles covered

in silk brocade and set with gems that complemented the latest of Worth's designs. This successful collaboration with fashion provided Cartier with introductions to the international elite of Europe, America and Russia.

Art Deco jewellery

BY THE START of World War I, the popular Garland Style was beginning to wither. This was compounded by the unavailability of platinum which had a more important role to play in the production of explosives. A second influencing factor of the war was that women's clothing became more streamlined, tighter fitting and practical.

Below
ART DECO EARRINGS
FRENCH c.1920

This laid the foundations for the next important fashion, Art Deco. Images from Egypt, India, China and Japan epitomized the Deco style and were adapted in an angular and sometimes architectural way that was clean-cut and harmonious with 1920s dress.

Colour was of the utmost importance, being an integral part of this new design. Charles Jacqueau (1885–1968) was Cartier's chief designer at this time. His passion for the mystical East was reflected in his extraordinary jewellery designs that were imitated throughout Europe and America for nearly 20 years. Coincidentally, and of great good fortune for Cartier, Howard Carter discovered Tutankhamun's tomb in 1922. The world marvelled at the vibrantly coloured treasures that poured forth serving to underline and add impetus to Cartier's Deco designs.

The 1940s and 1950s

THE ONSLAUGHT OF World War II brought Art Deco to a natural conclusion. Trade routes were closing, demand declining and many jewellers abandoned their work tools to take up arms. It was a time of economy and this was reflected in the shop windows of jewellers. Extravagant

Above
**VAN CLEEF AND ARPELS
ART DECO BRACELET**
FRENCH c.1925

gems were no longer in evidence and patrons adjusted to colourful semi-precious and synthetic stones and a zealous use of gold. Most jewellery from the 1940s in Europe and America took its inspiration from machinery. This may partly have been owing to the intense production of war machines that jewellers were temporarily caught up in.

Below
WAR-TIME SPRAY BROOCH
ENGLISH c.1940

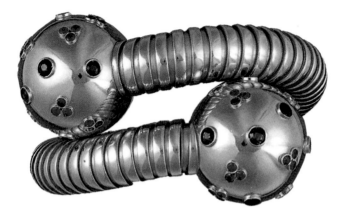

Above
**COCKTAIL BRACELET
GAS-HOSE AND BALL
BEARING DESIGN**
ITALIAN c.1945

Caterpillar tracks, variations of stylized wheels and discs, screw threads, ball bearings and gas or hose pipes all found a place in 1940s 'cocktail jewellery'.

The war altered far more than current jewellery designs. Forty years of French domination of the market came to a resounding halt as the Nazis invaded France, Belgium and the Netherlands. Jewellery manufacturers, retailers and diamond cutters alike fled to the relative safety of Britain and Switzerland, but more significantly to America. This great influx of expertise and the wealth of raw materials that the jewellers brought with them to America, was responsible for shifting the centre of the jewellery industry permanently away from Europe. For the first time America led the market.

One of many exciting young designers to settle in America was a Sicilian duke, Fulco di Verdura (1898–1978). He had worked with Coco Chanel in Paris before opening his own New York based business in September 1939.

Below
HARRY WINSTON
DIAMOND SPRING BROOCH
AMERICAN c.1950

The expanding wealth and opulence of American post-War society, helped by glamorous Hollywood images, encouraged Americans to spend more money than ever before on jewellery. This inspired the 1950s 'all diamond look'. Purveyor of the most valuable gemstones of the world and ideally located at his 5th Avenue premises, Harry Winston wooed the world's wealthy with his all-diamond jewellery.

At the same time European jewellery design was enjoying the input of established sculptors and artists such as Giacometti, Picasso and Braque, the latter experimenting with textured gold. Salvador Dali, the great Spanish surrealist, created melting watches and pulsating ruby hearts.

The antique jewellery of the future

THE TONE OF the 1960s was altogether whimsical. Jungle animals by David Webb (1925–75) in bright enamels and semi-precious stones were high fashion in New York. Cartier produced the popular ladybird in coral and black enamel, while seashells set with precious gems mounted in gold were Falco di Verdura's amusing offerings.

When Neil Armstrong stepped onto the moon in 1969, interest in lunar jewellery resurfaced, in the abstract style of the 1970s.

BULGARI GOLD NECKLACE
ITALIAN 1980

Above
DAVID WEBB
ZEBRA BRACELET
AMERICAN c.1965

Women now required jewellery of a more versatile nature, to wear by day or night, at any occasion. The travel explosion of the 1970s and 1980s found many people continually on the move, and preferring to travel with relatively inexpensive but sophisticated jewellery. The Italian firm, Bulgari, with a major outlet in New York, designed internationally acclaimed jewellery that met this demand. Simple rounded settings in warm 18 carat gold held cabochon-cut coloured gemstones. Antiquities in the form of coins and engraved gems were the focal point of chain link necklaces.

Above
STAR BROOCH
ENGLISH 1970

Left
FALDO DI VERDURA
SEASHELL EARRINGS
AMERICAN c.1965

FANS

BY SUSAN MAYOR

Although fans are as old as hot weather, the second half of the 17th century is where today's collectors might aspire to start their collections. Rarely do more than two 17th century fans appear on the market each year, whereas hundreds of 18th century fans are sold.

Fans can be made from almost every conceivable material. They can be dated from the shape and carving of their sticks and guardsticks, and from the painting on the leaves or mounts. The painting can be compared to contemporary portrait miniatures, watercolours and oil paintings, to give both date and country of origin. Dating the costume of the figures is also very helpful. The subject matter on fans varies considerably. From the beginning of the 18th century one tends to find classical and Biblical subjects. From the mid-18th century pastoral subjects become predominant, painted as two or three shaped vignettes. From the third quarter of the 18th century charming *trompe l'oeil* fans from England, Germany and Italy are found.

In the early 18th century lacquered brise fans called 'Vernis Martin' were popular and again in about 1900, when pastiches of the earlier versions were produced.

Above
RACING FAN
ENGLISH 19th C.

Printed fans

Printed fans, often commemorative, make an appearance from the 1720s onwards as fanmakers felt a necessity to expand their trade and produce cheaper pieces. Some of the English fans printed after the 1734 Copyright Act still have their publication lines with the name of the fanmaker, and/or engraver and his address and date of publication. Although printed fans were cheap at the time, they were ephemeral and are now much sought after.

Some with rare and interesting subjects such as the 1727 coronation, the Battle of Colloden in 1745, and a New Game of Piquet in 1733 have fetched almost as much as comparable painted fans. Some subjects are amusing and entertaining, such as Conundrum fans. Most 18th century fans are etchings but all other types of prints do appear on fans: aquatints, stipple engravings (wooden brise fans are often applied with stipple engravings in the 1780s), and even very rarely mezzotints or woodcuts. By the 19th century many fan leaves are printed – particularly in the 1830s to 1870s, when fan leaves were frequently hand-coloured lithographs, often pastiches of 18th century fans with pretty mother-of-pearl sticks. Chromolithographic fans appear in the 1860s to 1880s, some printed on silk and linen. They make a fresh appearance in the 20th century as amusing advertising

Right
LITHOGRAPHIC FAN
ENGLISH c.1851

Fans from outside Europe

MOST SURVIVING EUROPEAN fans are folding fans, with sticks. These were in fact introduced in the 17th century from the East where they had been held in high esteem, sometimes with leaves painted by distinguished artists. It is rare for the collector to find a mounted Chinese or Japanese fan from before the late 18th century but then fans and leaves of lesser artistry but great charm were made for export to the West. Exported paper leaves were similar in size and subject matter to European fans. From the late 18th century we find Cantonese carved ivory brise fans like European fans they were smaller in the early 19th century, and the Chinese soon added tortoiseshell, mother-of-pearl, enamelled filigree metal, some gilt lacquered wood and sandalwood. From Japan the collector can find fine ivory brise fans lacquered and decorated with Shibayama work from the 1880s. Most other cultures produced fans. As yet only one from Rarotonga in the South Pacific have fetched big money. Other ethnographic fans commonly found are: rigid hide ones from North and West Africa, beech bark and feather fans from the Huron Indians in North America, feathers mounted with humming birds from Brazil, and West Indian folding fans of pressed ferns

fans for grand hotels, restaurants and scents. These were mainly French and are often designed by well-known decorative artists and illustrators such as Bernard de Monvel.

The fans of the very early 19th century are mainly very small brise ones of ivory or horn. A few late 18th century and early 19th century brise fans were extremely well painted in the manner of Angelica Kauffmann. From the 1850s to 1890s some very fine lace fans were produced, with mainly Honiton, Brussels, Chantilly or Carrickmacross laces.

Many fans from the second half of the 19th century are signed but often by little known decorative artists. However, some very fine fans were produced in the 1860s to 1890s by artists such as A. Solde and Callamatta. Billotey, who also painted on glass, painted fine fan mounts on silk gauze of flowers and insects for the well known fanmakers Duvelleroy. A number of traditionalist genre

Above
CARVED IVORY BRISE FAN
CANTONESE, CHINA c.1820

....

painters like Olivier de Penne in France and Richard Doyle in England painted mounts for fans. Compared with leaves by fan painters these are still very reasonable in price, unlike fans painted in the Art Nouveau style. In the 1890s Duvelleroy produced very fine double-sided fans depicting romantic subjects for the English market.

From the 18th century onwards fans often incorporated novelties. One finds middle 18th century double image fans, with three or four different scenes and when opened the wrong way, from right to left, a hidden scene is revealed. Some fans of this type are painted with risque images. There are also double-image brise fans from the 1820s, spy-hole fans, fans with carved handles and telescopic fans, parasol fans and collapsible fans.

TEXTILES

Above
EMBROIDERED PICTURE
ENGLISH 1770

TEXTILES

BY DIANA FOWLE

Tapestry

NEARLY EVERY TEXTILE except felt is produced by weaving, the interlinking of the warp and weft thread on a loom. However, some are patterned during this process and some are decorated afterwards either by a needle, as in embroidery, or by painting or printing. Tapestries are perhaps the best known of the woven textiles. Technically the term tapestry describes the weaving process as well as the actual hanging: the pattern is worked during weaving by the weft and not embroidered by a needle. Tapestries are normally large scale wall hangings and are composed of coloured wool or silk wefts and undyed linen warps.

It was not until the 13th century AD that tapestry weaving seems to have become a European industry. Paris and the Low Countries, in particular Arras, were very important centres of production. Wealthy aristocracy required tapestries to decorate their castles and demonstrate their wealth. Tapestries were very practical items; they could be relatively easily transported and re-hung in each castle by an itinerant court to give colour and warmth.

Medieval designs

THE STYLISTIC DEVELOPMENTS of tapestries closely follows that of paintings. There is little spatial recession and the figures seem to be piled vertically on top of each other, producing a crowded wall of colour. The weavers rendered each detail with great care and it is possible to date tapestries by examining the details of the costume. Hunting and processional scenes were popular, for example, the Devonshire Hunting Tapestries, woven in Burgundy in circa 1450, now at the Victoria and Albert Museum in London. Tapestries without figures were also made; the *millefleur* tapestries are particularly attractive as they depict fields of flowers.

Later tapestries

BY THE 16TH CENTURY the effects of the Renaissance were beginning to be felt in tapestry design. This change was underlined by the Raphael cartoons, which were produced by the artist for Pope Leo X in 1515 and were woven in Brussels. The cartoons depict the Acts of the Apostles, with real figures in three dimensional receding

Below
TAPESTRY
SWISS c.1430–44

landscape skyline has been lowered producing an impression of well ordered rational space. These developments in the rendering of perspective continued throughout the century, as did the gradual increase in the colour range used; by the 18th century as many as three hundred different dyes were used in tapestries so that realistic shading could be achieved.

During the 17th century Brussels continued to remain a tapestry centre; however workshops in both England and France became serious rivals. The Mortlake workshop in London was set up under James I's patronage in 1619 and made

Right
GOBELINS TAPESTRY
FRENCH
Early 18th C.

Below
RAISED WORK CASKET
ENGLISH c. 1660

many large sets. France began to rival Mortlake after the creation of the Gobelins and Beauvais workshops by Colbert for Louis XIV; the production at Aubusson was also re-organized.

The Gobelins was the Crown's personal factory, directed by the artist Charles Le Brun (1619–90), who produced many important tapestries intended to increase the Sun King's prestige. Beauvais and Aubusson were smaller centres producing less grandiose tapestries for private clients.

English weavers from Soho were also producing tapestry during the 18th century, although not on the same scale as France. John Vanderbanke and Joshua Morris were two of the best known. Morris produced colourful pieces often with decorative sprays of flowers and exotic parrots; Vanderbanke produced a famous set of Chinoiserie scenes.

Above
FORMAL SAMPLER
AMERICAN 1812

The Gothic revival

BY THE END of the 18th century the fashion for tapestries had virtually disappeared and it was not until the Gothic revival that they once again became popular. The Arts and Crafts movement encouraged the re-examination of the old textile crafts. William Morris (1834–96) established a tapestry workshop at Morton Abbey where extremely successful re-interpretations of early tapestries, such as millefleurs and verdures, were produced, as well as figurative tapestries.

Embroidery

WILLIAM MORRIS ALSO produced other types of decorative textiles, in particular printed and embroidered hangings. Embroidery has been used for furnishings for a long time. Although it requires much skill, it is easier to produce domestically than a tapestry and is cheaper. Since the late 16th century well-to-do school-girls were taught embroidery. They practised various stitches and recorded new patterns on their sam-plers. In the 16th and 17th century these took the form of long narrow strips of cloth, normally of linen, worked in a random manner as a form of reference which would serve to remind the embroiderer of previous works. Some are dated and worked with the embroiderer's name and age.

By the late 17th century samplers had lost much of their practical value and came to be admired for their decorative appeal. They were often framed and were seen as a type of embroidered picture show-ing off the skill of the worker. Gradually the design of samplers became standardized and by the late 18th to early 19th century, they follow a set pattern, usually consist-ing of a religious verse, with spot motifs of flowers, birds, animals and architectural features below with a floral border.

Another form of popular embroi-dery was the needlework picture. Although there are earlier examples, it was not until the 17th century that they seem to have become wide-spread. At this period they were normally worked in coloured wools highlighted with silks, or silk on silk, and often depict religious or mytho-logical subjects. English embroidery from this period is particularly attractive as it is often worked with strange details such as carefully observed insects and animals. These were copied from pattern books or from herbals which were full of botanical drawings.

Above
LONG SAMPLER
ENGLISH EARLY 17th C.

Once the needlewoman finished her sampler and embroidered picture she often progressed to a needlework casket. These were boxes with the outside covered with embroidery and usually with two doors at the front opening to reveal small drawers, sometimes with secret compartments at the back. They were used to store treasures such as jewellery, lace and letters.

Berlin woolwork

BY THE SECOND quarter of the 19th century the craze for Berlin woolwork began to take over contemporary needlework. This was a type of embroidery worked on wide mesh canvas often in cross stitch in wools. The wools were dyed in Berlin and the patterns were printed there. Many embroidered pictures, fire screens and cushions were produced. Recognized by the bright colours of the wools, sometimes highlighted with beads or in plush stitch. The subjects are often of medieval scenes or flower arrangements.

Embroidered furnishings

THE AMATEUR NEEDLEWOMAN also turned her hand to more practical domestic objects, in particular furnishings. In the 18th century many chair backs and seats were embroidered by amateur and professional alike. They were usually in tent stitch on a linen ground and show subjects similar to those in embroidered pictures. Cushion covers were also popular as were large coverings for tables, known as table carpets. These are normally characterized by a non-directional central panel framed by a border which was intended to hang round the edge of the table. These were popular during the 16th and 17th century and were sometimes worked with the family coat of arms.

The other important domestic furnishings were bed hangings and covers. The four poster bed required several pelmets and curtains which were often elaborately decorated. During the 17th and 18th century crewelwork was popular for bed furnishings. This was wool embroidery on a linen tabby or cloth weave ground.

Below
EMBROIDERED CHAIRBACK
ENGLISH. Early 18th C.

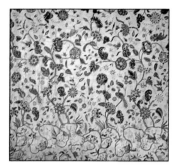

Above
CREWELWORK HANGING
ENGLISH Late 18th C.

Quilting

IT WAS NOT until the 19th century that the patchwork quilt became widespread. A quilt is a very practical way of providing a warm covering as it is composed of two layers of material sandwiching a layer of wadding, often wool; the three layers are sewn together with decorative patterns. The term 'patchwork' refers to the top cover, which was composed of scraps or patches of material joined together in elaborate designs to form a complete cover. This economical bed covering was popular in North America where many different and often dramatic designs were produced.

Collecting tapestries and needlework

PRICES FOR TAPESTRIES vary greatly depending on condition, subject matter, age and whether the price is complete or merely a cut down section. Very early tapestries rarely come on the market and attract very high prices; even good 18th century tapestries may reach six figures at auction.

Antique needlework can also command high prices, 16th and 17th century samplers could reach thousands of pounds at auction, but attractive 19th century samplers can be obtained for a few hundred. Embroidered caskets are particularly sought after.

Quilts are now among the most collectible items in the textile world, particularly in the United States where they fetch thousands of dollars.

Printed fabrics

PATCHWORK QUILTS ARE mainly composed of scraps of printed cotton dress material. Printed cotton was popular for both dress and furnishing fabrics from the early 18th century onwards. Originally printed and painted cottons, or chintzes, came from India where the process of dyeing clothes with permanent bright colours had been known since at least the 17th century. These Indian cottons were highly valued in the West as their exotic designs and

Right
PATCHWORK QUILT
ENGLISH
c. 1840
....

strong colourfast dyes were not available in Europe. They were used as bed hangings, covers and also for dress fabrics. It was not until 1752 that a method for producing high quality printed cottons was available in Europe with the invention of copper plate printing by Francis Nixon in Ireland, which substituted the old block printing method.

Silk

THE LATE 18TH century fashion for printed cotton dress fabrics seriously damaged the silk industry. Previously the finest costume had been made from elaborate figured silks, brocades and damasks. These were woven on a drawloom by skilled weavers copying a pattern produced by designers such as Philippe De Lassalle or Anna Maria Garthwaite. Lyon in Southern France was the most important centre of production

and her designers led the silk fashion, creating new patterns for each year. In the 18th century it was the pattern of the fabric, rather than the cut of the clothes that counted among the fashion conscious. Silk designs changed regularly and followed a clear trend. Early in the century bizarre silks with strange abstract patterns were popular; these were followed by lace pattern silks, then silks with lush naturalistic motifs and by the end of the 18th century silks with rows of ribbons or garlands were popular: these eventually developed into a neoclassical stripe. Fashions in furnishing silks changed more slowly; the large scale damasks with formalized flowering plants dominated this period's upholstery. Other woven fabrics such as velvet were also popular.

Smaller scale printed cottons were produced for dress rather than furnishing fabrics.

LACE, SHAWLS AND COSTUME

BY DIANA FOWLE

Lace

LACE-MAKING HAS a very long history; the simplest techniques and oldest known laces consisting of motifs darned on to a knotted or woven net (*lacis*). The most common are knotted filet and then woven ground Buratto. They are known to have origins in medieval times and have remained largely in the same format into the 20th century.

Other early laces from Italy arose from the need to decorate the newly visible line partlets and shirts. Seams were joined by plaited silk stitches and small holes were cut into the fabric and finished with either self or brightly coloured silks (cutwork or *Punto Tagliato*). Another form of decoration known as drawn thread work or *Punto Tirato* was formed by pulling bunches of threads together to form holes. The holes thus formed by cutwork became larger and larger, leading to decorative needlework infilling

based on the original threads of the ground. This is known as *Reticella*. Patterns are necessarily geometric and angular. The next development in the late 16th century was to discard the linen fabric and pin thread to a parchment pattern on a pillow. In this way, curved lines could be formed, with a buttonhole pattern built up on them. This lace is known as *Punto in Aria*, literally, stitches in the air. It was used to trim linen and the newly fashionable ruff.

European lace-making centres

THE MOST IMPORTANT trading cities in the late 16th and early 17th centuries were the centres of the lace industry. Venice was a specialist in needle laces of creamy white fine linen thread. Typically, it has a large padded outline to the damask-like floral patterns, often edged with loops (*picots*). This lace is known as *Gros Point de Venise*.

Another lace of distinction

arose as a result of royal patronage of Louis XIV under the direction of Colbert, his brilliant finance minister. In order to stem the flow of capital abroad to buy Italian and Flemish braids and laces, the French court were ordered to wear only French laces. The towns of Alençon and Argentan benefited enormously from this monopoly. This lace was known as *Point de France*. By the turn of the century Alençon and Argentan were diverging, with Alencon retaining a hexagonal, twisted ground and Argentan developing a mesh encased in buttonhole stitching.

Below
BRUSSELS LACE
FLEMISH 1730–40

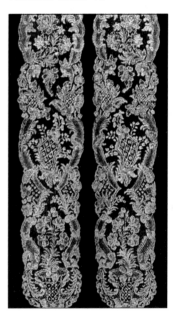

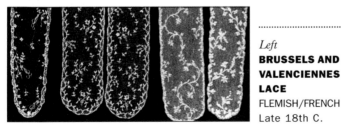

Left
BRUSSELS AND VALENCIENNES LACE
FLEMISH/FRENCH
Late 18th C.

Valenciennes lace owes much to France but also to Flanders. As it is made in one piece on the pillow, unlike Brussels bobbin lace where the flowers are made separately from both the ground and raised work, it is technically very complex and demanding. It was well established in the 17th century but like many laces reached a high point in the early 18th century with the popular demand for lappets and caps.

Flanders had an advantage over other lacemakers in Europe in having the damp climate best suited to spinning flax. The finest linen thread was widely exported to England and Italy. Brussels lace used it to advantage. In the 17th century the town produced a variety of bobbin and needle laces, sometimes pictorial but more commonly with plant motifs, with the beginning of the characteristic bunched thread outline. The needle lace is known as *Point de Gaze*.

English lace

ENGLAND WAS AN important consumer and producer of lace. It is thought to have been made in the 17th century, but research is still in progress to identify surviving pieces.

Much lace was produced in the East Midlands in Buckinghamshire. An indication of how large an industry existed is given by the large numbers of turned bone bobbins in circulation. Hollie Point is a particularly charming English speciality –

although samplers also exist. With the widespread adoption of machine laces towards the middle of the 19th century, laces became much more standardized throughout Europe and the strong regional flavour of hand made laces was lost.

Shawls

KASHMIR SHAWL WEAVING techniques are very similar to those of tapestry weaving. The special quality of Kashmir shawls lies in the use of goat down, harvested in the spring in the Himalayas. Attempts to farm the Kashmir goat have been unsuccessful as the goats fail to produce down unless temperatures match those in the Himalayas .

Kashmir shawls were certainly being imported into Europe by the 17th century. Shawls of that time are very simple, composed of a monochrome field with both ends woven with bands of elegant flowering shrubs usually based on indigenous flowers, such as the poppy or iris. This floral border does not usually exceed 12in in depth.

During the 18th century, motifs became more stylized and the naturalistic flowers made way for floral mosaics usually perched on a stylized urn. At the same time, striped and moon shawls (with a central medallion and four corner medallions) were also being woven, mainly for export to Arabia.

By the beginning of the 19th century, a typical shawl would

have end borders woven with approximately eight cones of about 12 inches high, usually composed of a myriad of smaller flowers forming a bush. As the century progresses, these bushes begin to tilt at the tip until by mid-century they are the typical Paisley cone shape so familiar to western eyes. By 1820 the ground between the cones is beginning to be filled with stray flowers and by 1830 the cones are indicated only by reserves of the ground. The woven borders begin then to fill the whole field partly as a response to European demand for more Oriental motifs.

A simple method of spotting early shawls is based on the fact that the taxation system current in the mid-19th century allowed tax collectors to cut shawl fragments from the loom as soon as possible to avoid the possibility of a weaver dying with unpaid taxes owing. Skilful embroiderers later sewed the fragments back together again.

The Indian market catered not only for indigenous demand but was skilful in supplying Europe with designs especially tailored to suit European taste. Agents from France and England dictated patterns and exported shawls to meet the demand for this perfect accessory to the Grecian modes then prevalent. The Empress Josephine is said to have owned 60 Kashmir shawls, some costing as much as 12,000 Francs.

European shawl weaving

PARELLEL TO THE Indian industry, the French, English and Austrians began to weave copies of Indian shawls. The main difference between Kashmir and European shawls is one of technique – European shawls are woven on a Jacquard loom, leaving floating wefts on the reverse, which are usually clipped to a rough surface. All threads run parallel to the shawl ends. On the reverse of Indian shawls, threads run in all directions from one area of colour to the next.

One of the earliest shawl manufacturers in France was Guillaume Ternaux (1763–1833), producing shawls with marked European motifs. He considered the Indian motifs 'barbarous'.

Nineteenth century shawls

DATING EUROPEAN SHAWLS of the first half of the century can be done by comparing Indian patterns. The field is generally monochrome with the shawl ends woven with cones. In 1837 a relatively short-lived fashion for 'turnover' shawls bloomed. These were sewn together in such a way that when folded diagonally both borders showed right side up. Towards the middle of the century shawls became smaller and square with very narrow borders. Until the second quarter of the century narrow ribbon borders were sewn on the length of the shawl. After this time they are woven as a piece with the shawl. The shawl fields gradually gave way until in the 1860s the whole shawl was covered with

cones with only a residual central medallion. With the 1870s and the introduction of slimmer silhouettes, the days of the shawl were numbered. They continued to be given as wedding presents to wealthy brides, but were no longer worn.

Men's costume

SEVENTEENTH CENTURY MEN'S costume is really only found in museums, although occasional pieces do turn up. Eighteenth century costume, however, is relatively plentiful. Throughout the century men's costume was basically a suit, comprising breeches, waistcoat and coat. But fabrics, trimming and embroidery however changed with the fashion. The cloth quaality and trimming were status symbols.

At the beginning of the century coats reached well below the knee, almost completely concealing the

very roomy breeches. They stopped above the knee until the 1730s and were worn with stockings rolled over them. They were often of the same fabric as the coat. The coat was collarless and with stiffened side pleats echoing the shape of ladies' panniers. Cuffs were flared and deep almost to the elbow (boot cuffs). Waistcoats were often sleeved and could be of contrasting fabric.

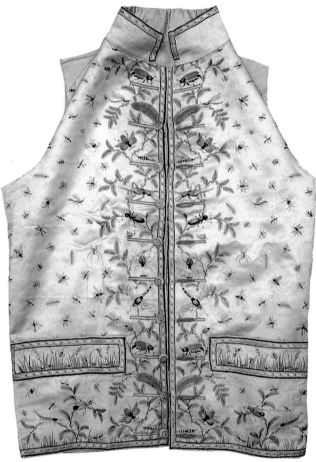

Left
GENTLEMAN'S EMBROIDERED NIGHTCAP
ENGLISH c.1600

Right
MAN'S WAISTCOAT
ENGLISH c.1780

Below
MAN'S DOUBLET
FRENCH OR ITALIAN
Early 17th C.

The last two decades of the 18th century saw changes in fashion epitomized by the *Incroyable,* with his tight fitting short coat with high collar, dazzling waistcoats and raffish appearance.

The early 19th century saw the coat being cut back at the front and the introduction of a waist seam about 1820 and trousers make their first appearance. Surviving men's dress from the 1840s and 1850s is rare as it was worn out in service.

Women's costume

VIRTUALLY ALL COSTUME predating the 17th century is now in the possession of museums and collections. Even 17th century costume is so rare that, when auctioned, it can command five figure sums. Little has survived, partly because of the early 17th century fashion popular until the 1630s for decorative slashing of costly brocades, which weakened the fabric. Several exam-

ples survive of the later fashion of embroidered linen bodices, elaborately worked with scrolling foliage, birds and insects. An exception to the scarcity of 17th century costume is the number of fine linen shirts and chemises.

It is far more common to find 18th century costume, of which far more has survived, if rarely unaltered. Women's costume can be divided roughly into two basic shapes, both being worn over stays, rather than having boned bodices. One shape developed from the T-shaped nightgown of the late 17th century. This evolved into the loosebodied 'sack' dress, or *robe a la française*. These dresses required vast lengths of material and were therefore usually immensely expensive.

The second basic shape evolved from the mantua of the 1690s – a robe pleated to the waist, with a train for formal occasions, but without one for everyday use. The characteristic of a mantua is the elaborate pinning of the skirts to the waistline. Both types of dress were worn over hoops.

Eighteenth century robes are dated by various means – the silk used can usually be accurately placed by its design – and then also by the accessories, trimming and sleeves. The basic shape does not alter greatly until the 1780s. The late 18th century saw the first radical change in dress , as portrayed so successfully by

Gainsborough. The waistline rose, the tight bodices with a characteristic diamond-shaped panel at the back. Small jackets, known as Spencers, became popular. Hoops disappeared.

The nineteenth century

EARLY 19TH CENTURY dress was heavily influenced by the taste for Grecian culture. White was the most fashionable colour, with dresses having a high waistline reaching its highest point just below the bust by 1815. It reaches a more natural position in the late 1820s. New fabrics for these figure-hugging fashions include fine Indian muslins, often worn with expensive Kashmir shawls.

The waistline dips to a V-shape from the late 1820s onward to a pronounced 'V' in the early 1840s. Fabrics are predominantly heavy wools and silks. The 1850s see skirts made of lighter silks, and sleeves form bell shapes. By the 1870s, the skirt is being pulled to the back and bodices are tighter and longer to emphasize the curve of the back, underlined by the bustle. This marked slimming of the silhouette continues in the 1880s, with a profusion of trimmings and exotic feathers. The Naughty Nineties see exaggerated puffed sleeves until 1895 when they deflate as quickly, with the skirt mirroring this movement which helped to balance the silhouette.

The use of the Couturier

THE MID-19TH CENTURY saw the emergence of the Couturier, beginning with Charles Worth in Paris in 1858, creating dresses for Empress Eugenie and the courts of Europe. Early in the 20th century two names stand out from the mainstream – Poiret and Fortuny. Poiret's creations were heavily influenced by Bakst's Ballet Russe designs and his love of oriental fabrics and fashions. His designs were very probably the first to be worn without corsets. Mariono Fortuny, working in Venice, created his patent silk 'Delphos' dresses, the secret of whose pleating has never been discovered. His stencilled velvets after 15th and 16th century models are masterpieces and are widely collected. Coco Chanel (1883–1971) also contributed to the freeing of the female form by the use of cuts from the world of sport and the golf course.

Paris has always been the centre of the haute couture industry. Patou, Paquin, Vionnet and Lanvin all worked here, with Schiaparelli's surrealist creations standing out from the crowd. Later, Dior and Balenciaga must also be mentioned. The influential New Look of the late 1940s made a break with pre-war fashion. Balenciaga's contribution to women's fashion is of prime importance, creating a highly sculptured look which remains immensely inspirational today.

PAINTINGS

Above
THOMAS MORAN
MIST IN THE CANYON
AMERICAN Late 19th C.

OIL PAINTINGS

BY JEREMY HOWARD

Painting is one of the oldest and most venerable of the arts. Since the Renaissance it has enjoyed the status, along with sculpture and architecture, of 'fine' as opposed to 'applied' art.

Up until the end of the 15th century painters were regarded as craftsmen on more or less the same footing as goldsmiths. Indeed, many of the architects and painters of the Italian Renaissance received their first training as goldsmiths. The great altarpieces which adorned the Italian churches were collaborative efforts involving a team of craftsmen, of whom the carpenter who made the frame was generally paid more money than the painter who decorated it. There was very little scope for spontaneous strokes of genius by the painter. The whole notion of artistic individualism was also held in check by a highly organized guild system which was only gradually replaced with the growth of the art academies in the late 17th century in France.

Painting can be divided into two basic categories: mural painting and easel painting. For obvious reasons the collector will be primarily concerned with the category of easel painting.

The earliest easel paintings were altarpieces. The most important were large and highly complex works of art, but the

Above
JACPO DI CIONE
VIRGIN AND CHILD
ITALIAN Late 14th C.

collector may also encounter smaller-scale paintings, such as the diptyches which were painted for private devotion and were designed to be portable.

Early Italian altarpieces were invariably painted on a wood support covered in gesso (a mixture of size and plaster of Paris) over a ground colour of a greenish substance known as *terre verte*. The medium used at this period was tempera, not oil paint, the distinction being that in tempera painting the pigments are suspended in egg rather than linseed oil, and water is used as a solvent. The most important artistic centres in Italy in the late Middle Ages were Siena, where in the late 13th century Duccio (active 1278–1319) founded a great school of painting whose principal masters were to be Simoni Martini and the Brothers Lorenzetti, and Florence, where at the same moment Giotto's work was to be the basis of the main tradition of Western European painting. Sienese painting is characterized by great grace and lyricism, but the achievement of Giotto (c. 1267–1337) was that he managed to break away from the flat Byzantine style and invest painting with a new realism and sense of three-dimensional space. The discovery of perspective itself did not come about until later in the 15th century, although naive attempts at suggesting recession can be found in 14th century Italian painting, and it was not until the time of Masaccio in the 1420s that the lessons of Giotto seem to have been adopted into the mainstream of Florentine painting.

Meanwhile, in Northern Europe a flourishing Flemish school of painting centred on Bruges, Antwerp and Ghent produced such masterpieces of realism as Jan Van Eyck's *Marriage of the Amolfini* (1434) and the intense spirituality of his altarpiece, *The Adoration of the Mystic Lamb* (1432). It was Van Eyck (d. 1441), who was credited with the invention of oil painting.

Portraiture

ONE OF THE most revolutionary developments of the Renaissance period lay in the realms of portraiture. In the Middle Ages portraits tended to be rather generalized and hieratic, but the interest in antiquity in the Renaissance led to rediscovery of Roman portrait sculpture. The sculpture and painting of the 15th century in Italy, partic-

Right
LUCAS GRANACHI
PORTRAIT OF JOHANN FRIEDRIC
GERMAN
Early 16th C.

....

Below
SANDRO BOTTICELLI
PORTRAIT OF GIOVANNI DI PIERFRANCESCO DE'MEDICI
ITALIAN
LATE 15th C.

ularly in Florence, became highly realistic. As well as oil painting Antonello da Messina (c. 1430–79) introduced some of the lessons of Flemish realism into Venetian painting. Subsequently, a convention developed of painting bust-length portraits, probably the most distinguished practitioner being Giovanni Bellini (c. 1430–1516). This North Italian tradition of portraiture continued in the 16th century in the work of Titian (c. 1485–1576). Meanwhile, in Germany Albrecht Durer (1471–1528) and Hans Holbein (1498–1543) gave a new intensity to the Northern European portrait tradition.

Titian's influence was felt most clearly in the 17th century by Rubens and Van Dyck in Flanders, and Velazquez in Spain. In his portrait of Charles V at Muhlberg (1548) Titian had developed a new convention of the equestrian portrait, which was to be emulated most notably by Van Dyck in his famous portraits of King Charles I on horseback. A further innovation pioneered by Titian, dating from his early portrait of *The Young Man with a Glove*, was the pose of aristocratic nonchalance (the Italian word, derived from was sprezzatura) which became almost a cliche of portraiture from Van Dyck to John Singer Sargent.

In Holland, a more bourgeois system of patronage meant that the conventions of the Grand Manner did not really take root. Although there is bravura to be found in the work of Frans Hals (see in particular his famous *Laughing Cavalier* of 1624), the prevailing tone was one of sober realism, as is evident in the portraits of the Rembrandt School. Van Dyck's arrival in England in the 1630s determined the future course of portrait painting for the next two centuries. His example was consciously emulated in the 18th century by Sir Joshua Reynolds, who not only borrowed poses from Van Dyck but even dressed many of his sitters in Van Dyck costume.

Meanwhile, Reynold's arch rival Gainsborough adopted Van Dyck's feathery brushwork and his talent for capturing the textures of silk and satin.

Running at variance to the Van Dyck tradition in English portraiture was the more earthy, realistic and essentially middle-class style of portraiture of William Hogarth (1697–1764). Hogarth was the first native English portrait painter to emerge for over 100 years.

Portraits became fashionable as a form of interior decoration hung. Sir Peter Lely, painted a series of female portraits at Hampton Court, known as the Windsor Beauties (many of these beauties were, in fact, the

mistresses of Charles II. The logical extension of this idea of painting series of portraits was to group them all together in one picture, and so at the beginning of the 18th century a type of convivial group portrait developed which was known as 'the conversation piece'. One of the finest earliest examples is Hogarth's *The Graham Family*.

Hogarth was professedly anti-French but ironically the convention of the conversation piece almost certainly at first developed at first in France as a reaction to the formal tradition of the grand style of court portraiture. During the period of Louis XV's regency a new refreshing sense of lightness of touch comes into French painting, found in the work of De Troy, and above all in Boucher (1703–70). Even with grand sitters such as Madame de Pompadour, Boucher includes amusing details such as the jumble of objects on her side-table.

Above
NICOLAS DE LARGILLIERE
PORTRAIT OF A GENTLEMAN
FRENCH
Late 17th C.

....

Left
SIR ANTHONY VAN DYCK
PORTRAIT OF SIR THOMAS HANMER
ENGLISH
Early 17th C.

In the 18th century two strains run through the history of portraiture. The first is the 'paint me warts and all' tradition of realism found in the work of Durer and many of the greatest Renaissance masters, in Hogarth in the 18th century, and subsequently right through to Lucien Freud today. The second tradition assumes that the function of the artist is to flatter the sitter. This is the tradition of the so-called Grand Manner, which culminates in the work of John Singer Sargent (1856–1925). However, the Edwardian era was the swan song of the Grand Manner, and many of the most talented artists turned to a more realistic style of portraiture later in their careers. The 20th century has on the whole seen the triumph of the realistic school in portraiture.

Landscape

LANDSCAPE PAINTING IS found sporadically from earliest times.

Above
JOHANN ZOFFANY R.A.
GROUP PORTRAIT OF FAMILY OF LORD WILLOUGHBY DE BROKE
ENGLISH Late 18th C.

A delight in the countryside, for example, is evident in Roman frescoes; but landscape as a separate genre of painting emerges surprisingly late in Western art. The reasons for this were partly to do with

part of Europe was that the effect of Reformation deprived artists of their principal source of patronage, the Church, and they therefore started to paint pictures which would appeal to a secular audience.

Joachim Patenier (c.1485–1524) and Paul Bril (c.1554–1626) were among the pioneers of the new genre. Bril's example was followed by Adam Elsheimer, a painter from Frankfurt who settled in Rome in the first decade of the 17th century and whose example was to be enormously influential on Rubens and Claude Lorraine.

In the 17th century, three separate strains in the tradition of landscape can be seen. The first was that of the heroic landscape, pioneered by Annibale Carracci and Domenichino.

patronage. Throughout the Middle Ages and even early Renaissance, most commissions was for religious paintings where landscape performed merely an ancillary function. But there was also an element of artistic snobbery. Landscape was considered to be a rather lowly genre of painting because it was thought to appeal primarily to the senses rather than to the intellect. Around that same time, an independent tradition of landscape painting was emerging in Holland. One of the reasons why the landscape tradition seems to have taken root in that

Above
JAN BAPTIST WEENIX
**A BEGGAR BOY IN AN
IMAGINARY LANDSCAPE**
DUTCH Mid 17th C.

Right
FRANCOIS BOUCHER
LANDSCAPE
FRENCH Mid 18th C.

the Venetian vedutisti. Canaletto's works were thought to be so life-like that many people considered he must have used a 'camera obscura', although in reality he took so many liberties with Venetian topography that this theory is no longer generally accepted.

Meanwhile, landscape was pursued by Richard Wilson, and at the start of the 19th century by John Constable and the painters of the Norwich School.

Pierre-Henride Valenciennes (1750–1819) was the high priest of the Neoclassical French school of landscape painting, although he anticipated by almost 100 years the achievements of the Impressionists in his oil-on-paper sketches done from nature in the Roman *campagna*. One painter who was strongly influenced by Valenciennes was Corot. The Barbizon School of painters not only found sources of inspiration in Dutch painting but were also pioneers of the Klein air approach to painting. Meanwhile in England the ageing Turner was moving in the last 20 years of his life towards an abstraction and a sense of pure colour which was to be

Their realism was modified by experiences of Italy and Italian-based painters, and consequently their landscapes are suffused with a golden light.

In France the stern landscape tradition of the 17th century gives way to a whimsical approach in the following century, when Boucher, Fragonard and Hubert Robert painted landscapes in a magical never-never land.

A dramatic contrast to these poetic confections were the more-or-less contemporary, but far more pragmatic townscapes of Canaletto (1697–1768) and

Above
CANALETTO
**VIEW OF THE
GRAND CANAL**
VENETIAN
Early 18th C.

Left
JOHN
CONSTABLE
**LANDSCAPE WITH
FLATFORD MILL**
ENGLISH c.1825

highly influential on the work of Monet.

Ironically, as with so many art historical terms, Impressionism was first coined as a term of abuse. Impressionists are now the most popular and sought after landscape painters of all time.

Still Life

STILL LIFE, IN the opinion of the majority of academicians, was the lowliest of the genres. Like so many areas of painting, it did not really evolve as a separate category until the 17th century. The changing nature of patronage in the Netherlands then and the increasing specialization of studio practice encouraged certain artists not only to specialize in still life, but even to take certain types of still life as a sub-speciality. One thus has a situation where a painter such as Jan Leemans painted little

else but still lives of birdcages, and where specialists in flower painting such as Jan Breughel the Younger or Daniel Seghers would collaborate with a specialist in *trompe l'oeil* marble painting such as Erasmus Quellinus, or in figure subjects such as Hendrick Van Balen.

Certain categories of the genre have fallen out of favour in modern times. These include those with dead game. The

most popular category though, then and now, was probably the flower and fruit still life, which reached a peak of perfection in the Netherlands in the 17th century which has never since been attained. Leading exponents were Jan Van Huysum, Van Os and the painters of the Bosschaert dynasty.

Outside the Netherlands the tradition of still life painting was particularly strong in Spain where a type known as *bodegones* (a sort of kitchen still life with figures) became popular, particularly in Seville, as can be clearly seen in the early paintings of Velazquez (1599–1660). Spanish still lives of the 17th and 18th centuries are marked by their austerity as seen in the work of Melendez. In Italy the still life was strongest in Naples, where Michelangelo Merisi de Caravaggio (1571–1616), was a major influence.

Left
WILLEM CLAESZ HEDA
**STILL LIFE WITH BANQUET
AND OYSTERS**
DUTCH c. 1625

Below
HENRI FANTIN-LATOUR
BANQUET AND OYSTERS
FRENCH 1876

Looking at a painting

THE ART OF appraising a picture requires not only considerable knowledge of the history of styles but also an understanding of the basic techniques and materials. Whether oil or tempera based, a painting will have a support which can be made of wood or metal or canvas, onto which is laid a ground, the principal layers of paint, and finally a varnish which may incorporate glazes.

The support will tell the collector a great deal about the history of the picture, which is why one of the first things that an expert does when he looks at a picture, is to turn it over and inspect the back! If it is wood then the type of wood may give a clue as to the painting's country of origin. As a general rule, oak was used in Northern Europe, whereas soft woods such as poplar were favoured south of the Alps. Other clues may be given, if the picture is on canvas, by far the most common surface, by the type of canvas used. Venetian canvases, for example, have a herring-bone pattern, which one can observe in the surface of paintings by Tintoretto. Flemish canvases on the whole tend to be of much finer weave, and a number of early Flemish pictures are painted on linen.

Examination of the back of the picture will also throw up other clues such as the nature of the stretcher: collectors' marks, seals or labels. It will also tell you whether the picture has been relined or not, that is, transferred onto a new backing canvas. This process should not always be regarded with suspicion since most paintings have to be relined every 100 years or so in order to prevent flaking.

The condition of a painting is not easy for a layman to assess, but ultra-violet lamps help to detect the presence of recent overpainting by a restorer. When examining the front of the picture you should also look out for *pentimenti*, the tell-tale signs of where the painter has changed his mind, which are usually a guarantee that the painting is autograph work and not a copy. The final criterion in assessing a picture is quality, and a sense of this can only be acquired by years of attentive looking.

DRAWINGS

BY JEREMY HOWARD

Drawings provide one of the most challenging and rewarding areas for the collector.

Early drawings

THE ORIGINS OF drawing begin in the medieval monasteries. The art of illuminating manuscripts reached such a high point in the late Middle Ages that the major artistic developments north of the Alps may be said to have taken place in the field of illustration, rather than panel or wall painting. It was not until the 15th century in Italy that drawing began to play a central role in all areas of artistic activity. The reasons for this were partly practical. Until around the middle of the 15th century paper was not available in large supply and the alternatives, vellum or parchment, were too expensive to be used merely for roughing out ideas.

As paper became cheaper and more plentiful, these stock images were replaced by studies from life and drawing became more empirical. Artists were encouraged to study anatomy, and life drawing, both from the nude and clothed model, became *de rigueur*. Careful drapery studies were then made. These drapery studies reached their highest point in the work of Leonardo da Vinci (1452–1519).

Drawing became the essential medium of communication between the master and his assistants and the artist and his patron in the 16th century. On being given a commission, the usual sequence was as follows: first, the artist sketched out a rough idea which was known as the *'primo pensiero'*. Next, detailed studies were taken from life, the assistants or *'garzone'* being used to pose for the various figures in the composition. Studies of drapery and of the heads and hands of the

principal figures would then be made. Where exotic figures or animals were to be incorporated, these were often copied from the studio pattern books. These elements were then assembled and a more finished drawing was provided for presentation to the client before work began on the preparation for painting. This drawing would be highly detailed, and since it often had the status of a legal contract, would normally be on a high-quality support such as parchment or vellum.

Once the client's approval had been given, drawings would be squared up for transfer on to canvas or on to a wall. Squaring up involved drawing a grid which then the composition could be blown up into lifesized cartoons, a famous example of which is the Leonardo cartoon in London's National Gallery.

Left
NICOLO DI GIACOMO
DA BOLOGNA
ITALIAN 1351–1403

Right
FEDERICO BAROCCI
THE MADONNA DEL POPOLO
ITALIAN Late 16th C.

Drawing comes of age

There was a fundamental shift in the 16th century towards draughtsmanship. With the advent of Mannerism, drawings ceased to be merely functional and virtuoso draughtsmanship became an end in itself. The first academies of drawing were founded in the mid-16th century in Florence and Bologna and the formation of the first important collections of drawings, the most notable of which was that assembled by Giorgio Vasari (1511–74). The care he took in the presentation of his *'Libro dei desegni'* reflects the new importance given to drawings as works of art in their own right.

North of the Alps, portrait drawing developed in France in the work of François Clouet (c.1510–72), and in Germany in the work of Hans Holbein (1497/8–1543). German draughtsmanship of the period showed a curious mixture of innovation and conservatism. The invention of printing allowed the dissemination of Mannerist ideas throughout Europe, and Michelangelo's drawings, through the engravings of Raimondi, entered into the stock repertoire of Northern artists.

When the reaction to the Mannerist style set in in Italy, it was centred on Bologna. This led to the revival of life drawing, and the birth of landscape sketching from nature. Drawing again became a medium for

Above
GIORGIO VASARI
PAGE FROM LIBRO DE'DISEGNI
ITALIAN Mid 16th C.

working out ideas on paper, allowing the artist to change his mind, and a more tonal approach is apparent in the drawings of the sculptor Gianlorenzo Bernini (1598–1660) and Guercino (1591–1666), where the forms are modelled more sculpturally. In Genoa, the Flemish influence of Van Dyck and Rubens led to certain pioneering experiments.

Below
PIETRO BERRETTINI
CALLED PIETRO DA CORTONA
STUDY OF A HEAD
ITALIAN Mid 17th C.

In the Low Countries the late survival of Mannerism centred on Haarlem gave way to an emergent landscape tradition in the drawings of Roelandt Savery (c.1561–1639) and Paul Bril (1554–1626) who used a form of aerial perspective. This landscape tradition was continued by the Northern artists who settled in Rome in the 17th century, most notably Claude Lorraine and Nicolas Poussin.

In the 18th century France began to rival Italy as the artistic centre of Europe, although the continuing importance of Venice is shown by the brilliant drawings of Francesco Guardi (1712–93) and Antonio Canaletto (1697–1768). The most important artist of the early 18th century in France was Jean-Antoine Watteau (1684–1721), whose technique of using either two crayons (red and black) or three crayons (red, black and white), was to be much emulated. These were often presented in the *eau-de-nil* mounts of the period, and such was their popularity that a crayon manner method of engraving was invented which enabled highly deceptive reproductions to be produced.

The 18th century in France also witnessed the development of the pastel, which became popular for portraiture. But a reaction to the *ancien régime* set in with the French Revolution, reflected in the Neoclassical movement. The greatest Neoclassical draughtsman was undoubtedly Jean-Auguste-Dominique Ingres (1780–1867). At the opposite end of the pole were the dashingly romantic drawings of Gericault and Delacroix.

Above
JEAN-AUGUSTE-DOMINIQUE INGRES
PORTRAIT OF THE HONOURABLE MRS FLEETWEOOD PELLEW
FRENCH Mid 19th C.

Master drawings – techniques and materials

ALTHOUGH PAPER WAS manufactured in China from the 2nd century onwards, it was not readily available in Europe until the early 15th century. Medieval and Renaissance drawings were generally made on either parchment or vellum, materials made from animal skins. Vellum was the more expensive material and was made from the skins of calves, lambs or young goats. The surfaces of the skins were rubbed with pumice, ground bone or chalk, and it was then generally coated with a preparation of lead oxide and ground bone-meal. After about 1450 vellum and parchment were largely superseded by paper in Italy except for legal documents, model books and highly finished drawings which were made for presentation, although it survived well into the following century north of the Alps. Use of vellum was briefly revived in the 19th century by the Arts and Crafts movement.

Paper first appeared in Europe in the 12th century but was not readily available until after 1400. Until the 19th century, artist's paper was made from pulped rags, and came in two basic types, laid paper and wove paper. Laid paper was made by dipping a grid consisting of fine meshed horizontal wires and wider spaced vertical wires into a mould containing liquid pulp. In laid paper these vertical lines are easily discernible by holding the paper up to the light. Wove paper, was manufactured by dipping a much finer meshed grid into the pulp, which gave the appearance of a woven fabric.

During the early Renaissance coloured papers became fashionable, particularly for metal point drawing.

Above
JOST AMMAN
HEAD OF A BEARDED MAN
GERMAN Late 16th C.

The Venetians were among the first to import blue paper known as *'carta assura'* and shades of grey and fawn were also popular in northern Italy. The first paper-making machine was not invented until 1799 and it was not until the 1840s that wood pulp was introduced into paper manufacture.

Metal point

METAL POINT WAS used from the Middle Ages until the second half of the 15th century in Italy and later north of the Alps. A two-ended stylus made of gold, silver or lead was used on a prepared ground, and left a deposit on the skin of the support. The technique allowed artists little flexibility and was therefore ill-adapted to preliminary sketching. It was superseded in the 15th century in Italy by other media, and lead point was replaced entirely with the invention of cased pencils in the mid 16th century.

Pen and Ink

TWO TYPES OF pen were used in the Renaissance, the reed pen and the quill pen. Quill pens gave greater flexibility but reed produced a more powerful effect, and was favoured by Van Gogh and Rowlandson. Metal nibs were were not widely used for drawing until the 19th century. The ink most commonly used in the Italian Renaissance was iron gall ink which had the disadvantage that the gallic acid tends to eat into the paper and the ink turns from black to brown with age. A more satisfactory ink was carbon ink derived from soot, or bistre which was also derived from soot but was more browny-yellow in colour – it was favoured by Tiepolo. Sepia, a brownish ink which is derived from cuttlefish, was the last to be adapted by artists. Inks can give important clues for dating; for example, bistre and carbon inks were not generally in use until the 16th century and sepia did not appear as a drawing medium until the 18th century.

Chalks, Charcoal, Pastel

Black chalk was little used before the end of the 15th century. Red chalk, also known as sanguine, appeared later than black chalk, Leonardo being the first major artist to use it.

Charcoal was the preferred medium for sketching large-scale mural compositions in free hand from the time of the Greeks and the Romans, but was not widely used on drawing paper until the 16th century. The ease with which it can be erased made it a popular medium for preliminary sketches.

The closest drawing medium to painting is pastel. It consists of sticks of variously coloured powdered pigments mixed with white. Pastel did not become widely popular until the 18th century and was also favoured by Degas in the 19th century.

Watermarks and collectors' marks

ONE OF THE first things a connoisseur does when appraising a drawing is to hold it up to the light. This gives him important information about the nature of the paper and the watermarks, as well as revealing the presence of any restoration. In the case of English 18th century paper, dating is very easy since the date will normally be given underneath the paper manufacturer's name. When it comes to Old Master drawings, the watermarks for most of them can be identified by consulting Bricquet's dictionary, *Les Filigraines*. On the face of the drawing, normally in the bottom left or right hand corner, there will often be a collector's mark, which may give an important clue to the drawing's provenance.

Copies, reproductions and forgeries

COPYING HAS A long and distinguished ancestry and only an intimate knowledge of the work of an artist makes it possible to tell the difference between his hand and that of a good studio copyist. Faking has an almost equally long ancestry, although it did not become generally current until the 18th century.

The collector should also be aware of reproductions. In the mid to end of the 18th century various techniques of engraving were developed, which then produced highly successful imitations of drawings, among them crayon manner and soft ground etching.

Although knowledge of the various media and inspection of such indicators as watermarks and collectors' marks is helpful, the ultimate test is that of quality. A couple of examples will demonstrate: of the two drawings on this page, one is by the great French master, François Boucher, the other by an unknown artist working in his studio. In the case of the drawing by the unknown artist, the sheet passes most of the criteria on the check list. The paper is 18th century and the use of the three coloured chalks is highly characteristic of Boucher. The drawing is connected to and

Above
FRANCOIS BOUCHER
VENUS AND CUPID
FRENCH 1759

....

Below
CIRCLE OF BOUCHER
LA SULTANE LISANT
FRENCH Mid 18th C.

is probably a preliminary study for an engraving which then appeared in a book published in the 1740s. There is even a tantalizing inscription on the back which identifies the name of the collector to whom the drawing once belonged, an 18th century Englishman who had a distinguished collection of Old Master drawings. What is sadly lacking, though, is the great sense of volume and fluency that is apparent in the other illustration. The line is somewhat hard and hesitant and the fingertips do not taper to the same extent. Although it is doubtless a very pretty and interesting 18th century example, this drawing is considered to be one of three known copies of a lost work by Boucher.

WATERCOLOURS

BY JEREMY HOWARD

In origin, watercolours are not really a separate category but a branch of drawing. The art of watercolour developed along independent lines and it is treated as an autonomous art form with its own distinct conventions.

Technically speaking, the term watercolour is somewhat misleading since the medium is in fact gum-based, rather than water-based. The pigments are bound to each other. The water is used as a solvent in the same way that turpentine is used in oil painting. Whereas oil paint takes many hours to dry, watercolour is a much faster-drying medium.

The peculiar beauty of watercolour lies in its translucent effects, which allow colour washes to be laid on top of each other, and the whiteness of the paper to shine through.

The watercolour tradition in England begins with portrait miniatures, which were the most important vehicle of artistic expression at the Tudor Court. The most famous of the Elizabethan 'limners', as the miniaturists were called, was Nicholas Hilliard (1547–1619). The tradition was continued in the 17th century in the work of Isaac and Peter Oliver and, most notably, Samuel Cooper (1609–72), whose famous 'warts and all' miniature of

Oliver Cromwell has passed into the history books.

During the 18th century pastels were a favoured medium for portraiture. The technique of pastel drawing originated in Italy and was greatly popularized by the Venetian pastellist Rosalba Carriera who visited Paris in 1720. Her *'sfumato'* technique was much admired by English pastellists in the mid-18th century, such as Francis Cotes. Cotes' pupil John Russell was the most talented pastellist of the Regency era, developing a technique of deliberately smudging his pastels to sweeten the outlines.

Landscape and topography

THE MAINSTREAM TRADITION in English watercolours is the landscape tradition which first developed in the 17th century. Landscape painting in watercolour grew out of an essential practical activity – topography – and, right into the 19th century it retained a connection with the skills of map-making and surveying. Thomas Sandby, one of the more distinguished topographical painters, was an instructor in military surveying at Woolwich.

However, the founders of the English topographical tradition were all foreigners. Wenceslaus

Hollar was the first of these, a Bohemian artist who arrived in England in the entourage of the Earl of Arundel in the 1630s. He was followed by the Flemish artists Jan Kip and Leonard Knyff, who both published bird's eye views of the English landscape. Both these artists were essentially cartographers, but one native English watercolourist who was strongly influenced by Hollar, Francis Place (1647–1728), produced a number of watercolour drawings which have earned him some claim to the title of father of the English school of landscape painting.

In the 18th century the topographical watercolour was given further impetus by the visit of Canaletto in 1746, whose most notable English followers were Samuel Scott. Paul Sandby (1730/1–1809), another follower of Canaletto, used a mixed technique of gouache and watercolour in emulation of another Venetian painter, Marco Ricci, and is best known for his views around Windsor. A ready market for topographical watercolours grew up at the end of the 18th century, spurred by the fashionable antiquarianism and the impact of the French wars which effectively prevented English travellers from visiting the Continent and encouraged domestic tourism in its place.

A reaction against what was known as the tinted drawing, the carefully washed outlined drawings of Dayes and Malton, was inevitable. It came about partly as a result of technical experimentalism, and partly in response to the burgeoning Romantic movement.

Successive English artists visited Italy in the second half of the 18th century. The first of these was Alexander Cozens (1717–86), who developed a highly individual technique of sepia wash drawing, using a system of apparently haphazard ink blots. This duly earned him considerable ridicule and the nickname 'Sir Dirty Didgit', but he was an influential drawing master who did much to liberate watercolour from the straitjacket of topography. Another great innovator was Thomas Gainsborough (1727–88). He used a similarly experimental technique of chalk drawing rubbed with white lead, which was then dipped in skimmed milk and finished off with watercolour.

The experiments of Alexander Cozens bore fruit in the work of his son, J. R. Cozens (1752–97). He was greatly admired, not only by Constable but also by Turner and Girtin who, as young men, were employed by a benevolent amateur, Dr Thomas Munro, to copy the Cozens watercolours in his collection. Both artists had been trained in the 18th century topographical tradition where the outlines of a watercolour were neatly inked out and coloured washes then laid in. The impact of Cozens' example

Top Left
THOMAS GAINSBOROUGH
LANDSCAPE WITH CATTLE WATERING
ENGLISH 1770s

....

Left
JOHN ROBERT COZENS
A VIEW FROM SIR WILLIAM HAMILTON'S VILLA AT PORTICI
ENGLISH
Late 18th C.

....

Below
THOMAS GIRTIN
VIEW OF THE VILLAGE OF JEDBURGH
ENGLISH 1800

Above
J.M.W. TURNER
**A STUDY OF THE SEA AND SKY
THOUGHT TO BE MARGATE**
ENGLISH 1844

was revolutionary. Of the two, Thomas Girtin (1755–1802) was the first to break away from 'the neat precision of Malton and his school' and he pioneered a technique of rendering landscape with a loaded brush on a rough cartridge paper capturing the effects of light and atmosphere.

In the late 1790s, Turner himself began to move away from his early Edward Dayes manner, but, despite the increasing freedom of handling, Turner's watercolours never quite lost sight of their origins in the topographical tradition. Towards the end of his life, though, some of Turner's watercolours became almost abstract colour notes which have been seen as foreshadowing Impressionism.

This movement towards pure colour and almost abstract form was paralleled in the work of the leading artist of the Norwich School, John Sell Cotman (1782–1842), particularly in his

Yorkshire landscapes of the area around the River Greta, Peter de Wint (1784–1849), whose wash technique almost entirely abandons the use of line, and David Cox (1783–1859). At the same time a much more mystical approach to landscape was demonstrated by Samuel Palmer (1805–81) and his group of followers, George Richmond, Edward Calvert and Francis Oliver Finch, who became known as the Shoreham 'Ancients'. Meanwhile, the topographical tradition was continued in the work of Samuel Prout and William Callow, who recorded the Gothic architecture of Continental Europe, with loving, if rather prosaic, industry. The reopening of Europe after the Napoleonic Wars encouraged a fruitful interchange

between French and English artists in the 1820s and 1830s.

In the 1840's the formation of the Pre-Raphaelite brotherhood was witnessed and its championship by Ruskin. Both Ruskin and the Pre-Raphaelites favoured a detailed meticulous technique and an almost photographic intensity of vision which was emulated by watercolourists like William Hunt. Ruskin's enthusiasm for Turner found pictorial expression in the watercolours of Albert Goodwin and Hercules Brabazon, and his encouragement helped the success of a whole school of watercolourists.

Below
WILLIAM HENRY HUNT
BIRD'S NEST WITH WHITE ROSES
ENGLISH Mid 19th C.

Left
HERCULES BRABAZON
VIEW OF THE CHURCH OF SANTA MARIA DELLA SALUTE, VENICE
ENGLISH

The late 19th century saw the development of a distinctively American school of water-colourists, most notably Winslow Homer (1836–1910), and John Singer Sargent (1856–1925) and James McNeill Whistler (1834–1903), showed how watercolour could rise to the challenge of Impressionism. In the 20th century the influence of the age of watercolour has been felt in the works of John and Paul Nash, and the Neo-Romantics, Graham Sutherland and John Piper, demonstrated how the romantic watercolour can be adapted to the themes of the present day.

Materials and media

AS A GENERAL rule, the earlier the watercolour, the simpler the technique. Many 17th century watercolours are just brown wash drawings in the Dutch-Flemish manner. Towards the end of the 18th century the availability of commercially manufactured colours and in the early 19th century the introduction of a wide range of new pigments, made for greater technical complexity.

Artist's paper in England was generally of rather poor quality in the 17th century. Brown and blue paper were often used. In the 18th century, high-quality white paper was more readily available.

Reproductions and copies

THE CONNOISSEURSHIP OF English watercolours is complicated by the fact that although there are few early forgeries, copying was extensively practised. Drawing masters would give pupils their watercolours to copy. There are thus a large number of copies by amateurs dating from the end of the 18th century. Even more of a problem is to distinguish between the work of two professional artists working in the same manner. Rowlandson and Gainsborough were both forged in their own lifetime, but not until the 20th century were watercolours sufficiently prized to attract the attentions of the forger, most notoriously Tom Keating who faked a substantial number of Samuel Palmers.

Advice to the collector

PRICES OF THE very best English watercolours are now into the several hundred thousand pound bracket, but affordable work of quality can be found if one collects unfashionable items. Victorian watercolours, which were cheap, plentiful and almost invariably signed, have now become very expensive, and 18th century watercolours represent a much better buy. Figure drawing tends to be much cheaper than landscape. The collector should be even more aware than with Old Master drawings of the condition of watercolours, since they are very prone to fading and this can radically affect the value of their resale.

AMERICAN IMPRESSIONISTS

BY LAUREN RABB

The influences of French Impressionism were not felt immediately in America, because in the latter part of the 19th century America was still a provincial country and not yet able to provide much serious study of art. Young artists in America were trained as draughtsmen, and completed their studies by travelling abroad. In Paris they attended the Academies, where the traditional methods of painting were still taught and their initial training as draughtsmen was reinforced. In general, form and line were maintained, as Americans insisted on the integrity of the object; but the bolder palette of the Impressionists and a looser brushstroke were accepted. Americans Impressionists differed from the French in their interpretation of subject matter. The French worked to produce spontaneous, literal, objective views of nature. American Impressionists celebrated the human figure, did not dissolve the lines of animate objects, and often used figures to create a sense of nostalgia or a pastoral quality. The innate beauty of American Impressionist paintings has a tremendous appeal to the collector.

The first American Impressionists worked mostly abroad.

Mary Cassatt, (1845–1926) perhaps the most important of these, became friends with Edgar Degas in 1874 and basically remained in France the rest of her life. She was instrumental, however, in persuading her American friends to collect the French Impressionists, thereby introducing these artists to the United States. John Singer Sargent became famous for his portraits, but his landscapes are celebrations of the new Impressionist freedom of style. James Abbott McNeill Whistler, another expatriate, experimented tremendously with Impressionism and its aesthetic implications. And Theodore Robinson, another early American Impressionist, spent most of his career abroad, and was one of the first generation of American artists who 'discovered' the French Impressionist Claude Monet's Giverny countryside and made it his home.

The 'Ten American Painters'

AMERICANS BACK HOME were officially introduced to American Impressionism by the first exhibition of the 'Ten' held on 31 March 1898 at Durand-Ruel in New York. These ten artists had all studied abroad,

Top
FREDERIK CHILDE HASSAM
IN THE GARDEN
AMERICAN 1889

Above
FRANK WESTON BENSON
CHILD IN SUNLIGHT
AMERICAN Early 20th C.

and were united by a dissatisfaction with the Society of American Artists – a point which links them spiritually with the original French Impressionists who organized their early exhibitions in protest against the Paris Salon. The 'Ten' created the group to escape the conservatism of the Society.

The Ten American Painters were artists mainly from New York and Boston: Frederick Childe Hassam, J. Alden Weir, John Twachtman, Willard Metcalf, Edmund Tarbell, Frank Benson, Joseph De Camp, Thomas Dewing, Edward Simmons and Robert Reid. (Winslow Homer, who never considered himself an Impressionist, was invited to join, but declined.) When Twachtman died in 1902 his place was taken by William Merritt Chase. All of their lives bridged the 19th and 20th centuries. They were all committed to the Impressionist aesthetic, although in practice each artist differed greatly, and over the course of the next twenty years they continued to exhibit annually in New York and often in Boston. Their influence on American art was far-reaching and profound.

Although American Impressionism changed the course of American art forever, it soon became outmoded itself, and new movements inspired the next generation of artists. As American art moved from the Impressionists to the urban real

ism of the 'Ashcan School', Impressionism gradually lost its dominance not only among artists but among collectors as well. During the 1970s a few foresighted collectors began quietly amassing American Impressionist collections, but it was not until the 1980s that American collectors significantly rediscovered Impressionism, and in that decade prices skyrocketed. The market for American Impressionism began the 1980s with a huge supply of high quality paintings. Except for Sargent and Whistler, whose best works have long been in museum collections, excellent examples of works by Mary Cassatt, Winslow Homer, and all members of the 'Ten' were plentiful. In December of 1989, Christie's of London sold a Hassam entitled 'The Fourth of July'.

Collectors soon discovered the regional schools of American Impressionism, which remain more affordable than the 'Ten' and their circle.

As the recession of the early 1990s affected the American pocketbook, prices were expected to come down some, but this was seen as an adjustment of the market, and certainly not a decline in popularity for these artists and their paintings, which remain very much in demand. The American Impressionists will probably always be priced well out of reach for most antique collectors.

19TH CENTURY AMERICAN LANDSCAPE

BY HOWARD REHS

The Hudson River School

THE NAME HUDSON River School was coined to group together a large number of American landscape artists who were working between 1825 and 1875. These artists spanned several of the most important periods in American history, painting through the Jacksonian Era, Civil War, Secession and the Abolition of Slavery. They were contemporaries of such important writers as Irving, Cooper, Emerson, Thoreau, Whitman, Melville and Stowe and were not only familiar with the works of these authors, but at times heavily influenced by them.

The name, applied retrospectively, refers more to an attitude and style (showing the American wilderness in all its glory and detail) that these artists favoured rather than to a specific geographical location that they painted; though it is true that many of the older members drew inspiration from the Catskill region north of New York City, through which the Hudson River flows.

The School took root in 1825 when John Trumbull, Wiliam Dunlap and Asher Brown Durand first saw the work of Thomas Cole (1801–48) – the British born artist who is credited with its founding. Cole's early landscapes were spontaneous, capturing the boldness and majesty of the American wilderness. However, he could never completely give up his need to create large allegorical works; producing many important paintings in this vein including his famous series: 'The Course of Empire' (now in The New York Historical Society) and 'Voyage of Life' (now in Munson Williams Proctor Institute).

After Cole's death in 1848, Asher B. Durand (1796–1886) emerged as the central figure of the movement. Durand's work was more lasting in the scope of American Art and his aptitude for detailed, realistic scenes, influenced by the 'Truth to Nature' philosophy of John Ruskin, made him very popular with an America that needed an escape from its growing cities. Durand glorified the American landscape with his ability to express Nature convincingly in all its forms. His belief in open-air oil sketching allowed him and his followers to study and record, in colour, the true effects of sunlight on the landscape. However, like Cole, Durand's choice of colours was somewhat limited – preferring shades of green and brown. This has had a marked effect on the value of Durand's work.

Above
THOMAS COLE
LAST OF THE MOHICANS
AMERICAN Early 19th C.

Left
WILLIAM LOUIS SONNTAG
AND ARTHUR FITZWILLIAM TAIT
SUMMER MORNING, N.H.
AMERICAN Mid 19th C.

'Luminism'

BY 1850 THE natural progression of the interest in landscape and sunlight culminated in what is now called 'Luminism'. The works consist of small brush strokes, vast low horizons and subtle light, all combining to create the illusion of warm pervasive sunlight and serenity.

Jasper F. Cropsey (1823–1900), was a staunch advocate of direct study from nature. Cropsey received greatest acclaim for his paintings of autumn which are highly sought after.

During this period many other artists began working in styles closely aligned with the ideals of Thomas Cole. Included in this group are: Sanford R. Gifford, Worthington Whittredge, David Johnson, William Louis Sonntag, George H. Durrie, Martin Johnson Heade and Frederic E. Church. Some of these artists continued painting in the 'Hudson River' style, while others began to experiment with new ways of depicting the American landscape.

Fitz Hugh Lane (1804–65) is considered to be the leading member of this movement. Lane spent the first half of his artistic career in Boston working as a lithographer. By the early 1840s he had become known as a painter in oils. In the late 1840s he painted full time in the Luminist style.

This new style of painting was expanded on by Martin Johnson Heade (1879–1904). The early works show an affinity towards the Hudson River ideals, but by the 1860s Luminist traits began to show through. Heade's most noted works in the Luminist style were his marsh scenes.

Left
FITZ HUGH LANE
**THE ANNISQUAM RIVER LOOKING
TOWARD IPSWICH BAY**
AMERICAN Mid 19th C.

By the late 1850s John F. Kensett and Sanford R. Gifford (1823–86) had also made the transition from the Hudson River ideals to Luminism. Presently, it is their Luminist works that are most highly sought after.

In the late 1860s, with the close of the Civil War, the whole continent became available to the American artist. The mood that prevailed was one of patriotism and heroism, and with the expansion of American territories westward, artists found new subjects in the yet untouched frontiers.

One of the most important artists of the period was Frederic Edwin Church (1826–1900). The only true student of Thomas Cole – studying with him in the mid 1840s – Church never became a Luminist in the pure sense of the word; however, his monumental painting entitled 'Niagara' had a great impact on the works of Heade and Gifford. Church favoured large canvases and painted scenes of places as far south as the Andes and as far north as the Arctic. It was Church's brilliant arrangement of colour that was to have a profound effect on the Luminists. In recent years it has been the works of Church that have captured the passion of the present-day American collector.

There were many artists whose work touched on the ideas and ideals of the Luminist movement, the most notable of

Above
MARTIN JOHNSON HEADE
ORCHIDS AND HUMMINGBIRDS IN A BRAZILIAN JUNGLE
AMERICAN
1871–2

whom are Bierstadt and Whittredge. Albert Bierstadt (1830–1902), Church's chief rival, was mainly noted for his grand scale Western landscapes done with meticulous draughtsmanship. Even though many of his compositions hark back to the ideas of the Hudson River School, his effects of light are pure Luminism. The twilight dusk scenes of Worthington Whittredge (1820–1910) capture the Luminist light, creating the silent and eerie feeling of a vast vacant region. His well known series of works done on the beaches of Newport, Rhode Island were also painted in the Luminist style. Other artists of the period include William Bradford, Alfred T. Bricher, William Trost Richards and Francis A. Silva all of whom favoured views of the sea.

Collecting American landscape artists

IT IS INTERESTING to examine the fluctuating popularity of the 19th century American landscape artists. For the first half of the 19th century the Hudson River School dominated the art scene. They founded and controlled the National Academy of Design, placing many of their members in key positions. Their paintings were highly sought after and commanded impressive prices. By the mid 1860s the first New York Galleries had opened–showing works by European artists – so by 1875 the demand for American artists had peaked.

For the next 80 years many of the works by these artists found their way into storage rooms, basements and attics. It was not till the 1960s that prices started to rise. Today works by these artists can command high prices.

ART OF THE AMERICAN WEST

BY HOWARD REHS

American Western art is a stylistically diverse genre of the North American frontier. Western art has served in turn as a catalyst in the evolution of American popular culture.

The earliest artists

The first wave of artists in the 1820s included Samuel Seymour (c.1775–1823) and Titian Ramsay Peale (1799–1885), both skilled water-colourists, who provided Eastern and European viewers with the first glimpses of the Rocky Mountains. Today these rare works are precious historical documents as well as art objects.

The 1830s and 1840s saw the arrival of George Catlin (1796–1872), Karl Bodmer (1809–1893), and Alfred Jacob Miller (1810–74). Catlin's style is tempered by the urgent need he felt to document the Native Americans before the inevitable wave of change overtook them. Bodmer was the first to render Native Americans with ethnographic accuracy. Miller provided visual documentation of the fur trade.

Seth Eastman, John Mix Stanley, Rudolph Friedrich Kurz, William de la Montagne Cary, and Peter Rindisbacher were among the first generations to record the frontier and its native inhabitants.

The land became a national symbol of wealth, majesty, and dominion. Landscape artists, including Albert Bierstadt (1830–1902) and Thomas Moran (1837–1926), created exhilarating visions of the 19th century.

The work of Henry F. Farny (1847–1916) exemplified a continuing desire to depict the Native American accurately.

Left
ALBERT BIERSTADT
SUNSET IN THE ROCKIES
AMERICAN
Late 19th C.

Right
GEORGE CATLIN
THE MANDAN INDIANS
AMERICAN
1871

Artists in the South-west

LATE IN THE 19th century, the South-west became a mecca for American artists. Many of the country's most innovative artists visited the area – among them Marsden Hartley, Robert Henri and Stuart Davis – but the artists whose work is most associated with the South-west are those who came to stay.

Above
HENRY F. FARNY
ON THE TRAIL IN WINTER
AMERICAN 1894

The most renowned of these formed groups known as the Taos Society of Artists and Los Cinco Pintores.

The artists of the Taos Society strove to create a distinctively American art. E. Irving Couse, Joseph Henry Sharp, Ernest Blumenschein and Victor Higgins, provided sympathetic interpretations of individual Native Americans.

In the early 1920s, Fremont Ellis, Willard Nash, Wladyslaw (or Walter) Mruk, Jozef Bakos and Will Shuster formed Los Cinco Pintores, their work ranges from the traditional to radical abstract.

Others from the South-west include John Sloan, Andrew Dasburg and Georgia O'Keeffe.

Fact and fantasy in the 20th century

THE MYTH OF the West developed very quickly. Through the illustrations in popular novels, magazines, and posters, artists like Harvey T. Dunn, W. H. D. Koerner, Norman Rockwell, Frank Schoonover, Charles Schreyvogel and N. C. Wyeth catered to demands, helping to form the stereotype of the Wild West that many Americans still cherish.

Illustrators expressed the character of the West by the cowboy. The cowboy eventually became as rigidly stereotyped in art and in the popular imagination as the Native American.

The most renowned Western artists are Charles M. Russell (1864–1926) and Frederic S. Remington (1861–1909). Russell's narrative imagery expresses an empathy for other creatures and a sense of humour. Remington is the most widely known and influential of all the artists of the American West. His work ranges from large canvases, heavy with narrative detail, to nocturnal scenes. His mastery of the depiction of dramatic tension is most evident in his bronzes.

Collecting American Western art

IMPORTANT WORKS IN this field are mainly handled by the major auction houses and there are several specialist galleries in New York City and the Southwest. Exclusively Western oriented auctions are also held in the United States, such as one that is held every Spring in Great Falls, Montana.

Below
FREDERIC S. REMINGTON
THE CHEYENNE
AMERICAN 1901

ENGLISH PORTRAIT MINIATURES

BY CLAUDIA HILL

The word miniature implies any small object, but it has altered its meaning over the ages. It derives from the Latin word 'minium' meaning red lead, or vermillion, the pigment used on the illuminated manuscripts of the middle ages. The verb 'miniare' denotes the process, and the person who did this work was called a 'miniator'. Thus the word originally described a process and not the object.

A miniature is a portrait or scene. The paintings are usually executed on a small scale, although many are larger than small oil paintings. Miniatures can be painted in any medium, and whilst the earliest examples are painted on vellum, those of the 18th and 19th century are on ivory.

The miniature portrait originated in the early years of the 16th century. Before printing was invented, manuscripts were illustrated by the medieval limner. It was not until the time of Henry VIII, that any effort was made to paint portraits of living persons.

The medal was a Renaissance revival of an antique art when they tried to capture the true likeness of the sitter. They were modelled with great care and were designed to be worn by the recipient. They were housed in small circular containers which covered with glass. From the medal the portrait miniature took its circular shape and size.

Miniatures fall into two types, the portrait miniature and cabinet miniature. The former is usually circular or oval, and worn as a piece of jewellery. The latter is generally square or rectangular in shape and designed to sit on top of furniture or to hang on a wall.

Early portrait miniatures

THE EARLIEST SEPARATE portrait miniature is believed to be Jean Fouquet's self-portrait painted in enamel, circa 1460. The substance used for enamelling is a combination of a simple flux which contains silica, nitrate of potash and powdered glass, together with different metallic oxides which, when mixed together, produce a variety of colours. This compound has then to be placed on a metal surface. Fouquet's is an isolated example, for the art of enamelling did not flourish until the 17th century.

In England the miniature as a small portrait in watercolour emerged during the reign of Henry VIII, circa 1520. It was formerly believed that Hans Holbein (1497/8–1543) was the leader in this field, but it is now

Above
NICHOLAS HILLIARD
A GENTLEMAN
ENGLISH c.1600

known that Lucas Hornebolte (1490/5–1544), taught Holbein the art of limning.

All the 16th century miniatures, except those in oil, were painted on vellum stuck onto cardboard; playing cards were usually used for the backing as they were thought to provide the strongest support.

The earliest portraits by Hornebolte and Holbein were circular, but Nicholas Hilliard (1547–1619), made the oval popular. Hilliard, limner and goldsmith to Queen Elizabeth and King James I of England, continued to use a blue background but he also introduced a crimson curtain. He also painted rectangular miniatures against a landscape or the interior of a room and encouraged the use of gold leaf and gem like colours to give a rich and precious effect. His work is highly sought after, and as quite rare.

Hilliard had many pupils, the most notable being Isaac Oliver (1556–1617), but whose work was artistically more advanced. Oliver's features are better modelled and the characters were portrayed with more insight.

At the turn of the 17th century James I and other noble patrons began to show a preference for small limned copies of prized Old Master oil paintings, rather than for original compositions.

Above
SAMUEL COOPER
BARBARA VILLIERS, COUNTESS OF CASTLEMAINE
ENGLISH 1664

Artists of the 17th century such as John Hoskins (d. 1664/5), and his nephew Samuel Cooper (1609–72) were particularly influenced by Anthony van Dyck, the Flemish artist who worked at the court of Charles I. They abandoned traditional colour schemes and brushwork, in favour of a palette, and produced works of a new depth and vitality.

Cooper was so highly regarded that he was patronized by Charles II and by Oliver Cromwell. He was a great innovator in the field of miniature painting. He painted his flesh tint in a warm reddish brown tone, in place of the pink over white hitherto used in the English school of limners. Cooper explored the effects of indirect illumination and shadow and usually signed with the initials SC in separate letters or monogram followed by a date.

Many of the miniaturists working during the the 17th century were greatly influenced by Cooper. Ornate inscriptions, were replaced with simple block signatures and frequently dated. By the end of the century a form of stippling or dotting was introduced in shading the face and sometimes the backgrounds.

Enamelling

THE 17TH CENTURY saw a major development in enamelling. Previously, enamel portraits had been created by painting directly in enamel, and a metal division had been necessary to keep the colours from running into each other. Jean Toutin (1578–1644), a French goldsmith, discovered the method of applying colours onto a thin ground of previously fired white enamel, which enabled the portrait to be re-fired without damaging the tints. Opaque colours could be laid onto enamel like watercolour upon vellum.

A school of enamellers emerged. The Swiss artist Jean Petitot (1607–91) introduced the art of enamel painting into Britain, having learnt the art from Jean Toutin (1578–1644) and the Swede Jacques Bordier (1616–84). Petitot was employed by Charles I to make rings, jewellery and to paint enamel portraits.

The art of enamelling portraits was not firmly established in England until the Restoration, when Swedish miniaturist Charles Boit (1662–1727) encouraged a new interest. He came to England in 1687, and for many years after his arrival court patronage was disposed to favour enamel painting. In 1696 his abilities were recognized by William III, who appointed him Court Enamellist. Technically Boit's enamels are excellent and are often pink and yellow in colouring.

Boit taught Christian Frederick Zincke (1683/4–1767), who came to England in 1706 and was in great demand. His enamels are not quite as smooth as Boit's and often a red stippling can be observed on the face. One great difference between the two artists is that Zincke's enamels almost always have a smooth enamelled back to the miniature, whilst Boit's tend to be rough. One feature that distinguishes him from most other enamellists is that he did insist on making his enamels from life. There are many examples of his work around today.

Plumbago miniatures

DURING THE LATTER part of the 17th century plumbago miniatures and drawings came in vogue and were popular until about 1720. These are finished drawings, executed with graphite or black lead. The word is derived from the Latin *plumbum* for graphite, a pure mineral. The portraits were executed on vellum or paper, and were not usually stuck on to a support, as in the case of miniatures painted in watercolour.

There were several artists working in plumbago in England during the late 17th century, the most notable being David Loggan (1633-97), Thomas Forster (b. 1677) and Robert White (1645-1703). Characteristic of these plumbagos is their extreme attention to detail, particularly that of the sitter's costume.

Ivory based miniatures

AT THE TURN of the 18th century a major development took place which greatly affected the history of miniature painting. Rosalba Carriera (1675-1757), an Italian miniaturist, discovered that pieces of ivory or bone made a good base on which to paint. The first artist in England to use ivory as a base was Bernard Lens (1682-1740). His work appears to be remarkably fresh in comparison with his contemporaries like Peter Cross and Benjamin Arlaud.

'The modest school'

BY THE MIDDLE of the 18th century, there emerged what has now been classified as the 'modest school' of miniaturists, who flourished between 1740 and 1770. The miniatures of this period reflect a break from the ostentations of the Baroque age. This lack of pretension is reflected not only in the way the sitter's appearance and character are presented, but even in the size of the miniature, which would be about 30–40 mm ($1^{1}/4$–$1^{1}/2$ in) high. This small format made them most suitable to be worn as jewellery, either set in rings, bracelets or to be worn in a locket around the neck. Though they are by minor artists, the miniatures of this period are charming and very accessible today. They mastered some of the technical difficulties and paved the way for some more notable masters of the end of the century.

It is sometimes difficult to discriminate between individual styles of this period by the very nature of the size and modest approach to the portrait. Fortunately a sufficient number are signed enabling the collector to recognize them. An influential artist of the modest school was Gervase Spencer (d.1763). His miniatures bear the initials 'G.S.' and are dated between 1745 and 1761. He practised both in enamel and on ivory, as did many of his contemporaries Nathaniel Hone (1718-84) was

Above
RICHARD COSWAY
A LADY
ENGLISH Early 19th C.

a prolific artist whose miniatures are signed with 'N.H.', dated between 1750 and 1770.

Several artists of this time had the same initials and signed their work accordingly, for instance Samuel Cotes and Samuel Collins.

The heyday of miniature painting

BY THE END of the century ivory was the most popular base for miniatures, and it was Richard Cosway (1742-1821) who first discovered its true potential. His early works are often small but as larger ivories became popular, circa 1785, so his style developed. He learnt that by floating transparent pigments on to the ivory, one could leave the material itself to suggest the light. He adopted the method of painting hair in soft masses and introduced a background of blue clouds. The use of Antwerp blue is very typical. Occasionally he signed his works in full on the reverse.

Jeremiah Meyer (1735–89), produced a large number of miniatures. As his work is rarely signed, it may go unrecognized, but his work can be identified by studying the treatment of the sitter's face. The mouth, nose and eyes are slightly angular looking, in comparison with Cosway's more lucid approach. His backgrounds are usually soft, pale and uniform in colour as opposed to Cosway's cloud effect.

Richard Crosse gives the mouth prominence in his art, but his system of colouring is quite unique. His small portraits always seem to be pervaded by a greenish blue tint.

Arguably the most sought after artist of this period is John Smart (1742/3–1811). He formed the style of adding his signature to a cursive 'J.S.' and date. Between 1785 and 1795 he visited India; miniatures done during this time are easily recognizable for he added a capital 'I' after his signature.

Unlike many miniaturists his style and technique were fully developed at the beginning of his career. He favoured a background of uniform grey buff colour and used a red brick colour for the complexion. The eyelashes are so carefully drawn that one can sometimes count each individual one. Perhaps one of the reasons his work achieves such a high reputation today, besides being very attractive and beautifully executed, is that the details of the costume are in flat bodycolour and consequently have not faded.

These sketches, which Smart probably kept in case repetitions were required, are works of art in themselves, and are the same size as the miniatures for which they were intended.

Another artist of considerable ability was George Engleheart (1750–1829). Regrettably many of his works have been exposed to light causing the greens and carmines to fade. Nevertheless, his work is desirable, particularly those he painted after 1780. Characteristics of his miniatures from this period are the linear massing of hair, diagonal grey strokes at the corner of the mouth and zigzag outlining of the drapery in opaque white. He favoured the use of blue backgrounds drawn in diagonal strokes. He excelled in painting women and children and often portrayed them wearing large straw hats entwined with bows and ribbons.

After 1800, Engleheart often used the rectangular format in place of the oval one: these examples are usually signed with a 'G.E.' Engleheart's fee books from 1775 to 1813 are an astounding record of industry and indicate the prolific patronage which he had. It is known that he could produce up to 228 miniatures in a year. This vast quantity is indicative of the great demand for miniature portraits at the end of the 18th century.

One lesser artist whose work is plentiful is Andrew Plimer. His earlier works, of the years between 1785 and 1789, are signed 'AP' and dated, but lack the brilliance of his later work by which he has become known.

Samuel Shelley (1750/56–1808) was a late 18th century artist of considerable ability. His miniatures possess great charm. Characteristics of his work are a yellowish green flesh tint, and the enlargement of the pupil of the eye. Occasionally the miniatures are signed 'S.S.' on the front, but more frequently, the signature is 'Sam Shelley' on the reverse, followed by his address.

Left
JOHANN HEINDRICH HURTER
MRS MARY NESBITT
ENGLISH 1783

The enamel miniature continued in the second half of the 18th century by artists such as Henry Spicer (1743–1804), a pupil of Gervase Spencer, and by Johann Heinrich Hurter (1734–99).

19th century miniaturists

ANDREW ROBERTSON (1777–1845) at one time also intended to make a series of copies of Old Masters, but he changed course to that of miniature portraits from life. In place of the attractive but rather frivolous paintings of Cosway and other 18th century miniaturists, 19th century patrons were looking for more solid and richly painted portraits executed on a larger scale and more like the oil paintings and watercolours that were becoming so popular at this period. Robertson felt that miniatures ought to be oil paintings on a small scale, and his style reflected the change in public taste.

By 1814, Robertson employed Sir William Charles Ross (1794/5–1860) as his assistant to help paint in the backgrounds of his miniatures. Once Ross became known he too became a prolific artist in his own right, and he was appointed in 1837 as Queen Victoria's miniature painter. His miniatures are well designed. He had a great ability to paint full-length figures on ivory and compose them into charming pictures.

The demand for larger portraits, for displaying on the top of furniture or for hanging, meant that miniatures lost the intimacy that they had hitherto possessed. These larger portraits, good though many of them are, could not defend themselves against the cheaper method of photography.

There are certain subjects which prove to be especially popular today judging by the prices they reach at auction, namely examples of pretty ladies, children, soldiers or historical figures.

Below
ANDREW ROBERTSON
PRINCESS AMELIA
ENGLISH 1810

Collecting miniatures

COLLECTORS SHOULD NOT be swayed by fashion or taste, for these fluctuate, but it is advisable to buy what appeals and try to obtain those that are in good condition. Damaged miniatures, especially those on ivory, are difficult to repair. It is important to remember, however, that whether a miniature is set in a jewelled locket or in a simple frame, it is the quality of the painting that matters, regardless of the period in which it was painted.

The most obvious type of forgeries are those which are housed in ivory frames, made of old piano keys. These were made on the Continent at the end of the 19th century, and are still produced today. They have old paper from French or German books pasted on the back and are often signed with the names or initials of well-known painters, such as Reynolds or Gainsborough, and miniaturists such as Cosway, or Engleheart. Another form of forgery is to overpaint a photograph which is then offered as a genuine miniature. During the late 19th century when photography became popular, studios employed artists to hand-tint photographs. The result was a coloured likeness, but not a true portrait miniature.

PICTURE FRAMES

BY JAMES BRUCE GARDYNE

French and Spanish frames

Only in recent years has the art world shown an interest in this field. The picture frame has been continually neglected as an object in its own right. But the late 1980s saw a change in attitude which has resulted in a more educated approach.

It is generally accepted that the origins of the picture frame are in Renaissance Italy. The 15th century saw a change in the siting of paintings; instead of being a fixed part of the wall they could be a more moveable object requiring both a protective and structural support. As many of these pictures were housed in churches, it was not surprising that the earliest frames were derived from architectural elements, resembling window designs or even church facades.

By the 16th century the frame had been reduced to a

Above
CARVED FRAME
ITALIAN 17th C.

plain structure made up of four flat panels of wood known as the *Cassetta*. Its basic format was adhered to throughout Italy during the 16th and 17th centuries, although the gilding and painted decoration varied from region to region.

Later, the flat profile of the *Cassetta* was to develop into a distinctive baroque manner with complex sweeping silhouettes and pierced fruit and foliate carving. In Florence, the 'Leaf' frame variation had a curved, graceful, almost sculptural, outline with carved scrolls and foliage.

Left
CASSETTA FRAME
ITALIAN Late 16th C.

UP TO THE END of the 17th century the most influential centres of frame-making were in Italy. By the early 18th century, a geographical shift had occurred and French craftsmen had come to dominate the art. Louis XIII (1601–43) frames were characterized by a strict rectangular format with a tight bonding of decoration that did not interfere with the profile. Louis XIV (1653–1715) style, with corner and centre decorations but still retaining strictly defined boundaries, to the French Regency period (1715–23), where the corners and centre motifs come to dominate the frame, resulted in pierced scrolling tendrils and ribbons, with an ornamental silhouette.

The reign of Louis XV (1723–74), saw an abundance of naturalistic carving breaks and rectangular boundaries. This was later to subside into a formal simplistic style during the time of Louis XVI (1774–92).

The Spanish frames of the 16th and 17th centuries were influenced by those in Italy. They stuck to the basic flat *Cassetta* form, but adorned the centres and corners with high relief ornamentation. The heavy decoration gave the frames a three-dimensional quality that was sometimes lacking in their Italian counterparts.

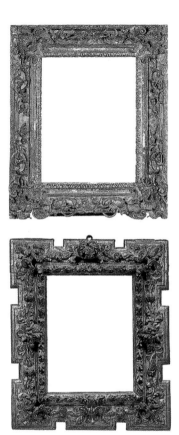

Top
FRENCH REGENCY FRAME
FRENCH Early 18th C.

Above
CARVED AND GILDED FRAME
SPANISH 17th C.

Frame-makers in the following century were not to attain the same level of imagination, and consequently designs were to change little in concept except to become heavier and more static in appearance.

The greater plainness of Dutch and English frames

The Dutch frames of the 17th century adhered to two basic designs. The most common form was the black or ebonized frame whose decoration lay in a shallow surface carving which produced a basketweave or ripple effect. A simpler way to achieve a similar effect was to decorate the frame with a tortoiseshell veneer.

An alternative to the ebonized or tortoiseshell frame was the 'Lutma'. It incorporated a relief-like form with swags of flowers, putti and stylized heads running from a cresting top to the base of the frame. This gave rise to a similar design in England during the 17th century, called the 'Sunderland' frame.

In England, frames were influenced by ideas from the Continent. Whilst the 'Lely' frame was inspired by the Venetian panel frame, the 'Carlo Maratta', was a variant of the 'Salvator Rosa' frame. Later the 'Swept' frame was to have its origins in the profiles of the Louis XV frames.

English 18th century furniture was dominated by Thomas Chippendale (1709–79). By the mid1700s the English neoclassical style created harsh outlines decorated with Vitruvian scrolls, volutes and egg-and-dart running patterns.

Throughout England and the Continent the 19th century was dominated by the composition frame, which enabled earlier styles to be reproduced in vast inexpensive quantities. The age of the individual framemaker and skilled craftsman had finally passed and its effect would only be recreated in plaster.

From its Renaissance, architecturally induced origins, through the flat surround of the *Cassetta* and culminating in the French 18th century, the frame had always been an important, if secondary component, to the painting as a whole. Consequently, it is worth remembering, that the cost of making a frame was often higher than that of the commissioned picture itself.

EUROPEAN SCULPTURE

IONA BONHAM-CARTER

Above
GIAMBOLOGNA
RAPE OF A SABINE
ITALIAN Late 16th C.

The field of European sculpture is a richly varied and expansive domain of antique collecting. Unlike the more utilitarian areas, such as furniture and carpets, the acquisition of sculpture has primarily been a luxury.

The Middle Ages

DURING THE MIDDLE AGES the Church was the main patron of sculpture. Churches were decorated not only with stained glass and frescoes, but also with richly coloured and gilded wood sculpture, finely wrought metalwork, enamels and reliquaries. To all the church goers of the day the atmosphere created by such surroundings would have been heavenly, and many of the works of art would have been narrative and consequently instructive to the illiterate majority.

The medieval and gothic sculptures and works of art of exceptional craftsmanship which survived the centuries of anarchy and religious turmoil are now mostly to be found in museums, and sometimes in church treasuries. When an important medieval enamel or ivory comes up for sale, the competition from museums and specialized private collectors is fierce.

The main workshops of enamels were in Limoges in France in the 12th and 13th centuries, where the art of enamelling became a highly sophisticated production. One can still purchase a 13th century

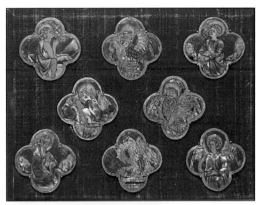

Left
TRANSLUCENT ENAMEL QUATREFOILS
SPANISH
Late 14th C.

....

Below
CARVED SANDSTONE FIGURES
ENGLISH
13th C.

Limoges enamel cross, although a complete reliquary casket would be very expensive. The rarer, and often finer, 12th century enamels from the Mosan region seldom appear on the market. Italy and Spain also produced fine translucent enamels in the 14th and 15th centuries, many of which adorned silver-gilt church plate. These can still be found on the market and are relatively inexpensive.

Due to the perishable nature

of wood, not many examples of early wood sculpture of high quality have survived. However, unlike the specialized skills required for enamel work, wood sculpture necessitated simpler talents and could therefore be carved locally. Examples of these provincial works also appear on the art market. On the other hand, medieval stone sculpture survives with greater ease, and is often still *in situ* decorating the exterior of cathedrals for example. Secular stone carving of this date is rarer.

The Renaissance and Early Modern period

WITH THE GROWTH of the wealthy merchant classes in the 14th and 15th centuries, the demand for secular art increased, though the burghers also commissioned religious sculpture, but of a size more suited to their homes rather than to an abbey.

Italy had both a powerful church, and wealthy merchants, whose commissions of sculpture influenced their northern counterparts. An example of early Italian sculpture to come on the market recently was a marble relief of the Virgin and Child attributed to the Master of the Marble Madonnas, dated to the second half of the 15th century. This sculpture illustrates the relationship between the ecclesiastical and secular patrons of the early Renaissance, but may have been commissioned by a merchant to be placed either in his home or in a church he patronised.

The invention of printing had a big effect on the production of enamels, stained glass and marble, wood or ivory reliefs. A craftsman could enamel a plaque or carve a relief using as his inspiration a woodcut or engraving.

Above
MINIATURE WOODEN HOUSE ALTAR
GERMAN c.1500

Left
MASTER OF THE MARBLE MADONNAS
RELIEF OF THE VIRGIN AND CHILD
ITALIAN 15th C.

Facing page
NICLAUS WECKMANN THE ELDER
CARVED ALTER WING
GERMAN Early 16th C.

Above
IVORY CLOCK
GERMAN Mid 17th C

Left
GIAMBOLOGNA
A REARING HORSE
ITALIAN Late 16th C

Below
BARTHELEMY PRIEUR
**KING HENRI IV AND
QUEEN MARIE DE MEDICI**
FRENCH Early 17th C.

Secular art in the 16th and 17th centuries

WITH THE ADVENT of Humanism in the 16th and 17th centuries the great princes acquired important collections of secular art, including curiosities, such as ostrich eggs, coconuts and nautilus shells, which were mounted in silver or copper gilt, with enamels and jewels, and placed in special cabinets of works of art.

The presence in one place of many prominent artists created a distinctive style particular to an area. This was the case in Prague, where Rudolph II (1552–1612) attracted many of the great artists of the time. A particular style was generated by the fusion of major sculptors working for François I at Fontainebleau. However, the diplomatic exchange of prized works of art took place between the different European courts, thus disseminating styles. Giambologna, who worked for the Medici in Florence, influenced both the French and German courts through the portable medium of the small, highly finished bronze.

Left
MASSIMILIANO
SOLDANI-BENZI
BUST OF A YOUNG FAUN
ITALIAN 18th C.
....
Below
JOHANN ANDREAS THELOT
HOUSE ALTAR
GERMAN Early 18th C.

The bronzes produced by Giambologna's close assistants such as Antonio Susini, are highly prized. France, too, had highly prized court sculptors such as Barthélémy Prieur who worked for Henri IV and Marie de Medici.

The Baroque age

BAROQUE SCULPTURE OF the late 17th and 18th centuries was most prominent in Italy and Germany. In Germany and Austria in particular, the Baroque style was used as decoration in churches, and also in the palaces and libraries built by the nobility.

An interesting example of this association of Christianity and elaborate adornment is a lavish house altar in ivory, bone, silver, gilt copper and wood sold at Christie's in April 1991. It is a rare and splendid work of art of the typically Baroque taste.

With the 18th century and the settled monarchy in England, the English patronage of sculpture became established. As a result of continental travels, the English patronized the artists of Italy and France, and brought their acquisitions home. Artists such as Massimiliano Soldani Benzi of Florence received commissions for bronze reductions of celebrated sculptures from both English travellers and European royalty. His bronzes follow the Giambologna tradition of high finish and glowing, reddish gold patination.

Right
SIR ALBERT GILBERT
THE KISS OF VICTORY
ENGLISH Late 19th C.

The 18th and 19th centuries

TOWARDS THE END of the 18th century, the production of Grand Tour bronzes, often based on Antique Roman originals, had reached its zenith of industry. In Rome the Zoffoli and the Righetti workshops specialized in this commodity, executing small bronzes. These bronzes are still relatively inexpensive at auction. The 18th century also saw the enriching of English sculpture by the influx of foreign sculptors, particularly Huguenots and Flemings, who sought the stability and prosperity of English patrons.

The art of portraiture, mainly in marble, was revived and it became de rigueur for an Englishman of culture to have his bust done by one of the fashionable foreign sculptors of the day. On the other hand, by the late 18th and early 19th centuries, an extensive industry of portrait sculpture was established by sculptors such as Nollekens, which cost a fraction of this.

The early part of the 19th century continued the Neoclassicism of the late 18th. The most prominent sculptor of the period was the Italian Antonio Canova, outstanding not only for his own technical excellence and pure compositions, but also for

his widespread influence on the many gifted young sculptors from France, Scandinavia, Germany and England working in his studio. This style of sculpture was particularly popular in England, where it found generous patrons. John Gibson, for example, returned to England much influenced by Canova and treasured by the British. Towards the end of the century, a small group of English sculptors broke away from this academic tradition and formed a freer style known as The New Sculpture. This is typified by the fluid and romantic work of Frederick Leighton, Alfred Gibson, Alfred Drury and Henry Onslow Ford.

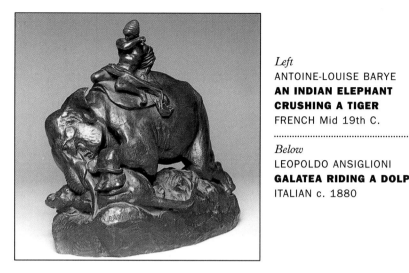

Left
ANTOINE-LOUISE BARYE
AN INDIAN ELEPHANT CRUSHING A TIGER
FRENCH Mid 19th C.

Below
LEOPOLDO ANSIGLIONI
GALATEA RIDING A DOLPHIN
ITALIAN c. 1880

On the continent, new trends such as the French '*Animalier*' school developed slightly earlier. Sculptors such as Antoine Louis Barye and Pierre Jules Mene enjoyed great popularity, both at home and abroad. Their charming bronzes of animals, which introduced a new naturalism to the subject, were produced in large quantities and varying quality, which is reflected in the diverse prices they now fetch. They remain, nevertheless, within reach of more modest collectors. Simultaneously, a romantic tradition imbued both private and public sculpture, firstly in France and then spreading to the whole of Europe. The range of subject matter and of sculptors was immense, and examples of these decorative bronze and marble works of allegorical, mythological, realistic and religious subjects can still be found at reasonable prices. The appearance of wealthy patrons, stimulated by the Industrial Revolution and the development of sophisticated and mechanical techniques, encouraged the production of these decorative sculptures. 'Galatea Riding a Dolphin' by Ansiglioni grandly illustrates the frivolous and charming aspect of much later 19th century sculpture.

DECORATIVE
ARTS
MOVEMENTS

Above
GILT BRONZE LAMP
FROM A MODEL BY RAOUL LARCHE
FRENCH Early 20th C.

THE ARTS AND CRAFTS MOVEMENT

BY LYDIA CRESSWELL-JONES

The Arts and Crafts movement originated in England as a reaction to the growing materialism of the 1850s. Despite the Industrial Revolution, the improved methods of manufacture and the employment of new materials, stylistically pieces were still echoing the themes of the past. As manufacturers adapted themselves to the new machinery, they began to lose sight of the aesthetic qualities of their products.

The need for a defined manifesto was recognized by a few pioneers, and William Morris (1834–96) was one of the main originators. Morris embodied the embryonic movement; a painter, poet, craftsman, lecturer and militant pamphleteer, he wanted to unify all the arts and crafts to bring about comprehensive reform.

William Morris

MORRIS STUDIED AT Oxford from 1853, and had developed an affection for the culture of the Middle Ages. He had also become familiar with the works of John Ruskin (1819–1900), who believed that a respect for materials and all their qualities was paramount to the craftsman. Writing in *The Seven Lamps of Architecture* (1849), Ruskin stated: 'I believe the right question to ask is simply this: was it done with enjoyment – was the carver happy while he was about it?'

Top
MORRIS HAND-KNOTTED CARPET
ENGLISH c. 1900

Above
WILLIAM MORRIS AND DE MORGAN TILE PANEL
ENGLISH c. 1876

Left
MORRIS THREE-FOLD SCREEN
ENGLISH 1889

At Oxford, Morris worked for two years in the office of the architect George Edmund Street (1824–81), where he met Philip Webb (1831–1915). In 1859 Webb designed the Red House at Bexleyheath for Morris and his bride, Jane Burden.

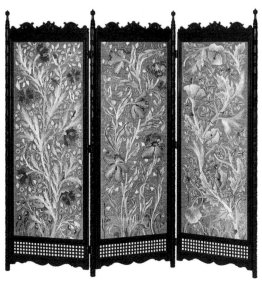

Groups of workers were involved throughout the building process. Together with Dante Gabriel Rossetti (1828–82) and Edward Burne-Jones (1833–98), Morris and Webb searched for function and originality in what they made.

It was partly the Red House project that inspired Morris to set up in business. The firm of Morris, Marshall, Faulkner & Co, Fine Art Workmen in Painting, Carving and Furniture and the Metals, was established in 1861 and was the first such collaborative venture in existence. The firm first showed at the 1862 International Exhibition at South Kensington in two classes – decorated furniture, tapestries and stained glass windows. They were awarded medals in both classes and, the stained glass was so good an imitation of medieval ware that, some competitors in the trade believed that they had used original glass.

Morris' followers

AS THE FOLLOWERS of Morris urged for the practical and less ornamental, so more guilds based on Morris' cooperative began to be established. In 1882, Arthur Heygate Mackmurdo (1851–1942) founded the Century Guild of Artists. Mackmurdo's friendship with Morris had been established by 1877, with the formation of the Society for the Protection of

Above
MACKMURDO MAHOGANY CABINET
ENGLISH
c. 1886

....

Right
VOYSEY HIGH-BACKED CHAIRS
ENGLISH
1898

Ancient Buildings. Through the Guild's magazine *The Hobby Horse* first published in April 1884, Mackmurdo questioned some of Morris' beliefs, but also acknowledged 'as an artist and craftsman, he is our master'.

Although not officially a member of Mackmurdo's guild, Charles Annesley Voysey (1857–1941) worked with it. Voysey had originally trained with the cabinet-maker, John Pollard Seddon, and the architect, Saxon Snell, but in 1881–82 he had decided to set up on his own as an architect. Voysey had travelled with Mackmurdo in Italy, and in 1883 started to collaborate with the guild on designs for wallpapers and textiles. His furniture designs soon became recognized by both the public and critics for their artistic merits.

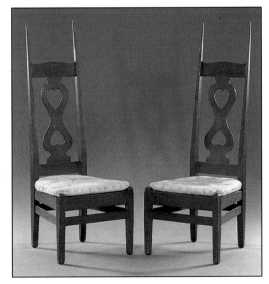

work. The guild produced silver and jewellery and delicate enamels, leatherwork and woodwork. The work had a distinctive style in design, including simple forms reminiscent of medieval silverwork. Many included semi-precious stones, and almost all had a hammered surface, stressing that the pieces were hand-made rather than manufactured. The guild furniture, always looked as if it was hand-crafted.

Left
VOYSEY MANTEL CLOCK
ENGLISH c.1895

Below
ASHBEE CABINET
ENGLISH c.1906

Charles Robert Ashbee (1863–1942) attended a meeting of the Hammersmith Branch of the Socialist League, and was struck by the ideas and beliefs of the group. He was living at an educational charity in London, where he was the only architect in residence. He started a Ruskin reading class and began to teach drawing and decoration. Ashbee founded the Guild of Handicraft in 1888, with three members and a working capital of £50. Its aims were to re-educate its members and train them for a specific industry. A s h b e e moved the guild in its entirety, in 1902, to Chipping Camden in Gloucestershire. By now it comprised 150 men, women and children, and the decision to relocate was taken by a poll of the members. Ashbee revived the educational aspects of his

By 1905 the guild was suffering financially. The constraints in terms of time resulted in pieces priced considerably higher than those of other local workers who were embracing the new machinery. Ashbee's trial and error methods, athough noble, were expensive, and as the strain began to show. Eventually the guild was forced into liquidation in 1907.

In 1890, Ernest Gimson, W. R. Lethaby, Ernest and Sidney Barnsley, Mervyn MacCartney and Reginald Blomfield founded the firm of Kenton & Company. Named after a street near their workshop in Bloomsbury, the group purposefully avoided an idealistic 'guild' title. Each member of the group contributed £100 towards the cost of setting up and turned their attentions towards experimenting with daring technical innovations and making one-off pieces of furniture rather than following a manifesto in the way that Ashbee had. However, the firm was to be short-lived, due to lack of capital. Nevertheless, at their first exhibition at Holborn in December 1891 and at the Arts and Crafts Exhibition Society show of 1890, they received much critical acclaim.

Lethaby is most relevant in the Arts and Crafts movement as a teacher and theorist. He founded the Central School of Arts and Crafts with George Frampton in 1896, which became the most advanced and dynamic art school in Europe until the foundation of the Bauhaus.

After the demise of Kenton and Company, Gimson and the Barnsley brothers wnet into partnership producing simple, strong pieces of furniture and metalwork, enriched with smoothly sculptural details, a style developed by the Dutch cabinetmaker Peter Waals, who collaborated with Gimson. The visitors to their workshops were many and the difficulty was only to complete the orders that they received.

Above

INLAID MAHOGANY TABLE DESIGNED BY W.R.LETHABY
ENGLISH 1890–91

Below
WILLIAM DE MORGAN
LUSTRE DISHES
ENGLISH Late 1880s–1900

The philosophy spreads

PUBLIC AWARENESS OF the Arts and Crafts movement was developed through exhibitions and competitions. Lectures on art and craft were given and mail order companies and speciality shops were established.

The Arts and Crafts Exhibition Society, was set up in 1888 to revolt against the exclusive view of art encouraged by the paintings-biased Royal Academy exhibitions. The work it showed included furniture by Edward Barnsley, Lethaby, Voysey and Walter Cave, silver and jewellery by Ashbee, Henry Wilson and Nelson Dawson, and glass by James Powell. The Society also held lectures and demonstrations as part of an attempt to publicize the aims of the movement. As similar problems of industrialization were recognized abroad, the theories of Ruskin and Morris began to reach a wider audience. In Vienna, Josef Hoffman and Kolomon Moser established the Wiener Werkstatte in 1903. In Germany, too, similar workshops were growing in the 1880s and 1890s. Whilst in America, a number of craftsmen began to adapt to the English craft ethic .

One of the main exponents of Arts and Crafts ideals in America was Gustav Stickley (1857–1942). He had trained as a stonemason and was deeply influenced by Ruskin and in 1898 travelled to England where he met Voysey and Lethaby, among other designers. On his return to America he began to produce his 'Mission' furniture, huge, yet simple oak pieces. His company was called 'The United Crafts' and the workshop was organized along the lines of the guilds in England.

In Chicago and the Mid-West the work of Frank Lloyd Wright (1869–1959) culminated in a movement now known as the Prairie school of architecture. The founder of the school, Louis H. Sullivan (1856–1924), was a revolutionary architect and pioneer of skyscrapers. As chief draughtsman from 1888 to 1893 Wright absorbed many of his theories, notably that 'ornament is mentally a luxury, not a necessary' and that 'it would be greatly for our aesthetic good if we should refrain from the use of ornament for a period of years'.

Wright's early designs in furniture showed him more as a sculptor. The stark exteriors of his buildings contrasted well with the uncluttered interiors, reflecting what became a life-long admiration of Japanese architecture.

As the Arts and Crafts movement developed into the 20th century it became apparent that a total rejection of the machine age did not spell long-term success. Their search for a standard of goodness and suspicion of anything new, did not represent a sound business ethic. The new society that Morris and his followers envisaged bore little resemblance to the reality of the Victorian industrial economy, and Morris' belief that he could 'never be contented with getting anything short of the best' often meant that it was only the wealthy who could afford to become his clients.

ART DECO

BY OLIVIER BROMMET

The Art Deco style draws its name from the Exposition des Art Décoratifs et Industrielles, held in Paris in 1925.

The exhibition included contributions from most of the industrialised countries, although Germany was excluded and the USA declined the invitation to attend. It was quite apparent that there was one prevalent style, that of the French exhibitors. The French were the most important exponents of the style, so much of the best of Art Deco is French in origin.

Above
SILVER-LEAFED WOOD COMMODE
FRENCH 1923

Left
ART DECO POSTER
FRENCH 1935

Furniture

ART DECO GOES back to when the fashion designer Paul Poiret (1879–1944) released women from the confinement of the corset, and shortened skirts. In the same year, Sergei Diaghilev and his Ballets Russes came to Paris for the first time inspiring Poiret to design brightly coloured exotic fashion accessories.

The following year the Salon d'Automne produced a similar turning-point in French furniture design. The German stand at this Salon shook French artists and designers who were still very much involved with Art Nouveau, while the Germans showed progressive modern Neoclassic styles.

Furniture design became more geometric and decoration was reduced to abstract motifs intended to break the symmetry.

Fashion designers were at the forefront of this change. Paul Poiret met Josef Hoffmann and Koloman Moser, the founders of the Wiener Werkstatte. Poiret created l'Atelier Martine, upon his return to Paris. This was a school and workshop combined, where girls were given a free hand to design textiles, rugs, wallpapers and furniture. L'Atelier Martine was a success, and later artists such as Raoul Dufy became associated with it.

The most important *ébeniste* (a French term which implies someone who combines all the skills of a master designer and cabinetmaker) of the period was Jacques-Emile Ruhlmann who established his own firm, Ruhlmann et Laurent. This was

to become the most prestigious decorating firm in France. Using expensive woods and hiring the best craftsmen to execute his designs, Ruhlmann effectively put his furniture out of reach of all but the rich. The middle classes also wanted modern furniture, so the big department stores set out to satisfy their needs. They provided modern furniture, and a whole range of accessories in a unified style, designed and manufactured in their own workshops. The first store to open such a workshop, was Le Magazin du Printemps, under the name Atelier Primavera. Galleries Lafayette followed three years later. The best Art Deco furniture is very expensive to buy. It is, however, still possible to pick up attractive pieces of quality furniture if one is prepared to go for lesser names.

Top
PRIMAVERA
PAINTED WOODEN TABLE
FRENCH 1925

Above
PIERRE LEGRAIN
AFRICAN-STYLE STOOL
FRENCH Early 20th C.

Left
JACQUES-EMILE RUHLMANN
ROSEWOOD AND IVORY DESK
FRENCH 1927

Glass

FRANCE HAD A long history of glassmaking, which peaked during the Art Nouveau period. Artists like Emile Gallé and Antonin Daum, revived many old techniques. Both men's factories participated at the 1925 exhibition, where Daum presented heavy glass vessels with deep, acid-etched geometric motifs.

These vessels were influenced by Maurice Marinot (1882–1962)who was originally trained as a painter. Marinot became attracted to glass in 1911 and started working with decorative enamels. As his understanding of glass working grew, he started to create heavy glass vases and bottles. He is best known for his use of hydrofluoric acid to cut deep geometric motifs in glass. Marcel Goupy and Auguste Heiligenstein were enamellers working in a similar vein, while Andre Thuret, Henri Navarre and Jean Luce were all influenced by his later work. Marinot's work is widely represented in museums but appears only rarely on the market.

The work of René Lalique (1860-1945), is more widely available and more collectable. Lalique was first a highly influential jeweller. His women with flowing hair or life-like insects, in gold and with precious stones, brought him worldwide acclaim. He became interested in glass and started experiment-

ing in 1902, creating glass jewellery. He started to create vases and figures in the lost-wax technique, hitherto only used for bronze. His first commission came in 1906 when he was asked to design scent bottles for the firm of Coty. Unlike Marinot, he did not concentrate on creating unique pieces, but used the latest technology for high quality mass-production, using a stamping press to press glass in a mould, he produced large editions of the same design.

Lalique's commissions included fountains for the city of Paris and glass decorations for ocean liners. Although widely copied no one was ever able to match his brilliance.

Another popular glass technique was *pâte-de-verre*. Crushed and powdered glass is mixed with a binding agent and metal oxides as colouring agents to create a paste, which then lines a mould in a kiln at a temperature high enough to vitrify the paste.

The most important and popular artists to work in this medium were François Decorch-

Above
DECO GLASS VASES
MAURICE MARINOT (left)
ANDRE THURET (right)
FRENCH Early 20th C.

emont, Almaric Walter and Gabriel Argy-Rousseau. but their styles were very different. Often using lost-wax technique, Decorchement produced heavy-bodied vases cast with natural or geometric motifs.

Almaric Walter, who started working in pâte-de-verre at Daum set up his own workshop in 1919, and is best known for heavy, opaque objects, small sculptures and vases. Gabriel Argy-Rousseau produced a semi-opaque substance, richly coloured and lightweight. His work consisted of bowls, panels, vases (see picture left), lamps and sculptures. His early work was decorated with classical motifs, but in the 1920s, and animals, mythological creatures and geometric patterns appeared on his work. This later work is very much in demand today.

Ceramics

ART DECO CERAMICS reflect the interest there was in Chinese, Islamic and Greek mythology. The two most important artists in the twenties were Emile Decoeur and Emile Lenoble. Decoeur worked in stoneware and porcelain. Around 1925 he created vessels covered in magnificent plain coloured glazes. Emile Lenoble on the other hand, put the emphasis on decoration.

André Metthey gave up stoneware as early as 1906 and worked in earthenware. Jean Mayodon became artistic director of the Manufacture de Sèvres. René Buthaud was technical and artistic director of the ceramics department of Primavera before taking up a senior teaching post at the Bordeaux Ecole des Beaux Arts.

The two largest factories were Havilland in Limoges and the Manufacture de Sèvres. Sèvres set up a *faience* department in order to prepare for the 1925 Exhibition by asking artists and decorators like Lalique, Ruhlmann, Dupas and many others to design for the factory. Theodore Havilland called on Suzanne Lalique (René's daughter) and Jean Dufy.

England produced some very good work in ceramic in this period. Royal Doulton ceramic sculptures designed by Richard Garbe as well as their 'Sung' and 'Chang' wares are widely collected today. Probably the most sought-after English 'Deco' potter today is Clarice Cliff. Her brightly coloured 'Bizarre' wares, introduced in 1928, are widely available. Much rarer are her creations decorated after designs by well known artists including Duncan Grant, Laura Knight, Ben Nicholson and Frank Brangwyn.

Susie Cooper painted strong cubist and abstract patterns in bright colours and eventually became a leading designer for Wedgwood.

It is still possible to buy quality ceramics at reasonable prices if one looks for the lesser known names. The French factory of Robj produced a range of novelty bottles in the shape of figures dressed in bright costumes. These are amusing and attractive. One can also find very attractive objects by Shelley potteries of Staffordshire, England

Metalwork and lacquer

THE INTERWAR YEARS saw a great demand for decorative metalwork. New technology made the manufacturing of metal easier; new alloys and patinas were also discovered at this time.

Edgar Brandt was the most successful of the metalworkers. He was responsible for the Porte d'Honneur at the 1925 exhibition, and also for a room in the Pavilion d'une Ambassade Française. Many public commissions came his way, including the Tomb of the Unknown Soldier and its eternal flame under the Arc de Triomphe in Paris. He also created a variety of light fixtures, fire-screens and radiator grills, the light fittings often in conjunction with glass shades by Daum. Other successful metalworkers were Gilbert Poillerat, Paul Kiss, Jules and Michel Nics and Richard Desvallieres.

Jean Dunand (1877–1942) concentrated on *dinanderie*. In this process a single sheet of copper is hammered into a shape, and then decorated by means of patination, embossing or the inlay of other metals.

Dunand is more famous for his lacquer work which he applied on to metal vases. He moved on to screens, panels and furniture, which he decorated using colour pigments in the lacquer, by incising motifs, by inlaying mother of pearl or crushed eggshell. He lacquered furniture created by designers such as Printz, Ruhlmann and Legrain.

Left
EDGAR BRANDT
WROUGHT-IRON MIRROR
Les Jets d'Eau
FRENCH Early 20th C.

Below
JEAN DUNAND
CRUSHED EGGSHELL AND LAQUER WOOD PANEL
FRENCH c. 1928

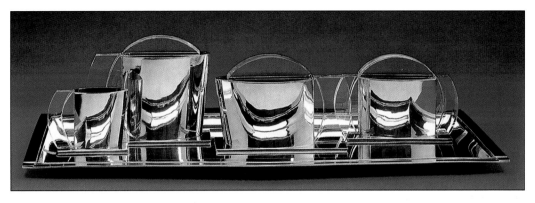

Silver and jewellery

THAT GEOMETRIC MOTIFS and clean lines of Art Deco appeared early on in silverwork is largely due to the metalwork company Christofle, which commissioned artists such as Paul Follot and Gio Ponti to design for it. It was also responsible for most of the tableware on the prestigious ocean liner, *Le Normandie*. This tableware was electroplated, a process Christofle had introduced in the mid-19th century and made its speciality.

The leading silversmith of this time was Jean Puiforcat (1897–1945). He came from a family of silversmiths, and first exhibited his own work in 1921. Puiforcat designed objects of geometric design with plain surfaces, doing away with the decoration and hammered patterns that had been popular for so long. He combined silver with hardstones such as lapis lazuli, rock-crystal and jade, and with rare woods like ebony.

One of the major exceptions to French domination of Art Deco was Georg Jensen (1866–1935). His designs are both classical and modern, and were so popular that he opened retail outlets in Berlin, Paris, London, New York and Stockholm between 1908 and 1930. Jensen's stylish but cheap silver jewellery has remained so successful that most of his designs are still in production today.

The changes in fashion also had an effect on jewellery. Women cut their hair short so there was no longer any need for combs or tiaras. Large hats were replaced by small cloche hats, making hatpins obsolete. Short hair encouraged a fashion for long ear pendants. Dresses with deep necklines, open backs and short sleeves were ideal for showing off long necklaces, set with diamonds, pearls, onyx, enamel, carved jade or coral.

Above
JEAN PUIFORCAT
SILVER AND GLASS TEA AND COFFEE SERVICE
FRENCH 1925

Below
GEORG JENSEN
'MAGNOLIA' TEA AND COFFEE SET
DANISH Early 20th C.

Long gloves disappeared and were replaced by bracelets and bangles or wristwatches. Cigarette cases and powder compacts became exquisite works of art, and decorated with finely carved plaques of jade, coral or rock-crystal set in gold boxes and highlighted with enamel, mother of pearl inlay and coloured stones.

The important jewellery firms making these were Cartier, van Cleef and Arpels, Janesich, Lacloche Frères, Boucheron and Chaumet. Apart from these large firms, a few individuals managed to make their mark, particularly Jean Fouquet, Raymond Templier, Gerard Sandoz and Paul Brandt. Their work could be seen as sculpture rather than jewellery. Coco Chanel's costume jewellery became very popular during this period.

Modernism

MODERNISM RAN PARALLEL with Art Deco. Modernists thought that objects and interiors should be devoid of any unnecessary decorative clutter.

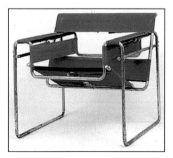

Right
JEAN DUFY
LIMOGES PORCELAIN 121 PIECE DINNER SERVICE
FRENCH c.1928

Left
PIERRE CHAREAU
CARD TABLE
FRENCH c.1920

Below left
MARCEL BREUER
'WASSILY CHAIR'
GERMAN c.1920

Below
EMILE DECOEUR/P.GAUCHER
SEVRES PORCELAIN VASE
FRENCH 1946

Unlike Ruhlmann, they wanted to make modern design accessible to everybody. Tubular steel combined with glass and wood was widely used for furniture. Some classics of design still in production today continue to have a modern feel, for instance Marcel Breuer's tubular steel cantilevered chair designed at the Bauhaus in 1924. In France, a group of artists formed an organization called L'Union des Artistes Modernes. René Herbst, Francis Jourdain, Helène Henri, Robert Mallet-Stevens and Raymond Templier were its founders, soon to be joined by other major artists of the time.

ART NOUVEAU

BY JANE HAY

Art Nouveau is above all a 'look'; a visual style so distinctive as to be instantly recognizable, easier to describe than to define. Spanning the period from 1880 to the outbreak of the First World War, it was part of the great reaction to industrial machine age ethics which took place in the West at the end of the 19th century. Although its roots are to be found in Britain, it swept across Europe as the fashion style *par excellence* of the era.

Celts, Japanese and maidens

IN BRITAIN DURING the 19th century the Pre-Raphaelite movement was one of the precursors of Art Nouveau. Two members of this group, Edward Burne-Jones and Dante Gabriel Rossetti, made lavish use of the image of the maiden to convey purity and innocence: this image was attractive to exponents of Art Nouveau as it confronted the facelessness of industry with the language of love and poetry. A bi-product of Pre-Raphaelite medievalism was the introduction of Celtic *entrelac* motifs, intertwining linear cartouches of serpents or foliage, for example, which were also to become leit-motifs of the new style.

In 1859, Japan opened its doors to the West for the first time in over 100 years, and at the 1862 London International Exhibition a stand was mounted displaying new wares from the East. The company of Farmers and Rogers had a trade licence with the Japanese government and, at the close of the exhibition, one of its employees, George Lazenby Liberty, purchased the remaining stock and opened a shop in Regent Street, London. There was also a shop in Paris selling similar products: blue and white porcelain, textiles, bamboo work and prints. The well-known American painter James McNeill Whistler was seduced by these new aesthetics, while the architect E. W. Godwin decorated his home in the Japanese style in 1862. As we can see, *japonaiserie* was introduced by a combination of retailers, artists and designers.

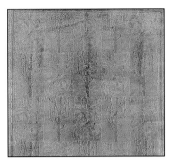

Above
ART NOUVEAU CARPET FROM LIBERTYS
ENGLISH 1890s

One cannot overemphasize the impact of Japanese design and aesthetics on the West. In general terms it introduced new spatial concepts and new attitudes to light, rhythm and harmony.

For Art Nouveau this meant pale colour schemes; flowing, rhythmic and organic patterns derived from Japanese textile designs; the use of vertical lettering; and a certain delicacy of execution.

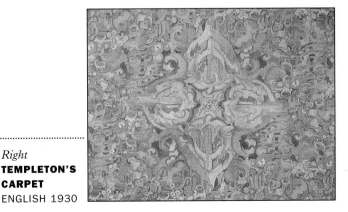

Right
TEMPLETON'S CARPET
ENGLISH 1930

The marriage between Japanese sinuous linear patterns and Celtic *entrelac* motifs combined to produce what is now known as the whiplash motif. The Western Symbolist movement in painting reinforced Oriental attitudes to organic design, with the result that foliate patterns were to become not just decorative but also meaningful. Three Art Nouveau motifs, the maiden, the whiplash and organic design, can therefore be traced back to these influences.

....

Below
C.R.ASHBEE
ART NOUVEAU JEWELLERY
ENGLISH Early 20th C.

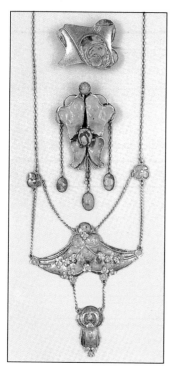

British Art Nouveau

THERE WAS A considerable amount of crossover between Art Nouveau and Arts and Crafts, especially in Britain, where one evolved from the other. Where the Art Nouveau response was primarily on an emotional level, Arts and Crafts sought political solutions. Art Nouveau was concerned with the visual expression of a piece, while Arts and Crafts placed emphasis on production itself. For Morris and his followers this was not just a style but also a way of life, and they rejected Art Nouveau as merely decorative. They were not afraid to adopt its motifs in their work, and when one considers British Art Nouveau, one must include the work of many who were actually wedded to the Arts and Crafts ideal.

While the maiden, whiplash and rhythmic foliate patterns were three essential components of Art Nouveau, they were only one aspect of it. At the other end of the spectrum was a rectilinear and geometric formal style introduced by the Scottish architect Charles Rennie Mackintosh. The Glasgow School, under the aegis of Mackintosh, offered a solution in the geometry of forms, which represented a radical departure. Opinion differs as to whether it falls within Art Nouveau. However, the Glasgow School had such a great impact on developments in Europe, it would be difficult to separate them entirely.

Above
ARCHIBALD KNOX
LIBERTY PICTURE FRAME
ENGLISH Late 19th c.

....

The movement was made popular through three major retail outlets: Liberty in London, Tiffany in New York which opened in 1878 and, from 1895 Siegfried (commonly known as Samuel) Bing's Maison de l'Art Nouveau in Paris. It was Bing's establishment that gave the movement its name. *The Studio*, a British arts magazine, was also to play a vital role in educating public taste and providing a platform for ideas. This debt to Britain was acknowledged abroad in such names as 'Style Anglais' or 'Style Liberty', in every country where it took root architects, designers and artists worked together in the new style, developing and ultimately transforming it.

Arthur Heygate Mackmurdo (1851–1942), co-founder of the Century Guild in 1882, introduced sinuous foliate tendrils into furniture and textiles, and through his magazine *Hobby Horse*, provided a showcase for graphic arts. Aubrey Beardsley (1872-98) was an important innovator in book designs and illustrations for the medieval epic *Morte d'Arthur*, Oscar Wilde's *Salome*, and the first issue of *The Studio*. The illustrator Walter Crane (1845–1915) introduced the new style into ceramics at Pilkington's, with larger factories such as Doulton and Minton following suit.

The architect M. H. Baillie Scott (1865–1945) designed furniture which was decorated with foliage in bright colours. He worked briefly with Archibald Knox (1864–1933), before being commissioned to decorate the palace of the Grand Duke of Hesse in Darmstadt, Germany. In his capacity as designer for Liberty's ranges of metalware marketed under the names 'Cymric' for silver and 'Tudric' for pewter, Knox did much to popularize the *entrelac* motif. The store churned out relatively inexpensive items for the middle classes.

French organic motifs

IN BELGIUM GROUPS and magazines had been proliferating since 1881, forming the 'Libre Esthétique' in 1894. Under the influence of Victor Horta (1861–1947), Henry van de Velde (1863–1957) and Gustave Serrurier-Bovy, Belgium was to move towards a more refined curvilinear and abstract style. This is notable in the architecture and metalwork of Horta, while the furniture designed by Serrurier-Bovy and Van de Velde was sophisticated and elegant, divested of floral motifs.

It was in France that Art Nouveau undoubtedly found its spiritual home, where rococo design combined with the new aesthetic ideals. Bing's Maison de l'Art Nouveau became the focus for the decorative and applied arts with designs contributed by Hector Guimard, famed for his Paris Metro buildings. By now any simplicity left over from Arts and Crafts had completely disappeared, replaced by elegant curves and the total integration of flora and fauna into form and decoration. Famous women of the day became icons. The commercial artist Alphonse Mucha (a Czech by birth) was inspired by the actress Sarah Bernhardt.

Left
AUBREY BEARDSLEY
SALOME
ENGLISH 1894

Above
**ALPHONSE MUCHA
LA PEINTURE**
FRENCH Early 20th C.

Right
DAUM TABLE LAMP
FRENCH Early 20th C.

In the provinces the creative hub was at Nancy, where Emile Gallé (1846–1904), the Daum Brothers and Louis Majorelle all had their factories. Gallé specialized in acid-etched and carved cameo glass decorated with landscapes, flowers and insects. His great rivals Daum produced some very fine work of their own. Gallé also designed furniture decorated with marquetry panels, but it is the decoration rather than the structure of these pieces which is their main appeal. The best École Nancy furniture came from Louis Majorelle (1859–1926).

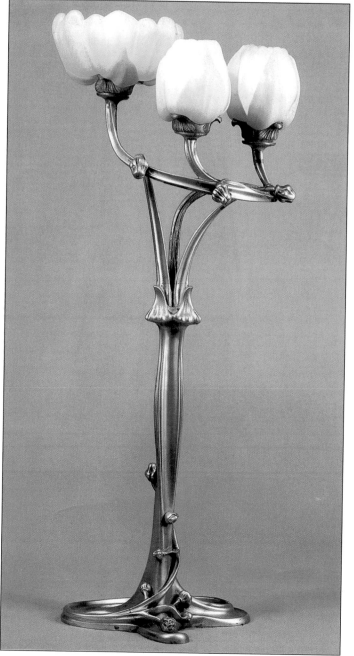

Right
**SUITE OF SILVER
FURNITURE**
FRENCH
Early 20th C.

René Lalique (1860–1945), the most famous jeweller of his day, combined precious metals and stones with glass and natural materials such as horn to produce the most fantastic and sumptuous pieces. All of this, however, was decorative arts for the exclusive and moneyed classes and this excellence in design did not often survive translation into mass-production.

Formalism and Geometricism

IN SCOTLAND THE architect Charles Rennie Mackintosh (1868–1928) designed his most famous commissions between 1896 and 1906, namely the Glasgow School of Art and the Cranston Tea Rooms. Mackintosh worked with his wife Margaret, her sister Frances and brother-in-law Herbert McNair:

this was the nucleus of the 'Glasgow School' which included George Logan, E. A. Taylor, George Walton and Jessie M. King. Furniture designs by Walton, Logan and Taylor were executed by Wylie and Lockhead; they were usually in plain oak set with stained glass panels of curvilinear motifs, often including a rose, while Mackintosh favoured white painted wood and maidens.

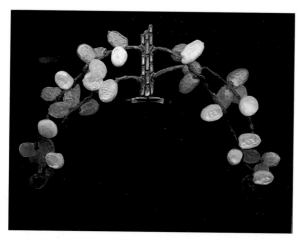

Left
RENE LALIQUE
DIADEM
FRENCH Early 20th C

Art Nouveau spreads into mass-production

WHEN ONE CONSIDERS the manufacturing side of decorative arts in Germany and Austria certain names spring to mind. In glass the firm of Loetz specialized in curvilinear forms in iridescent glass, although it also produced many pieces by Werkstatte designers. The great porcelain factories of Dresden and Meissen would take on the work of new designers to add to in-house designs. Iridescent decoration was also produced by the ceramic factory Zsolnay Pecs in what is now Hungary. Other factories such as Royal Dux and Amphora mass-produced centrepieces decked with Art Nouveau maidens in flowing robes and surrounded by curvilinear foliage. In metalwork the firm Wurrtembergerische Metal Fabrik (WMF) followed their example by mass-producing inexpensive pewter items decked with romantic maidens. This contrasts with the output of rivals Kayserzinn and Huecke, who preferred the abstract curvilinear design of Behrens and Olbrich, while the jewellery company Theodor Fahrner produced pieces at both ends of the stylistic spectrum.

Margaret and her sister worked in metal, stained glass, textiles, jewellery and graphics. Jessie King (1875–1949) specialized in delicate but detailed line drawings, but she also designed jewellery for Liberty.

The geometric formalism combined with heavy symbolism of Mackintosh's circle was not well received in England and we must look to Austria for its true impact.

In Vienna, in 1898 Gustave Klimt led artists, designers and architects to form a group which could show its work independently. Notable among the 'Wiener Sezession' (from which Austrian Art Nouveau derives its name) were Otto Wagner (1841–1918) and his pupils Joseph Hoffman (1870–1956), Koloman Moser (1868–1918) and Joseph Maria Olbrich (1867–1908).

Olbrich moved to Germany, but Hoffmann and Moser went on to form the Wiener Werkstatte (Vienna Workshop) in 1903. The Wiener Werkstatte developed an uncompromising geometric style popularly known as 'chessboard'. It executed architectural commissions and designed mass-produced bentwood furniture, manufactured by Thonet Brothers. Included in this group were Dagobert Peche, Michael Powolny and Otto Prutscher, and their trademark was a stylized rose within a square.

In Germany, Jugendstil (youth style) began with organic and symbolist motifs and progressed to the geometric after the Glasgow School had shown its hand at the 1900 Vienna exhibition. Germany was fortunate to have a wealthy enthusiast in the form of the Grand Duke of Hesse who funded a school of art and design at Darmstadt, inviting both Behrens and Joseph Maria Olbrich to take part.

Tiffany

LAST OF ALL we must consider the work of Louis Comfort Tiffany (1848–1933) who stands apart from the rest in America, where Arts and Crafts dominated. He was much influenced by changes in Europe. Today he is chiefly remembered for his leaded glass windows and light fittings depicting flowers, insects and birds, and his 'Favrile' range of hand-blown iridescent glass vases.

The eclipse of the style

IN THIS SURVEY it is not possible to enumerate all the different forms of Art Nouveau, nor to examine its impact on every region. The principal themes and areas have been explored but they should not be considered exhaustive; some of the most interesting architecture, for example, is to be found in Spain in the work of Antonio Gaudi, whose fluid structures of poured concrete are still considered revolutionary today.

In many ways Art Nouveau was an anachronism, an attempt to reinvent romantic images of women and organic design in an era when the telephone, motor car and electricity were part of a snowballing technological culture. It is ironic that the forces which generated it, mass-production and mechanisation, were also the ones which ultimately led to its eclipse: the work of Art Nouveau designers

Above
WIENER WERKSTATTE
THE 'SITZMACHINE'
AUSTRIAN Early 20th C.

was nearly always exclusive and expensive, and in the main failed to cater for mass consumption. On another level, because it did not have the intellectual foundation of Arts and Crafts, and once all the stylistic possibilities had been explored and exhausted, it came to a natural conclusion without leaving any obvious imprint on the next generation. Perhaps this is why it first fell into disregard and later into obscurity until it was rediscovered in the late 1960s. Nonetheless, it left behind many works of great beauty and

helped to sweep away the excesses of 19th century Rococo. One can trace Art Deco and Bauhaus back to these early attempts to create a new grammar of ornament, and in particular to the work of Mackintosh and the Wiener Werkstatte. They all contain the seeds of Modernism, and for all these reasons Art Nouveau is an important staging post in the history of decorative arts.

NORTH
AMERICAN
ART AND
ARTEFACTS

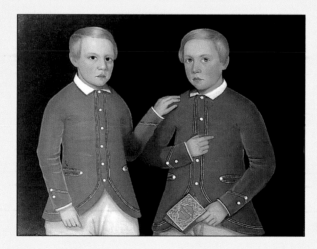

Above
AIMMI PHILLIPS
PORTRAIT OF TWO BROTHERS
AMERICAN c. 1850

NATIVE AMERICAN ARTEFACTS

BY JOE RIVERA

Early in the 20th century American Indian arts were considered the exclusive province of anthropology and natural history museums. However, during the last 25 years there has been a remarkable development of interest in Native American art. In the early 1970s, two of the greatest contributions to the popularity of Native American art among collectors were Sotheby's two sales of the Green Collection, and the Norman Feder exhibition at the Whitney Museum, New York. Among collectors, this art has become internationally recognized as an excellent investment because of the power of its aesthetic beauty, its historic significance, its inherent spiritual nature, and its rarity. Even so, it is still considered to be one of the best kept investment secrets in the fine art field.

The tremendous increase in the collection of Native American art by private collectors and museums has resulted in a rapidly increasing rise in prices. We have also seen the birth of a successful American magazine devoted exclusively to Native American art which has been a great tool in educating the general public in an appreciation of the Native American heritage.

Above
TSIMSHIAN PUPPET
NATIVE AMERICAN c.1850–70

Below
CROW WAR SHIRT
NATIVE AMERICAN c.1850

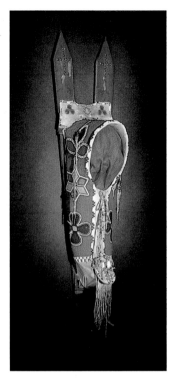

Above
KIOWA CRADLE
NATIVE AMERICAN c.1890

Below
ACOMA STORAGE JAR
NATIVE AMERICAN c.1885

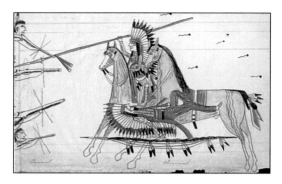

Native American art, which ranges from the Pacific Northwest to the Eastern Woodlands, can be enjoyed both for its visual merit and for the meaning it holds. The artwork was created by employing such skills as weaving, basketry, potterymaking, embroidery, and the applied arts of bead, quill and featherwork. The decoration not only made the piece more beautiful but also gave an object its significance.

Much of the art was made to emphasize the importance and rank of the individual who owned and used it. Many objects were made as gifts given at the coming of age of a young person, a marriage and the birth of a child. Others were made for religious purposes, and often decorated with representations of the spirits.

The coming of the white man brought not only new materials but also styles and objects that were incorporated into the clothing and artefacts of the Native American people. Venetian glass beads, brightly coloured silks, brass tacks, mir-

rors and commercial blankets are only a few of these new materials. Vests, shoulder bags, epaulettes and gauntlets were all incorporated into Indian costume.

Wherever designs were taken from and whatever materials were used, the artefacts have always indicated the Indian belief in the unity between art and life. Every creation expressed features of style that clearly identified and separated it from the art of any other part of the world.

Collecting Native American art

THE PRICE OF an American Indian artefact is determined by the age, condition, authenticity and rarity of the object.

Antique Native American art can be purchased from reputable galleries located in Sante Fe, New Mexico, which is the centre for authentic American Indian art. It can also be bought from well known auction houses like Sothebys, Butterfields and Skinners, during their Tribal Art Sales.

Above left
KIOWA LEDGER DRAWING
NATIVE AMERICAN c.1885

Above
NAVAJO WEARING BLANKET
NATIVE AMERICAN C. 1880

Below
WESTERN APACHE STORAGE BASKET
NATIVE AMERICAN c.1890–1915

AMERICAN FOLK ART

BY JOE RIVERA

The term 'Folk Art' as applied in America has been described as the art and artefacts of the common man, made by and for those individuals who first settled and nurtured what was to become the United States. And just as the United States has been termed 'a melting pot of society', the traits and differences which combine in creating the unique community which is America are exemplified in the best of American folk art.

Folk art was not restricted to rural communities, nor cut off by economic bounds. American folk art reflects and expresses the development and growth of the American middle class. Folk artists prospered throughout the country, from Maine to New York, to the Southern States and to the Midwest.

American folk art in countless variations was made by individuals who had a great gift and capability, an intuitive and an instinctive feeling for art, but not necessarily formal training. The exclusion of a formal guild

system in the United States, gave artists and craftsmen the independence and freedom to express themselves in ways that were unattainable to the academically trained or schooled artists. This peculiar environment enabled a number of folk artists to develop styles of artistic expression that often anticipated elements of abstraction encountered hundreds of years later by Modernist and other artistic movements in Europe and America.

The folk artists and crafts people were often required to

wear many expert hats. For example, Edward Hicks painted coaches and signs as well as his well-known paintings. In addition to being a working physician, Rufus Hathaway is acknowledged as a talented and prolific 18th century portrait painter. Skilled carvers produced sculptural pieces such as carousel animals, ship figureheads, or

Above
JOSEPH H. DAVIS
PORTRAIT OF DAVID C. AND MARY KNOWLES
AMERICAN 1836

Left
JOHN BREWSTER, JR.
PORTRAIT OF COMFORT STAR MYGATT AND LUCY MYGATT
AMERICAN c. 1850

Above
WILLIAM W. KENNEDY
PORTRAIT OF A LITTLE GIRL
AMERICAN c.1840

Right
EDWARD HICKS
THE PEACEABLE KINGDOM
AMERICAN c. 1838

architectural ornaments, and metalsmiths fashioned weathervanes, whirligigs, lighting devices or horse shoes. Sailors on board whaling ships would engrave whales' teeth and fashion canes and other decorative forms from whalebone and wood, as well as mending nets. Ladies and young girls, who were trained in the 'feminine arts' at home, produced delicate watercolours, stitched intricate samplers and embroideries, and made strikingly beautiful quilts, coverlets, hooked rugs and table covers as well as mending clothing and doing other routine domestic chores. There were the professional crafts people who plied their trades by specializing in the production of utilitarian objects, such as hardware, signboards, trade figures, painted and punched tinware, pottery, toys, fire buckets, ornamental painting, decoys, and weavings.

These objects share a boldness of form, a brilliance of colour, a sense of imagination and design ability which made the lack of technical proficiency almost irrelevant. As the famous Boston collector and noted connoisseur Maxim Karolik said,

'While the folk artist might lack the ability to describe, he does not lack the ability to express. We are speaking of poetry rather than prose.'

Folk paintings

PERHAPS THE MOST prolific and popular forms of American folk art are portraits, weather-vanes and textiles. Before photography in the 1850s, the pictorial record of most of the American people was recorded by folk artists. A small number of these artists have been identified and their work researched, the majority of the painters remain anonymous. Among the most famous folk painters of the 18th and early part of the 19th century is Winthrop Chandler (1747–90), who worked in Connecticut during the 1770s, painting portraits and over mantles. Significant works by Chandler have sold at auction and in private sales. Two folk portrait painters whose works can encompass a very broad price range are John Brewster, Jr. (1766–1854) and Ammi Phillips (1788–1865). Brewster was a remarkably talented deaf-mute artist who worked in Connecticut in the 1790s, and in Maine in the 1820s. Phillips was one of the most prolific and celebrated of folk painters whose work is very popular today.

During the 19th century a large group of folk portrait painters was active, including Joseph H. Davis, who specialized in watercolour profile portraits. Jacob Maentel was another watercolourist who executed profile as well as frontal portraits.

The most prolific folk portrait painter in the 19th century was William Matthew Prior (1803–73), and members of the so-called 'Prior-Hamblen School'. These painters worked in the New England states during the 1840s and 1850s. Prior-Hamblen portraits can be recognized for their 'flat' style of facial rendering.

The most sought-after folk paintings are the works of Edward Hicks (1780–1847). Hicks was a Quaker preacher and sign painter from Newtown, Pennsylvania. He is one of the most important and desirable of American artists of the 19th century for his delightful renditions of 'The Peaceable Kingdom' and 'Penn's Treaty with the Indians', both of which were taken from print sources.

Weather-vanes

ALTHOUGH THERE WERE a number of weather-vanes in 17th and 18th century America, the majority of the hollow bodied copper and cast iron weather-vanes were produced by small factories located in New England and New York during the second half of the 19th century.

Above
REARING HORSE WEATHER-VANE
AMERICAN c. 1860

....

Left
MINIATURE DEER WEATHER-VANE
AMERICAN c.1860

These makers included the firms of H. L. Washburn, J. L. Mott, Rochester Ironworks, J. W. Fiske, A. L. Jewell, and L. W. Cushing and Sons. One of the earliest and most acclaimed makers of factory-produced weather-vanes was J. Howard and Co. of West Bridgewater, Massachusetts. The weather-vanes produced by the Howard firm are highly distinctive, made with cast zinc front parts, with the balance of moulded hollow copper. The unidentified artist responsible for the designs of the Howard weather-vanes gave his creations a unique classical elegance, with highly stylized forms that may have been inspired by antiquities.

Copper weather-vanes are rare and those which retain their original gold leafing or green verdigris patination are highly prized. Many charming and desirable weather-vanes were 'homemade' created in rural communities utilizing materials at hand. An excellent example of this type is the silhouetted wooden rooster, with original painted decoration and leather cockscomb.

Bed 'ruggs' and quilts

THE EARLIEST FORM of bed covering made in the United States consists of the 'bed rugg', which is a form of heavy woollen bedspread. Most bed ruggs were produced during the 18th century in New England, one of the earliest being dated 1724. Fewer than fifty bed ruggs survive today; the majority reside in museum collections.

Pieced and appliquéd quilts have been produced in America since the mid-to-late 18th century. The majority of quilts date from the 19th and 20th centuries. Quiltmaking reached its all-time peak during the mid-19th century in Baltimore, Maryland.

One of the most splendid and best preserved examples of a 'Baltimore Album Quilt' is the example attributed to Mary Evans made for Mary and Sarah Pool, circa 1846. The superb quality of the appliquéd and stuffed elements combined with the density of the composition make this one of the supreme achievements of American textile folk art.

....

Above left
ROOSTER WEATHER-VANE
AMERICAN c.1840

Below
BED RUGG
AMERICAN 1806

Left
MARY EVANS
ALBUM QUILT
AMERICAN c. 1850

Samplers and needlework pictures

ONE OF THE most popular areas of collecting are samplers and needlework pictures. A sampler differs from a needlework picture by including the alphabet. The advanced scholarship in this area has made it possible to identify distinctive samplers and needlework pictures specific to schools, towns and regions. Samplers are often rich in biographical information, for example the Susan Rabsom sampler from Philadelphia, Pennsylvania, incorporates numerous stylized pictures in silk on a linen ground, inscribed 'Susan Rabsom Her Work 1789'.

Collecting American folk art

INTEREST IN COLLECTING and studying American folk art dates to the last decade of the 19th century. Among the earliest collectors and scholars in this newly emerging field was Edwin Atlee Barber, whose speciality was Pennsylvania German folk art. The recognition of folk art as a category of 'American art' began in 1924 with an exhibition organized by Juliana Force at The Whitney Studio Club, in New York City. Throughout the 1930s Holger Cahill assembled exhibitions at the Newark Museum, in New Jersey, and at the Museum

of Modern Art in New York City with folk art borrowed from the collections of contemporary artists of the day, including Charles Sheeler, Charles Demuth, Elie Nadelman, and Robert Laurent. These artists saw in this 'primitive' work an anticipation of the kind of abstract art that they were creating.

Cahill's exhibitions brought folk art to the attention of such early collectors as Abby Aldrich Rockefeller, whose collection now comprises The Abby Aldrich Rockefeller Folk Art Center at Colonial Williamsburg, Virginia. Electra Havemeyer Webb's collection now forms the Shelburne Museum, in Vermont. Henry Ford also collected and his collection has become the Henry Ford Museum in Dearborn, Michigan; finally Henry Francis du Pont's collection now forms the Winterthur Museum in Delaware. These private collections, which in turn became the nucleus for the public institutions which bear their names, did much to popularize a wonderful vernacular art form, and to bring this material to the attention of the public and scholar alike. The process of building up the public awareness of American folk art has been influenced by

Above
TRADE SIGN
AMERICAN c.1820

Left
HELEN RABSON
EMBROIDERY SAMPLER
AMERICAN 1789

museum exhibitions, scholarly publications, and the market-place. An entire generation of dealers, collectors and museum professionals has seen the market for the finest American folk art literally expand by leaps and bounds.

The development of the market

BETWEEN 1930 AND 1960, there were only a handful of dealer-specialists. The most dramatic expansion of the folk art market occurred in the mid-1970s and coincided with an exhibition at the Whitney Museum of American Art, in New York City, 'The Flowering of American Folk Art'.

The first of a series of seven auctions at Sotheby Parke Bernet in New York offered a superb group of folk water-colours from the renowned Garbisch collection. These folk art auctions attracted worldwide attention because of the rarity, quality and diversity of the pieces, and the fact that the audience for folk art had grown in both number and sophistica-tion. In the forty-odd-years since the Garbisches had begun to collect, the world of folk art collecting had made a quantum leap from simply being 'quaint decorations' to serious works of early American art.

The landmark auction sale of the Stewart E. Gregory folk art collection in 1979, at Sotheby Parke Bernet in New York, marked an escalation of prices for the best folk art that has yet to pause. Many auction records were set at this sale, and the US$1.3 million total was a record for a single owner auc-tion of American folk art. It was a breakthrough as a major event in the art world, creating an international awareness and monetary appreciation for American folk art. Numerous record prices were established at the Gregory sale.

Throughout the 1980s out-standing items entered the market through the disposal of folk art from a number of distinguished collections. Another record price seemed to be achieved at each of these auctions. At the four sales of the Barbara Johnson Whaling

Collection there were numerous records set for scrimshaw. The Pottery Collection of William E. Wiltshire III established many record prices, including a record for redware. At the sale of the Theodore H. Kapnek Collection of American Samplers a record was set when a Matilda Filbert sampler sold for US$41,800. At the Howard and Jean Lipman sale a record was set for painted furniture when a Pennsylvania decorated blanket chest brought US$41,000. At the Thomas G. Rizzo Sale a record was set when a weather-vane in the form of the Statue of Liberty brought US$82,500. At the M. Austin Fine Sale, a Baltimore Album Quilt sold for US$176,000.

The record for a sampler is now

Above
CAROUSEL GIRAFFE
AMERICAN c. 1900

US$198,000, paid for an 18th century Marblehead needle-work picture inscribed 'Ruthy Rogers'. A portrait painted by John Brewster, Jr., depicting a father and daughter, sold for $852,500.

THE ARTS OF THE EAST

Above
TANG DYNASTY
POTTERY HORSE
CHINESE 618–906

CHINESE WORKS OF ART

BY RODDY ROPNER AND PETER TUNSTALL-BEHRENS

Chinese Jade

JADE IS A generic term covering nephrite, a silicate of calcium and magnesium, and jadeite, a silicate of sodium and aluminium. Both are extremely hard stones, ranking 6.5 and 6.75 on the Mohs' scale. In its purest form, jade is white and translucent, but often partially coloured by inclusions of mineral impurities. It is the skill with which the lapidarist incorporates any of these natural flaws in his carving which is critical to its success.

Unavailable in China proper, nephrite was originally found in pebbles and boulders from two rivers in Khotan in the Taklamakan Desert until supplies were exhausted in the 18th century. Jadeite, imported from Upper Burma, has only been carved since the 18th century. For the Chinese, jade carries reverential auspicious symbolism, representing heaven, purity,

Below
CELADON AND RUSSET JADE BOULDER
CHINESE 18th C.

loyalty and intelligence for Confucius.

In the Neolithic and early Historical period, jade was carved for practical purposes. The mining of nephrite and accompanying technical developments resulted in larger pieces. Loose copies of archaic bronze vessels, vases and censers as well as smaller animal and figural groups were produced in large numbers during the great period of jade carving under the Emperor Qianlong (1736–95).

Chinese bronzes

THE ARCHAIC BRONZES of China (c.2000BC-500BC) saw the introduction and development of bronze tools, weapons and ritual vessels. Tin and lead were added to copper to reduce the latter's melting point (1083°C) and increase its hardness. Early bronzes were cast by pouring the molten metal into a gap between a central core and an outer casing of section moulds; the interior of these moulds could be incised with designs in negative image.

Rituals in the Shang dynasty (c. 16th–11th century BC) demanded sacrifices to ancestors, and bronze vessels were cast for these ceremonies. They included wine and food vessels.

Above
BRONZE WINE VESSEL AND COVER
CHINESE 11th–9th C. BC

Initially performed as state rituals, these sacrifices were later enacted by aristocratic families. Technically the vessels developed from the earliest thin bodied *jue*, a tripod wine vessel, with a narrow band of decoration, to storage vessels with ornate and dramatic decoration. The most popular motif was the *taotie*, a form of hybrid bird and beast probably used to ward off evil spirits.

Initially the Zhou dynasty (c.11th centuryBC–221BC) continued the rituals and bronze techniques of the Shang. There was less emphasis on wine vessels, as alcohol had been associated with the demise of the Shang. Inscriptions were now extended to lengthy passages explaining why the bronze was commissioned and extolling the virtues of the owners' ancestors.

New techniques were introduced and during the Spring and Autumn period (770–476BC) we find copper, turquoise, silver and gold inlays.

The lost-wax method of casting developed during the period (475–221BC). The significance of ritual vessels declined and a greater range of utilitarian wares appeared, including mirrors which were made in large quantities from the 4th century BC until the Tang dynasty. These were usually circular discs cast with one smooth surface and the reverse with detailed ornament.

Lacquer

LAQUER IS PRODUCED from the sap of the lac tree. It can be coloured with dyes and hardens in a warm damp atmosphere. Layers of lacquer are usually applied to a wooden or cloth core to give the object a light but sturdy foundation.

Below
TANG DYNASTY
SILVER-BRONZE MIRROR
CHINESE 618–906

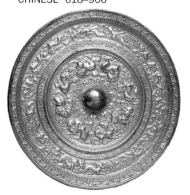

Right
FAMILLE ROSE ARMORIAL SAUCER DISHES
CHINESE
Mid 18th C.

Cups, bowls and boxes were painted with geometric designs or figures such as musicians. Production of lacquer increased dramatically during the Han dynasty. Lacquer inlaid with mother-of-pearl dates back to the Tang dynasty. Monochrome bowls and dishes were especially popular. The technique of carving through alternately coloured layers with the design of cloud scrolls, to produce what is known as Tori lacquer, was started during the Song dynasty and was widely practised during the Yuan.

Under the Ming and Qing there was a profusion of techniques including carved and inlaid lacquers in both monochrome and polychrome.

Chinese Export art

THE CHINESE BEGAN to export art to the West on a regular basis after the colonization of Macau by the Portuguese in 1517. The mainstay of the

China Trade comprised tea and silk, but the thin white body of porcelain found a ready market in the West. The Portuguese dominated activities for a century. Early pieces of porcelain which survive are Chinese or Middle-Eastern forms decorated in blue and white. Trade began in the 17th century under the Dutch East India Company. Roughly potted pieces decorated in blue and white with floral-filled panel designs were very popular in the West. These date from the mid-century and are known as 'Kraak porselein'. Cargoes of finer quality pieces dating from

Below
'QUAIL BOWL'
CHINESE Late 18th C.

Above
'KRAAK PORSELEIN' DISH
CHINESE Late 16th or early 17th C.

c.1650 and 1750, including the famous Nanking Cargo, have been recovered from sunken ships. These comprise both Western and Chinese forms, still decorated in blue and white, and include purely utilitarian objects such as teapots, teabowls and saucers and decorative garnitures of beaker vases and jars.

The 18th century witnessed the introduction of the English to the trade and the use of poly-chrome decorations labelled *famine rose, famine verte* and *famine noir.* These were used to decorate human and animal models and specially commissioned dinner services enamelled with family and Masonic arms and historical and mythological 'European subject' designs. As factories in Europe began to manufacture porcelain offering a cheaper and not inferior alternative, the China Trade slackened. Other examples of Export art include screens, sewing boxes and games boxes decorated in lacquer, wall-paper, silver, fans and furniture. A large number of paintings depicting views of the Treaty ports and watercolours accurately illustrating Oriental species or the manufacture of Oriental porcelain were sent back to families of the Traders and to museums and schools.

Below
BLACK LAQUER HARDWOOD SCREEN
CHINESE 19th C.

Chinese ceramics

THE HISTORY OF Chinese ceramics charts the progression from earthenware, pottery fired up to 1100°C, to stoneware, fired at 1200°C–1300°C to produce a vitrified body, and culminates with porcelain which in the West is considered to be a ceramic body achieved by combining kaolin or China clay with petuntse or China stone fired at 1280°C–1450°C to achieve a fine white-bodied vitrified ware. Chinese ceramics are discussed in detail on page 25.

Amongst the most refined of all Chinese ceramics are the stone wares and porcelains of the Song Dynasty. Their beauty is derived from simple forms and monochrome glazes. Many wares are associated with individual kilns from which they derive their names but are known to have been produced at a number of sites. These wares of Northern China include the ivory-white Ding, the green-glazed, grey-bodied, Yaozhou, the distinctive Jun with its turquoise glaze often splashed with purple and the simple grey-green Ru; at their finest all were produced for Imperial use. Contrasting with these were the boldly carved, incised and painted Cizhou pieces which formed the largest body of popular wares.

The flight of the Imperial Court south to Hangzhou in 1127 encouraged the growth of the southern kilns.

The most prolific wares of this period are the so-called celadons of Longquan which are typified by an opaque green glaze on a grey stoneware body which fires red where exposed in the firing. The pale blue *qing-bai* 'bluish white' porcelain produced at the Jingdezhen kiln complex.

Sophisticated blue and white porcelains were being produced at Jingdezhen by the mid-14th century. The colour blue is produced from cobalt oxide, painted onto the body which is then glazed and fired.

Blue and white came to be appreciated by the Chinese and reached its height in the 15th century. During the late Ming period, Imperial patronage of Jingdezhen declined. During the late 16th and 17th centuries the potters sought new markets. The mid-17th century, referred to as the 'Transitional' period sees a profusion of new shapes and subjects.

The Ming dynasty was overthrown by the Manchu Qing (1644–1912) dynasty and the emperor Kangxi (1662–1722) reasserted control over the Imperial kilns at Jingdezhen. They were responsible for producing perhaps the most technically perfect porcelain.

While blue and white porcelain forms the largest section of wares from China's last two dynasties, *famille verte* and *famille rose* were also produced, but only during the Qing dynasty.

Above
MING DYNASTY
BLUE AND WHITE DISH
CHINESE 1403–24

Below
YUANG DYNASTY
BLUE AND WHITE JAR
CHINESE 1276–1368

Buying Chinese works of art

As WITH OTHER antiques, there are two main methods for buying Chinese works of art, through the auction houses or through dealers. The main auction houses hold regular sales often devoted to either Chinese taste or export market works of art. The lots are normally on view for several days prior to the auction and provide the potential buyer with an excellent opportunity to study the pieces at leisure with the aid of a detailed catalogue description and estimate for guidance. Departmental staff are happy to provide further information and condition reports if requested. While dealers carry stock around the year, many hold specialized exhibitions and can offer an excellent individual service. Many dealers also exhibit at annual fairs held in major cities.

Chinese works of art vary in price considerably within any given category and is largely dictated by quality and condition. The quality can only be assessed by studying as large a range of examples as possible. The finer quality pieces will inevitably cost more but are more likely to hold their value. Condition is an equally important consideration. Chips, cracks and repairs can greatly reduce the value of most pieces, particularly ceramics, where a premium is currently paid for items in perfect condition.

ISLAMIC WORKS OF ART

BY JOHN CARSWELL

What is Islamic art? The term is so all-embracing that it is as well to define some of its parameters. Chronologically, it covers the 1,400 years since Muhammad revealed a new religion, Islam, in the 7th century, to the present day. Islam spread from Arabia throughout the Middle East and North Africa to Spain and the Atlantic, and eastwards to India, South-east Asia and China. Culturally, Islam is even more complex, for over the centuries the ancient, indigenous civilizations and dynasties of Central Asia and the Near and Far East were absorbed by conversion, but never entirely lost their own identity.

Can one identify anything specifically 'Islamic' in the art of these different peoples and times? There is a tendency to expression through the use of geometric forms and patterning, to such a degree of complexity that they become a metaphor for the infinite. But there is also a love of the natural world, with floral and faunal motifs tailored into lively arabesques. The old dogma which states that Islam prohibits the representation of the human form is simply not true; but figural representation belongs to the secular world, of manuscript painting and the minor arts, and certainly not the mosque. The one single most striking aspect

of Islamic art is calligraphy – the calligraphy primarily of the Qur'an, but also the Arabic and Persian inscriptions found on monuments, in manuscripts and throughout all the minor decorative arts.

Carpets and textiles

WHAT KIND OF Islamic art is one likely to encounter today in the West? Perhaps the most obvious form, and not immediately perceived as Islamic, is the carpet. Most carpets combine the two predominant Islamic themes – geometric forms and the arabesque – with infinite degrees of invention. This also applies to the rarer Islamic textiles – Persian silks and Turkish velvets. Carpet scholarship, is still marked by imprecision; for the buyer, the surest ally is a reputable dealer, and a careful perusal of literature on carpets and textiles, suchas the journal *Hali*.

Ceramics

AFTER CARPETS, ISLAMIC ceramics constitute a rich field for appreciation. Islamic pottery has been one of the predominant crafts since the 7th century, and in the early days of Islam represented a local response to the wonders of imported Tang dynasty Chinese porcelain. The

Below
SHRUB AND ARABESQUE CARPET
PERSIAN Late 16th–early 17th C.

Moslem potters added a number of innovations of their own to the history of world ceramics. In the early centuries they were renowned for the production of beautifully toned golden lustreware. Found in Mesopotamia, the technique then appears in Fatimid Egypt, and later still in 12th century Iran, where it was used for the decoration of vessels but also for star-shaped and moulded tiles. In 9th century Persia, a unique form of earthenware was produced, with a cream coloured slip decorated with symmetrically designed calligraphic inscriptions. This aristocratic ware was associated with the Samanids, and many examples were excavated by the Metropolitan Museum, New York, at Nishapur in North East Persia.

From the 14th century onwards, Chinese blue-and-white porcelain made its impact on the Middle East, and potters in Persia, Syria, Egypt and Turkey all came up with their own solutions to produce a blue decorated ware in the Chinese

Right
IZNIK
POTTERY DISH
TURKISH
c.1580
....
Below left
IZNIK TILE
TURKISH
Early 16th C.
....
Below right
MAMLUK
QUR'AN
EGYPTIAN
c.1488

style. These imitations were distinctly Islamic, and the asymmetrical Chinese forms were standardized. Particularly fine examples of hexagonal tiles in this style can be seen in the Murad II mosque at Edirne, the Ottoman Turkish capital on the European mainland in the 15th century, before the capture of Constantinople in 1453. In Turkey in the 16th century the famous potteries at Iznik initially produced tightly drawn designs for tiles and vessels in cobalt blue and turquoise; this monochromatic phase then evolved into a highly sophisticated combination of subtle colours and swirling, arabesque designs, and by the 1560s reached its peak with the introduction of a brilliant tomato red in relief.

Court art in 16th century Turkey was epitomized by its consistency of style. This was

because many of the patterns were produced by the *nakkashane*, or court designers, to be executed by craftsmen. One of the most characteristic motifs were *cintimani*, combinations of three crescents and pairs of tiger-stripes, these unmistakable Turkish designs can be found on ceramics, textiles and woodwork.

Woodwork and metalwork

WOODCARVING IN THE Islamic world in the early period survives in a series of panels with deeply cut arabesques. Fine examples can be found in Egypt, where the dry climate has helped preserve them. Mamluk manuscripts have an unmatched refinement of style, in calligraphy and decoration. Exactly the same idiom can be found on Mamluk woodwork, on the carving of mosque furniture and fittings, such as doors; on Mamluk stonework, such as the decorative domes of tombs and shrines in Cairo and Jerusalem; and even on leather, on the endcovers of Mamluk Qur'ans tooled with identical patterns. The Qur'an, indeed, may have been one of the major transmitters of style. Every year there was a great fair at Mecca at the time of the pilgrimage, and it is not difficult to imagine

Qur'ans changing hands on that occasion, to be dispersed throughout the Islamic world.

Mamluk metalwork – brass basins, platters, stands, lamps and other forms – was inlaid with silver and gold, with abstract geometric patterns and floral motifs often derived from Chinese sources such as the lotus, and figural medallions depicting rulers and courtiers, and scenes from Christian iconography. Parallel with it is the production of enamelled glass, beakers and hanging lamps.

Above
**ENAMELWORK
CANDLESTICK**
SYRIAN
13th or 14th C.

....

Left
**MAMLUK METALWORK
BRASS EWER WITH
INLAID SILVER**
EGYPTIAN
Early 13th C.

Western influences

INFLUENCES ON ISLAMIC art came not only from the East and Central Asia, but also from the West from the 16th century onwards. European goods filtered into the Islamic world, through Turkey, Syria and Persia. An English organ-builder, Thomas Dallam, took a mechanical organ, to Istanbul as a present from Elizabeth I to the Sultan. Gentile Bellini visited Istanbul and worked for several months for the Sultan Mehmet II in the late 15th century. French jewellers and European craftsmen are known to have been employed at the court of Shah Abbas I in Persia in the 17th century. In the 18th century and later, the emergence of an affluent middle class in the Islamic Near East meant that there was a new market for European textiles, and other goods.

In the 19th century western influences became stronger with the advent of mass tourism. There were numerous photographers practising in Istanbul, Beirut, Jerusalem and Cairo in the second half of the century. In architecture, a style evolved in Ottoman Turkey which combined local necessity with European forms, and 'Ottoman Baroque' was born.

JAPANESE WORKS OF ART

BY JOHN CARSWELL

Left
IMARI TUREEN AND COVER
JAPANESE c.1700

With Japanese art, we think first of Commodore Perry, the bluff American naval officer who in 1853 started the process which ended the two and a half centuries of peaceful seclusion for Japan. In fact, the West had begun to take note of Japan and its art had already long exercised its sway over the West.

Leaving aside Marco Polo, contact began with the missionary efforts of the Portuguese. They arrived in Japan in 1543 and were soon under the leadership of the Basque Jesuit Saint Francis Xavier. They were followed the Dutch through their East India Company, the famous VOC, or Vereenigde Oostindische Compagnie. The second half of the 16th century and the first part of the 17th thus formed a great trading period between Japan and Portugal and Holland.

Portuguese influence was largely responsible for the Momoyama style of decoration of this time. It mostly comprised animals and birds among flowering trees and shrubs, executed in gilt painted lacquer and shell inlay. To the Dutch the West also owes the vast importation of porcelain, made As well as the porcelain known as Imari, a finer quality was produced, called Kakiemon. These two art forms were largely intended for the export market and cannot therefore be called typically Japanese. To our recent forbears Japanese art would have been mainly confined to the Edo period (1603 –1868). The art of this period included painted screens and scrolls, woodcut colour prints, books, calligraphy, sculpture, ceramics, lacquer, costumes, armour and weapons.

The export market since the Edo Restoration

The Edo period was rich in the diversity and ingenuity of its art. The miniature, arts flourished, such as, the small lacquer boxes known as *inro* or seal containers, and *tonkotsu* or tobacco containers these were carried on the sash by means of a small carved toggle known as a *netsuke*. Small works of art such as these appealed greatly to collectors in Europe during the prosperous years of the late 19th century, and quite fortuitously it was at this time that the Japanese decided to discard such objects.

Commodore Perry's arrival served as a trigger in releasing pent-up opposition to the

Left
MOMOYAMA PERIOD
CHRISTIAN PORTABLE SHRINE
JAPANESE c.1590

Shogunate which ruled Japan in a tyrannical manner. The defeat in 1868 of the Shogunate and the restoration of real power to the emperor, began a fresh period marked by the government's decision to embark on complete westernization of the country. In the Meiji period, 1868–1912, vast quantities of objects which reminded the Japanese of their feudal past were labelled 'curios' and exported to the west. There they formed the bases of many collections of Japanese art.

Besides *inro* and *netsuke*, these exports included woodcut colour prints, looked on as a rather plebeian art by the Japanese, and swords and sword-fittings – after the prohibition of sword wearing these were sold in increasing numbers by the often impoverished *samurai class*. Collections were soon being formed of *tsuba*, or sword-guards, which, with *netsuke*, became extremely popular.

Some other very collectable swordfittings were the *kozuka*, or handle, of a small knife, the *kogatana*, carried in the scabbards of some swords; the *fuchikashira*, or paired fittings from each end of a sword's hilt, and the *menuki* – small metal fittings placed on each side of the hilt.

Above left
NETSUKE
GOD OF LONGEVITY
JAPANESE 18th C.

Below
INRO PIECES
INLAID WITH GOLD AND
MOTHER OF PEARL
JAPANESE 19th C.

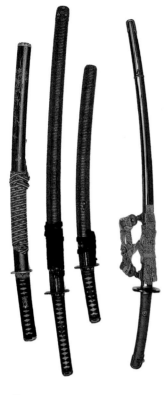

Above
JAPANESE SWORDS
14th, 15th and 17th C.

Since the Japanese were at heart a nation of potters rather than decorators of porcelain, pottery tea-bowls and other tea ceremony items were available in great quantity, and with them came beautifully decorated lacquer boxes, for example tiny ones to hold incense (*kogo*), larger incense boxes (*kobako*), writing boxes (*suzuribako*), document boxes (*bunko*, often made to match the *suzuribako*), and many others.

Above
SUZURIBAKO
JAPANESE 17th C.

But the import of these Japanese art objects is only a part of the story of this 'age of enlightenment', for, as if its antique arts were not enough, Japan now turned to the wholesale manufacture of art for the western world. To this period belong ubiquitous Kaga and Satsuma wares, vividly coloured cloisonné enamel plates, elaborately detailed ivory carvings and richly decorated bronze vases and similar objects decorated in high relief with birds, flowers, insects and the like, all done with the greatest realism.

The makers of this 'Meiji Art', as we call it today, were often the sword-fittings craftsmen and other artists who had lost their former employment and now turned to new enterprises. Some items of this type pre-date 1868, but it was in Meiji (1868–1912) and Taisho (1912–26) that the trickle became a flood.

Key terms

RESTRAINT WAS HARDLY ever a feature of this new export art, and much of it can be described by the Japanese word *hade,* meaning flowery or florid, the converse being *shibui,* meaning astringent or restrained. Some knowledge of these terms may be helpful to the student of Japanese art. Another which he will encounter is *yugen,* literally meaning profound or mysterious, but difficult to define precisely since it is applied to something that really lies beyond art and can only be sensed intuitively. Sometimes translated as 'occult', it is evoked by simple forms which have in them 'the lines of eternity'.

Another word is *aware,* originally an expression of delight but later meaning gentle pleasure tinged with melancholy, a sadness that comes from the knowledge that beauty soon passes away. The terms *wabi* and *sabi* are better known, the first meaning rustic simplicity and unpretentiousness, while the second is applied to things

Above
SILVER FILIGREE VASE
JAPANESE Late 19th C.

Above
SATSUMA WARE
JAPANESE Late 19th C.

Left
ANDO CLOISSONÉ VASE
JAPANESE Meiji period

that are old or imperfect, worn, tarnished or patinated.

Japanese art brings the pleasure that comes from learning something of the history and culture associated with an object, while it is always pleasant to know, that virtually all Japanese art collections have shown a steady increase in monetary value.

Many Japanese artists sign their work, often adding a date, so that another pleasure lies in developing the ability to read these inscriptions.

Finally, there is the subject-matter of Japanese art, where the beginner/collector enters a world of myth and legend, strange creatures with supernatural powers, yet a world where the Japanese artist shows his love of nature, his curiosity and his acute observation of the things around him. It would be difficult to find a form of art more satisfying to collect.

ARMS AND
ARMOUR

··

FRED WILKINSON

Above
DUELLING PISTOLS
ENGLISH Late 18th C.

Collecting arms and armour was a minority taste until after the end of World War II. It was probably the influx of American forces, many of whom were keen gun collectors, during the war which stimulated an interest among British collectors. Since then it has been a field that has constantly expanded with an increasing number of specialist dealers and books covering the many aspects of a fascinating and absorbing hobby.

Rising demand and value

As with any market the rising demand over the years has inevitably led to rising prices. This trend has slowed somewhat over the past year or so but in certain areas such as armour the upward rise continues. Good quality armour has more than retained its value even allowing for the rate of inflation and there is still a strong demand for good pieces. Next in popularity come antique firearms, followed by edged weapons and then, with a

Above
MEDIEVAL SWORDS
ITALIAN 1360–1400

Left
HEAVY CLOSE HELMET
GERMAN c. 1560

Right
THREE-QUARTER ARMOUR
EUROPEAN c. 1650

slightly smaller following, come sundry military objects lumped under the title of militaria.

No matter what is collected, knowledge is power and for those wishing to concentrate on arms and armour there are

many good, reliable books to help the amateur. Similarly, there are a number of specialist auction houses and dealers who can be most useful to both the beginner and the expert.

In practical terms, it is only possible to collect arms and armour dating from the 16th century onwards, although a few items of an earlier date may occasionally appear on the market. Most armour available to the collector is of the late 16th and 17th centuries. Swords from the Middle Ages and earlier periods do become available but the majority of edged weapons seen will be no earlier than the 16th century. Firearms have only been in general use from the 15th century.

The development of armour

ARMOURERS HAD TO offer protection which would allow the wearer to move with minimum restriction. The surface of the armour needed to be smooth so that there were no projections to catch an enemy's blade.

One of the earliest forms of armour was mail, made up of small metal rings intertwined to allow movement whilst protecting against a cut or thrust. Mail had limited protection as it was very vulnerable to the points of weapons. The armourer countered this by fixing plates to the mail, and as the process continued the body was more and more covered by plates until by the 15th century the warrior was protected by a complete outer skin of plate armour.

The head was protected by a helmet, the earliest are mostly of the late 16th century such as the close helmet which completely enclosed the head. The lighter, types were the morion and the cabasset which left the face unprotected. The most common 17th century forms were the burgonet and the pikeman's pot. The harquebusier or light cavalry man wore a helmet with a neckguard, two cheek pieces and a simple face guard. The pikeman's pot was usually plain with a broad brim. Nearly all 17th century helmets are made of two sections whilst earlier examples are fashioned from a single piece.

The body was protected by the cuirass, made up of a breast and back plate. Styles ranged from the fluted Maximilian style to the late 16th century peascod shape. Plates were tested by firing a musket at them and if the bullet failed to penetrate the subsequent dent demonstrated its strength.

By the 18th century most troops had abandoned armour. Although some cavalry retained a helmet and a cuirass, the arm defences and leg defences were no longer considered necessary. But armour was never completely discarded and a number of patented types were used during the American Civil War (1861–65) and its use is continued today with soldiers and police wearing body armour. Some armour was also retained for bodyguards and ceremonial units.

Helmets, cuirasses and gauntlets which protected the hand are the most popular items sought after by collectors. They are more accessible and easier to handle and display. Trench warfare in World War I led to the introduction of metal helmets for the troops and these can form an interesting and fairly cheap field of collecting.

Armour outside Europe

ARMOUR WAS STILL worn from the 17th century and was often a mixture of plate and mail. The helmets usually had only an adjustable bar to guard the face but the neck and sides of the

Above
SAXONY SWORD
GERMAN c. 1570

head were protected by a curtain of mail hanging from the rim of the helmet. Many of the troops carried a circular shield.

In Japan the armour was very different in construction, much of it was composed of small lacquered plates laced together into larger defences. The helmets, usually have a metal skull and a neck defence of lacquered plates.

Swords and spears

A FORMIDABLE ARMOURY of weapons existed to pierce the armour of soldiers. The spear and pike, were designed to make others keep their distance. Others, like the halberd, were a combination of axe and spear intended to chop and pierce.

The sword developed from a weapon intended mainly to cut, to one that was intended to thrust at undefended parts of the body or, to slash at foot soldiers from above.

Swords came in all sizes up to the large two-handed swords nearly six feet in length. These were intended as a slashing weapon swept around in circles above the head, although some were only carried in procession as a status symbol.

In the 16th and 17th centuries there was a marked change in use and the rapier was developed as a thrusting weapon. The sword-hand was protected by a metal bowl.

The rapier encouraged swordplay, and fencing schools were common during the 17th and 18th centuries. One style of fencing used a sword and dagger. The rapier was wielded in the right hand whilst the left hand held a short dagger.

The use of swords declined from the late 17th century and the rapier became more a costume accessory. They were worn by men of fashion until around the 1770s.

The military sword

THE SERIOUS WEAPON carried by soldiers was far less decorative and much more functional. The British infantry relinquished their short swords around the mid-18th century but officers continued to carry theirs. From the end of the 18th century, the design of the military sword was regulated by the government. This development took place throughout most of Europe and these 'official pattern'

weapons form a group on their own and are generally not too expensive. The type of sword differed for infantry and cavalry, and the pioneers, artillery and transport, had their own patterns.

The type of sword best suited for the military was long debated: a long, narrow-bladed thrusting weapon or a broad-bladed sword designed to slash and cut. Many swords were designed but nearly all failed to serve well in either capacity. By the 19th century new technology meant that in Europe the sword was not a serious military weapon.

In the East, the sword continued to play an important role. In India, the tulwar was probably the most common. The bladesmiths of Asia also produced a wide range of beautifully decorated daggers. The finest swords in the world were produced by the Japanese, but by the 19th century, even their warrior classes were forced to admit that the day of the sword had passed and the firearm was taking over.

Below
CEREMONIAL HALBERDS
GERMAN Early 17th C.

Early firearms

GUNPOWDER, A MIXTURE of sulphur, charcoal and saltpetre, was first discovered in China, probably in the 11th century. The secret of its manufacture reached Europe probably in the 13th century. The first positive proof of guns is found early in the 14th century. By the end of the 15th century many infantry were armed with muskets.

Muskets were loaded by pouring powder down the barrel and pushing the bullet down to sit on top of the powder. A small hole, the touch hole, was bored in the side of the near end of the barrel – the breech – and a small amount of powder was placed in a small pan adjacent to the touch-hole. This priming powder was fired by pressing the glowing end of a piece of smouldering cord (the match) into it. The match was held in the jaws of a pivotted arm

which was pushed down into the pan by pressure on the trigger. The flame from the priming passed through the touch hole and set the main charge alight which then exploded and the expanding gases drove the bullet along the barrel. The 'matchlock' musket was simple and cheap but the match had to be kept glowing.

In the 16th century a new ignition system was developed. Sparks were produced by friction between a piece of mineral, pyrites, and the roughened edge of a steel wheel. This mechanism, the wheel-lock, could be loaded and the mechanism set so that the weapons could be made ready to fire in an instant.

Gunmakers perfected the flintlock to generate sparks by striking a piece of flint down the face of a steel plate. The sparks fell into the priming and fired the weapon. The flintlock was efficient and continued in service for some two and a half centuries.

Development

A SCOTTISH CLERGYMAN, Alexander Forsyth, devised a chemical system known as fulminates to generate a flash to ignite the priming. When a small quantity was placed over the touch hole, and struck by a small swinging arm known as the hammer, it detonated, producing a flash and igniting the powder.

In the 1820s a simple copper cap containing some fulminate, the percussion cap, was designed. The mechanism was soon being used in a range of weapons, including revolvers. The idea of the revolver had existed but it was very difficult to produce an efficient flintlock revolver. The percussion cap changed this and American makers such as Colt, Smith and Wesson, and Remington were producing percussion revolvers. In Britain the leading manufacturers were Adams, Tranter, and Webley.

Opposite page top
**BREECH-LOADING
WHEEL-LOCK PISTOL**
GERMAN c.1560

....

Opposite page bottom
**PRUSSIAN FLINTLOCK
PISTOL**
GERMAN 1787

....

Right
FLINTLOCK BLUNDER BUSS
ENGLISH Late 18th C.

....

Below
PERCUSSION REVOLVER
ENGLISH c.1865

Militaria

MILITARIA RELIES LESS on its beauty and more upon its intrinsic interest. Medals obviously recall battles and bravery whilst the uniforms and headdress symbolize the glamour and colour of the past. One great attraction of militaria must be the range of material; books, medals, buttons, uniforms, maps, postcards, badges and equipment which can be collected at a cost well within the price range of most collectors.

C O I N S ,
M E D A L S   A N D
S T A M P S

Above
24 CENTS INVERTED JENNY
AMERICAN c.1918

COINS AND MEDALS

BY RICHARD BISHOP

Coins have been collected for many centuries. There are references to Greek coins in Roman literature, and the cabinets of Renaissance princes were crowded with ancient coins and medallions. A find of English silver pennies of the 12th century recently caused experts to wonder if a 'coin collector' had buried his collection to protect it from the bands of mercenaries devastating the country during the early years of the reign of Henry II. Printed books on coins date from the earliest years of printing.

In England the hobby has traditionally been the preserve of the parson, the academic and the country gentleman. Recently the appearance of investors and speculators, eager to spend large sums of money but not keen to devote time to serious study, has caused a few ripples. True coin collectors care less about commercial value than intrinsic historical interest but are prepared to pay for the rarest pieces.

The appeal of coins

ALL COINS LOOK much the same. Most are covered with illegible legends and indecipherable symbols, and have simple portraits. They are not easy to display and usually end up in a small box in the bank. The question is a fair one what makes numismatics such a fascinating subject, and coin collecting such an absorbing hobby?

Collectors all agree on one basic principle. The numismatist must be a student of history. The very word has its roots in ancient civilization and literally meant anything that was used as currency. *Nomisien* means 'to have in current use' and embraces all forms of wealth used in trade and for barter. The citizens of Sparta used heavy metal bars instead of coins. The early Romans used a bronze 'coinage', large blocks of bronze, cast in oblongs and simply decorated. They were exchanged by weight and quickly fell into disuse with the introduction of silver and gold. Numismatics includes forms of currency such as wampum,

shell or bead money used in North America, tea-brick money used in China, the many forms of shell and feather money used in the Pacific islands, and the massive, great stone money of the island of Yap. Each form of currency is an open door to a different culture, or an ancient civilization.

Numismatics is not about modern proof commemorative sets of coins, produced only for collectors and never intended to be used as currency.

The introduction of coinage

RECOGNIZABLE COINS MADE their first appearance in the Eastern Mediterranean in about 600BC. There is no exact time or place, though the kingdom of Lydia has long been regarded as the birth place of regular coinage. The speed with which precious metal coins ousted all other media of exchange was remarkable, and this has been the case whenever coinage has been introduced.

Top
DOUBLE DUCAT
Used throughout Europe from the 12th century onwards
DUTCH 1800

Left
ROMAN BRONZE COIN
Struck during the reign of the Emperor Caligula
ROMAN 37–41AD

Early collectors

THE EARLIEST COIN collections were almost exclusively ancient Greek and Roman coins. The demand for good quality Roman bronze coins was so great in Italy in the late 14th century that elaborate copies, or

Below
BRONZE MEDAL
ITALIAN c. 1655

Bottom
GOLD PRESENTATION MEDAL
GERMAN Late 17th C.

even fantasies, were made by professional medal engravers. Petrarch was one of the earliest of these Italian collectors, at the same time that great patron and collector, Jean Duc de Berry, was including coins and medals among his many purchases. During the 17th and 18th centuries medals became as popular as coins. As a means of communicating political or religious ideas, the medal was ideal, being durable, portable and relatively inexpensive to produce. The coin and medal cabinet became a natural part of the educated man's library.

Alongside the interest in history, there developed an appreciation of the artistic qualities of the best coins.

Collecting modern currency

IN THE UNITED STATES the criticism of 19th century coinage grew so that by the turn of the century it had become a matter of some urgency to find an acceptable series of designs for a planned new coinage.

Above
'HIGH-RELIEF' 20 DOLLARS
AMERICAN 1907

Below
MEDAL CABINET
FRENCH Mid 19th C.

Above
ANGLO-SAXON SILVER PENNY
ENGLISH Early 9th C.

The sculptor Augustus Saint-Gaudens was commissioned to design the gold 10-dollar and 20-dollar pieces, and his 'Indian Princess' and 'Standing Liberty' designs won universal approval. The 20-dollar was struck in high relief, in 1907. It was considered a coin which could rival those of the ancients in excellence of design and quality of workmanship. The experiment was too costly, and a much flattened version of the high relief coin eventually made its way into circulation. The modern coin however had taken its place among the best products of the ancients and the collecting of modern coins as a serious hobby was now accepted.

Collecting in Britain and Europe

IN ENGLAND THERE was less emphasis on artistic merit and more attention paid to historical context. Collectors were intrigued by the numerous issues of silver pennies put out by the Anglo-Saxon kings, their archbishops, and the Viking invaders who settled in the north of

England and issued their own coinage in imitation ot their southern neighbours. When the Gothic Revival in England finally made an appearance on the coins of Victoria there was an outcry, not against the heavily crowded Gothic design of the coins, but because the letters *D.G.* for *Deo Gratia* had been omitted from the 1849 florin. This so-called 'Godless' florin was quickly redesigned and the missing letters restored.

All over Europe coin collectors concentrated on the coins of their own countries. Coins reflect both a country's history and its aspirations and it was natural that collections based on place of origin should develop. Today the coin markets in the West, are distinct with domestic coins dominating. It is not uncommon for a large coin auction to be held in Germany or the United States in which every one of the thousands of coins on offer are exclusively of German or American origin.

Below
QUATRE LOUIS D'OR
FRENCH 1640

Above
GEORGE III HALF-GUINEA
Proof striking
ENGLISH 1787

Coin grading

OVER THE YEARS various systems of grading coins have developed. In America a numerical system based on a scale of 1 to 70 has been introduced, in which 1 is the lowest grade possible – the coin would be flat and with a hole in it to warrant this grade – and 70 is flawless, and so probably unobtainable. The European grades, verbal descriptions, correspond roughly to every ten of the American grades. Thus good = 20, fine = 30, very fine = 40, extremely fine = 50 and mint state = 60. Numerical grading has until recently been applied only to American coins, but the intention is that eventually these numbers will be used for all types of coins from all periods. To date there is no agreement among American numismatics about the detailed working of this numbered system and only the collector specializing in American silver dollars must worry about it. For the majority of coin collectors adjectival descriptions are sufficient.

Acquiring coins

THE COIN MARKET has grown rapidly since the 1970s. There have been several 'boom' periods, but also some corresponding slumps. Most experienced coin collectors are not seriously affected by these movements in the market. Nowadays, specialist markets and dealers provide an almost overwhelming choice, with every type of coin now available, and even the most obscure collecting interests catered for. The popularity of some types of coin is universal – ancient Greek and Roman are the most popular, while others are hardly in demand at all. This is the result of the recent growth in the economies, and the increase in the numbers of collectors, for example, Japanese coin prices have soared in response to increased demand.

The novice collector however need not be daunted by the wide range, both historical and geographical, available today through public auctions and dealers' lists. For most, the question of what to collect is answered automatically by a natural inclination to a certain type of coin, the gold sovereign, the silver coin or the copper token. Alternatively it may be an attraction to a certain period, such as the age of the 'Twelve Caesars' (the first century AD), or the Tudor and Stuart monarchs (the 16th and 17th centuries).

Roman gold coins are on the whole expensive, but Roman silver coins are affordable. Age is in fact not relevant when pricing a coin. What matters is how desirable is the coin, not necessarily how rare it is, and how many collectors actually want it.

Above
GOLD 20-YEN
JAPANESE 1880

Above
QUEEN MARY 30 GOLD SOVEREIGN
ENGLISH 1553–54

Above
CHARLES I GOLD UNIT
SCOTTISH c.1625

Left
THE MILLION POUND NOTE
ENGLISH 1948

The importance of condition

WHETHER HE SPECIALISES, or remains a general collector, the novice quickly comes to appreciate the importance of condition. The value of a coin can vary greatly according to its quality, and indeed some coins which are common in very worn condition are practically unobtainable in mint state. This is particularly true of base-metal coins, which were not precious enough to be carefully looked after at the time they were in circulation, and is less true of gold coins which tended to be handled with care from the moment they were produced. A collector who decides to concentrate only on the highest quality of anything other than modern issues must be prepared to spend a very long time building up his collection.

The best compromise between rapidly buying whatever is available and never acquiring a coin because the finest quality cannot be found, is to buy as good as you possibly can and be ready to up-grade whenever possible. All sale catalogues and dealers' lists offer coins that are graded, enabling the collector to buy with confidence. If the grade stated is wrong or misleading and the dealer is reputable, then the coins can always be returned.

There has been some concern among collectors recently about the increase in the number of

Above

THE PONTEFRACT UNITE
ENGLISH 1648–49

coin hoards being discovered. The sophistication of metal detectors makes hunting for 'buried treasure' a far simpler and more lucrative task than it was 20 years ago. Hoards of ancient and medieval coins are discovered in Britain and mainland Europe every week of the year.

Many of them contain hundreds, some even thousands, of coins. There is always the danger that what is rare and valuable today will be plentiful and inexpensive tomorrow. Underwater exploration has been developed to a point where wrecks can be located and examined, and even the contents salvaged, by remote control. Hundreds of wrecks around the world are currently being examined in this way.

None of this need worry the coin collector unduly if he has collected for pleasure, not for profit. The pleasure to be derived from finding and acquiring interesting and beautiful coins cannot be dulled by the activities of speculators or treasure hunters, and can only increase as the collection grows. The coins illustrated on these pages are all in extremely fine condition and in many cases are very expensive. It must be remembered that these are examples of exceptional quality. An excellent coin collection can be made for a fraction of this cost and the modest collector can find good examples of medieval or modern coins for under £50 (US$80). Coins can be collected at every level, and the history, religion, portraiture, heraldry, mythology and artistry of 2,500 years of civilization can be enjoyed by all.

Left

BADGE OF THE GARTER
ENGLISH Early 17th C.

STAMPS

BY TIMOTHY HIRSCH

The first adhesive postage stamp was brought into official use on 6 May 1840 and even at the time attracted considerable interest. One of the earliest chronicled stamp collectors in London was a solicitor, Robert Cole, working during the 1830s in Throgmorton Street and, from 1840, in Lothbury.

Robert Cole's collection, housed in a scrap book, comprised in part a number of first day cover cancellations including those for 5 December 1839 – the first day of the penny postage for the London District. More importantly, it contained a fine 'Penny black' used on a wrapper dated 6 May 1840 from Robert's daughter Augusta to her father, bearing his endorsement 'the first day of the use of postage stamps'. The collection was sold in a series of 29 lots at auction by Christie's in September 1986 and the 6th May cover realized £8,800 (US$14,000), from a total of over £20,000 (US$32,000) for the whole collection.

In many respects, Robert Cole was a collector of the future and was ahead of his time with his specialization and his emphasis upon postal history – the changing postal rates and postal markings. This aspect of collecting really developed as a separate discipline during the 1930s and only in more recent years has its full potential been realized.

For many Victorians, postage stamp collecting was generally unsophisticated and the aspirations of most were limited to gathering a collection of as many different stamps as possible from as wide a range of countries around the world. There was little degree of specialization and concepts of completion were of lesser importance. The primary concern lay with the design image and questions of paper type, perforation, watermark or shade were unnecessary complications.

Valuing stamps

MANY FAMILIES HAVE a collection of stamps which has been passed down, and frequently they hope that within such old accumulations there may be items of value and importance. However, the two key factors which must be carefully assessed are rarity and condition. Unlike most works of art stamps, in most cases, are prepared in essentially limitless quantities. For example, over 60 million 1d blacks were produced for use, so what gives it value is its condition or aspects of usage.

Left
PENNY BLACK
A first day cover of the first stamp
BRITISH 1840

A fine unused example with the original cement or gum on the reverse would bring over £1,000 (US$1,600); a premium would be paid for pairs, blocks or multiples of larger size. A similar emphasis upon condition also applies to the renowned triangular stamps of the Cape of Good Hope and the classic stamps of most other countries from around the world.

In other instances, rarity is the crucial factor in determining the value of a stamp. Rarity is a difficult concept to define as different collectors may look at it from a range of standpoints. What is rare to a young collector may simply be unobtainable with the limited means at his disposal whilst an experienced collector may consider a rarity to be a stamp which is unique or virtually so.

For example, for the 1d red stamps of Great Britain issued between 1858 and 1879, most are of minimal value but examples from plate 77 are worth around £50,000 (US$80,000)! There are nine recorded examples from this plate which was rejected at the time of printing because of the irregular spacing.

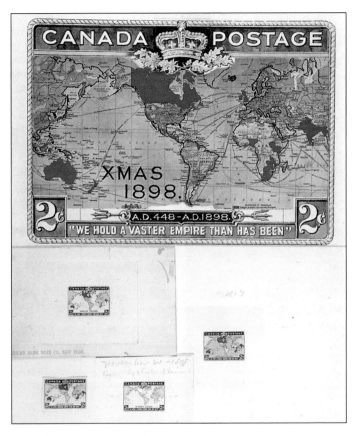

Specialized collecting

THE LAST 150 YEARS of collecting have resulted in a market of increased specialization, with most collectors today concentrating on the stamps of one country or a group of countries.

There is a greater emphasis on collecting proofs and essay material relating to the production of stamp issues, featuring items from the archives of the various security printers.

Above
**CHRISTMAS ISSUE
PROOFS AND ARTWORK**
CANADIAN 1898

Right
LARGE DRAGON COVER
CHINESE 1885

Errors and varieties

WITHIN TRADITIONAL PHILATELY, errors and varieties have always been popular and have achieved high prices at auction. Such errors may be variations of printing or perforating, or arise at other stages in the production of the stamps themselves. Whilst there may have been many hundreds of thousands, or in more recent times, many millions of a particular stamp printed, only a few examples might exist showing some error of printing or production.

With stamps printed in more than one stage, errors are more likely to occur in printing. The US Inverted Jenny may be a spectacular example, but other such inverts are known. These may not have achieved the same level of auction value, but have nevertheless still excited the interest of speialized collectors.

The 1920 one shilling stamp from Jamaica comprises two parts to the design printed in similar colours – orange-yellow and red-orange. In March 1922 about ten examples were found with the frame inverted, these being the remains of a half sheet of 30 stamps sent to Manchioneal Post Office. It is believed that the other half sheet was sent to Kingston GPO. Only about 20 examples in total are known. In May 1990 a mint example brought £13,200 (US$21,000) at auction in London.

Other mistakes may occur in the printing of multi-coloured

stamps. In 1964 a set of four stamps was issued by the Falkland Islands to commemorate the 50th Anniversary of the Battle of the Falklands. A single sheet of the 6d value was printed in error with the centre design showing HMS Glasgow instead of HMS Kent. The error was not noticed at the time of issue. A maximum of sixty examples exist and as yet the vast majority still remain to be identified.

Above
INVERTED FRAME 1SHILLING
JAMAICAN 1920

Left
COLLECTOR'S ITEMS
BRITISH 1840–7
From top to bottom:
An 1840 1d black,
plate 2 marginal block.

An 1840 1d black, plate 7,
block of four on thin paper.

An 1840 2d blue,
marginal block of six

An 1847 10d
mint corner block of four

Postal history

THE CONCEPT OF postal history and the illustration of the history of the postal service and the conveyance of mail has developed as an area of collection during the last twenty years. including airmail postal history or military mail. This might include covers from members of the British Armed Forces serving overseas, from the Zulu Wars in southern Africa or from the many conflicts in the Middle or Far East.

As an illustration, early pioneer flights have always captured the imagination of stamp collectors and the early attempts to fly the Atlantic are no exception. In 1919, Captain F. P. Raynham and his navigator Major Charles Morgan first attempted the crossing on 19 April in their aeroplane named 'Raymor'. A second attempt was made on 19 July but in both cases Raynham and Morgan only managed to fly a few hundred yards. So instead, on 21 July, Captain Raynham set sail for England on the *s.s. Grampian* taking with him the bag of mail salvaged from the 'Raymor'. The sixty envelopes were not delivered until January 1920, some nine months after they were posted!

Right

'PER AEROPLANE RAYMOR'
Handwritten overprint from the infamous early 'Airmail' delivery.
CANADIAN/BRITISH 1920

Of the 60 envelopes about 30 were franked with a special handwritten overprint *'per Aeroplane Raymor'*. An example, addressed to the Rt. Hon. Albert H. Illingworth, Postmaster General of Great Britain 1919–21, recently fetched £18,700 (US$30,000) at auction.

The appeal of stamps

THE ALLURE OF stamp collecting lies in the broad appeal of the hobby, the freedom which it gives to the collector to pursue his own line of acquisition, tailored to his own financial resources. In the long term, stamps have increased in value, reflecting not only inflationary pressures but also the vagaries of fashion and popularity. Some stamps today are cheaper than 10, 20 or even 50 years ago whilst others are worth infinitely more. The financial rewards from collecting stamps generally accrue to those who have formed a specialized collection.

Such a collection would include the major rarities and would have an even balance between stamps, production proofs and essays as well as the postal history of a particular country or subject. Narrow portfolios of generally unrelated items greatly increase the risk of a decreased investment, but as with most investments, stamps can move up or down in value.

During the late 1970s there was a rapid but unsustained increase in stamp values underpinned by investment speculation. In 1980, the market reversed and many prices never returned to earlier levels.

For many people, a collection of stamps from countries overseas may have been their first introduction to the history and geography of those territories. For most, the sense of collecting was far removed from the investment potential of their collection and ideally that is the basis upon which most people should pursue a collection of stamps.

CLOCKS, WATCHES AND SCIENTIFIC INSTRUMENTS

Above
**AUGSBURG MASTERPIECE
TABERNACLE CLOCK**
GERMAN c.1600

CLOCKS AND WATCHES

BY RICHARD GARNIER

The first mechanical clocks were made in the late 13th century for monasteries to call the monks to prayer, but by the mid 14th century most European cities had at least one public clock. These early clocks were sited near ground level and did not strike the hours. It was not until the mid 16th century that public clocks were first placed in towers, so that the sound of their bells could be heard over the city.

The earliest domestic clocks had been developed in Northern Italy, Switzerland, Germany and France. Made to be hung on walls, these chamber clocks were smaller than public clocks, but were still quite bulky. Of open-frame construction, they were decorated with Gothic pinnacles and crockets and surmounted by a bell housed within a spire.

Tower and chamber clocks were driven by weights. It was not until the late 15th century that the mainspring (a coiled driving spring) was made, making portable clocks possible. The earliest surviving examples date from the early 16th century.

The first watches were really just small portable clocks that could be slung on a cord round the neck. They originated in Nuremberg in the early 16th century. These early clocks and watches had drum-shaped cases made of engraved gilt-brass. By the end of the 16th century watches were often oval in shape, and after 1600 they could also be octagonal or modelled after objects and animals. These are known as form watches. The cases are constructed of gilt-brass, silver or gold, often set with rock crystal or gem stones, or are enamelled.

Early decoration

UNTIL THE EARLY 17th century enamelling was either in the Limoges tradition of painted enamel or of colours separated by dividing strips of raised metal. Around 1630, the goldsmith Jean Toutin of Blois developed the art of painting in coloured enamels on an opaque white ground. This technique produced exquisite miniatures of flowers, religious subjects or, portraits. The Blois enamellers did not sign their work.

The leading enamellists in the last quarter of the 17th century were the Huaud family of Geneva. Their subjects were generally copied from early 17th century paintings, but they achieved unsurpassed richness of colour in their watch-cases, which were signed on the band.

Some English makers produced a completely undecorated type of oval watch with bowed covers, known as a Puritan watch. At the same time, while weight-driven chamber clocks were declining in popularity elsewhere, the English developed a local form, known as the lantern clock.

Above
BLOIS FLORAL WATCH
FRENCH c.1650

Left
HUAUD WATCH
SWISS c.1680

These are of posted-frame construction but with turned columns rather than Gothic pillars. Pierced frets fill the space between the top of the frame and the bell above. The style was established in London by 1620, and they continued to be made there until about 1700, and in country towns their production continued up to the end of the 18th century.

17th century German clocks

WEIGHT-DRIVEN CLOCKS were more suited to the skills of the English makers. In Germany most clocks made in the 17th century were spring-driven. By 1580 most canister-cased clocks were square and in the 17th century many were hexagonal. The bases, which contained the bells, were hinged and stood on feet cast in the form of animals or fruit, but by 1620 were mainly of turned shapes. The tabernacle clock, made in the form of a miniature tower, with the dials on the vertical sides continued to be made until the end of the 17th century and hexagonal table clocks until well into the 18th century.

German fantasy clocks of the 17th century are the counterpart to form watches of the same date. Many being in the form of animals, urns or monstrances, others depict a Calvary with the crucified Christ flanked by two saints. Some of these clocks have an automaton action working in time to the strike of the hours.

English bracket and longcase clocks

NONE OF THESE clocks were more accurate than a quarter of an hour fast or slow in a day. Galileo first realized the likely effect of a pendulum, but it was the Dutchman Christian Huygens who, in 1656, first applied one to a clock. He then put Salomon Coster to making pendulum clocks under his patent. The Fromanteel family in London heard of the new invention and sent a son, over to Coster in 1657 to learn the art. On his return in 1658 the Fromanteels were able to advertise clocks that 'go exact and keep equaller time than any now made without this Regulater'.

The pendulum rendered clocks accurate to within three minutes a week and resulted in two new types of clock in England: bracket and longcase clocks. The first are spring-driven and intended to stand on pieces of furniture, but occasionally were provided with the wall brackets that have given them their name. Longcase clocks are floor standing weight clocks. The cases were made of wood, in contrast to the metal cases of most clocks previously. These cases had classical columns at the angles supporting a full entablature of frieze and cornice, topped by a pediment, and as a result the years

1660 to 1675 are known as the architectural period in English clockmaking.

By 1675, bracket clock cases had become a rectangular box with a base moulding reflecting the cornice and topped by a cushion-shaped moulding. Longcase clocks retained an architectural vestige in angle columns and a frieze and cornice. But their tops were no longer pedimented, being left flat or having a cushion-moulded caddy as with bracket clocks. A gradual progression occurred in the size of longcase dials, from 8 inches square in 1660 to 12 inches square after 1700. Then from about 1720 the basic square shape was augmented by an arched extension at the top, and this shape was repeated in the long door to the trunk about ten years later. Meanwhile, around 1720, the throat moulding between the hood and the trunk of the case was reversed from convex to concave.

Below
TABLE CLOCK
GERMAN c.1630

Left
**ARCHITECTURAL
LONGCASE
CLOCK**
ENGLISH
c.1675

Centre
**BRACKET
CLOCKS**
ENGLISH
1690–1790

Far right
**LONGCASE
CLOCK**
ENGLISH
c.1740

Bracket clock dials were initially 7 or 8 inches square, but by 1670 had shrunk to 5 or 6 inches square. Around 1710 the tops of bracket clocks developed an outline of two opposing curves known as an inverted bell top. These curves were reversed by 1760 into the shape known as the bell top.

The earliest longcase and bracket clock cases were of ebony or ebonized pearwood veneered on an oak carcass. Black finishes fell out of favour for longcase clocks, but remained fashionable for bracket clocks to the end of the century. By 1670, burr walnut was being used with parquetry inlay. Floral marquetry with pieces of green-stained bone, followed parquetry. Initially in oval or shaped panels on the case plinth and trunk door. This floral marquetry by 1685 has coalesced into one composition on the plinth and trunk door. Then seaweed marquetry came into vogue, and by 1710 had spread over the whole front surface of the case. There were more plain burr walnut than marquetry cases made, although some have been 'improved' with new marquetry in the late 19th century.

From 1700 marquetry decoration fell out of favour. The most popular japanning today are the bright colour examples. The most frequently found lacquer cases are of a dark colour. About 1750 walnut, was superseded by mahogany. By the end of the 18th century some cases were veneered with satinwood, and in the Regency and Victorian periods rosewood was frequently used.

Longcases had ceased being made in London by 1820, and died out in the provinces a few years later. Bracket clocks were made until around 1830, when they became smaller and are known as mantel clocks.

All through the 18th century English clocks and watches were considered superior to any others. In England, the clockmakers dictated the form of their cases, whereas in France it was the *ébenistes* (cabinetmakers) who controlled the piece. French clocks therefore follow closely the decorative fashions prevalent in furniture, metalwork and porcelain, without the time lag there is in England.

French mantel clocks were made in a profusion of fantastical designs in Louis XV's reign. Dials were commonly circular. A common type of clock has the movement and dial supported on the back of an animal. Others have cast ormolu or porcelain figures on rock bases surrounded by a bower of flowers in porcelain. Neoclassicism, led to a more sober style, characterized by rectilinear forms and architectural decoration. The 19th century saw an abundance of ormolu and porcelain mounted mantel clocks.

French clocks

THE FIRST FRENCH clocks were based on the Hague clocks developed by Huygens and Coster in Holland. These had rectangular cases with lunette crestings and velvet covered dials. In France this shape developed into more flowing forms, and by 1735 the bracket clock has a waisted form. By mid-century the ormolu mounts no longer fit closely to the outline of the case, being composed of openwork foliage at the hips, shoulders and on the cresting.

Much use is made of boulle (brass or pewter inlay in a tortoiseshell ground) in the Louis XIV, Régence and Louis XV periods. Louis XV's reign also saw other decorative finishes such as green-stained horn or *vernis martin* (a gilt imitation lacquer decorated with sprays of flowers).

Watches

THE INTRODUCTION OF the balance spring to watches had as revolutionary an effect on timekeeping as the pendulum had had on clocks.

Watches were often circular throughout the 17th and 18th

centuries. French examples of 1680–1720 are known as *oignons* because of the onion like shaped single cases, whereas in England slightly flatter watches were developed with a pair of cases. These pair-cased watches were the envy of all Europe and copied widely, especially in Holland.

Watch dials of the 17th century had a narrow chapter ring for the hour superimposed on a engraved plate, but from 1675 these were superseded by a champleve single sheet dial of gold, silver or gilt-metal.

....

Top left
BRACKET CLOCK
FRENCH Mid 18th C.

Top right
ELEPHANT MANTEL CLOCK
FRENCH Mid 18th C.

Left
SELECTION OF FRENCH WATCHES
FRENCH Mid 18th C.

From 1700 enamel dials began to be used in France, but not in England until the mid-1730s, from when many of the earlier watches with champleve metal dials were newly fitted with replacement ones in enamel.

Oignon cases could be either engraved or left plain. Pair-cased watches had a plain inner case and any decoration was applied to the outer case. Enamel decoration was quite popular in 18th century France, but was not much used in England. The English favoured *repoussé* decoration (embossed by hammering the inner surface) instead. Many of these repoussé cases have now been worn down or even pierced through on their highlights, unless fitted with a protective third case.

Genevan watch enamellers

EIGHTEENTH CENTURY ENAMELLING does not have the charm of the Huauds at the end of the previous century, and subject painting was reduced to an oval on the back of the case. From the 1760s increasing use was made of translucent enamel over an engine-turned ground, known as *guilloché* enamel. This frequently covered the whole back panel, which was then framed by a band of real or white enamel pearls. By the end of the 18th century the Genevan enameller's work surpassed French and English work and during the Empire period (to

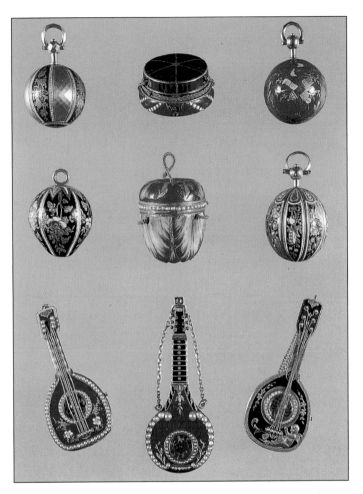

about 1835) they specialized in exquisitely enamelled gold and pearl-set musical watches and automata. The early 19th century saw the revival of form watches modelled after flowers or musical instruments.

Whilst the Genevan enamellers in the 19th century produced cases decorated with landscapes, portraits, bouquets of flowers or scrolling foliage in

Above
FORM WATCHES
Early 19th C.

abundance, it must be remembered that the majority of watches were cased in plain silver or gold. Watches had first been made thinner in fashion conscious France from the 1780s, and in the 19th century were universally of flatter, thinner form.

Above
CARTIER
ART DECO CLOCK
FRENCH 1920s

Right
CARRIAGE CLOCK
SWISS AND FRENCH 19th C.

The spread of mechanization

THE SWISS AND French introduced keyless winding via the crown button from about 1860.

The commonest form of English watch in the second half of the 19th century was the hunter, in which a glazed dial is protected from damage by a hinged cover. In a half hunter this cover is pierced in the centre in order to read the time without opening the watch.

The late 18th century saw the beginning of part making by home-based outworkers in Switzerland, while the watch was assembled at the watchmakers. Watchmakers in America seized on this idea of standardized parts, which they produced by machines from the mid-century, resulting in a cheap, reliable, mass-produced watch that was exported worldwide. As mechanization improved, the Americans, with all manufacturing processes of making a watch concentrated in single companies, lost their lead to the Swiss, where skilled specialized outworkers were the norm. The Swiss captured the quality market from the English in the early 20th century.

In France, the standardization of parts was applied to travelling clocks, known as carriage clocks, from around 1840. Over the next ten years their movements and cases were made to set sizes and quality of decoration. The simplest merely tell the time, while the most complicated strike the hours and quarter hours.

The carriage clock industry was completely disrupted by the First World War and the trade never really recovered. The Art Deco clocks of the 1920s were the last collectable timepieces of quality.

SCIENTIFIC INSTRUMENTS

BY JEREMY COLLINS

Interest in the art of science and the production of scientific instruments can be traced back to the late 15th and early 16th centuries, when the makers of instruments and experimental apparatus were among the more important artisans. No king, prince, bishop, or successful merchant at that time would have been without his cabinet of fine instruments, which would have demonstrated not just his wealth but his scholarly under-

Top
PLANETARIUM
ENGLISH 18th C.

Left
ASTROLABE
FLEMISH 1559

Below
POCKET ASTRONOMICAL COMPENDIUM
ENGLISH 1579

standing of astronomy, mathematics, surveying and the physical sciences. Makers such as Schissler, Habermel, Burgi, Coignet and others were in great demand, and the output of superlative, complex, instruments was prodigious.

To the tutored modern eye these beautiful creations should be seen and considered against their historical background. The energy and skill of those that made them are gradually, once again, being appreciated. Over the last two decades there has been an increase in interest in antique scientific instruments. Within the last decade prices have more than trebled for many items, and in some cases values have gone up by more than fivefold.

The tragedy has been that because of their one time low value and low regard, many instruments have been buffed up and polished.

All this is now changing and the major auction houses in London, Paris and New York have, with the understanding of the trade, have begun to repair the damage by producing a marketplace in which the very best can once again be purchased. Prices, in some cases, have risen dramatically.

Microscopes have always been of interest, particularly as they are of use in discovering the unknown, but have a certain decorative value.

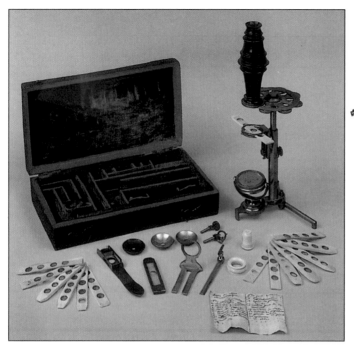

Interest in microscopy was at its zenith in the late 19th century, when many wonderful instruments and variety of slides were made for study in the home.

Surveying instruments, that is to say the level and theodolite, have always appeared in great variety. Collecting surveying instruments today gives the would-be enthusiast an enormous range of exciting, and eccentric instruments from which to choose.

Astronomy has always held a fascination for the professional and amateur alike, and since the days of Galileo, there have been many collectors of telescopes and astronomical instruments. When a particular astronomical event hits the headlines, prices tend to rise sharply. Once the phenomenon has passed, then prices tend to fall showing that interest can be of an ephemeral nature.

Fluctuating prices

THERE IS, AND always has been, a great interest in scales, weights and measures. However, since the establishment of a Standard measure in Britain, the variety of objects within this category has become legion. Many are marked with Borough coats of arms and maker's name, and if in their original condition, being both signed and dated, are sought after by collectors.

Left
'NEW UNIVERSAL' TELESCOPE
ENGLISH Mid 18th C.

Above
BINOCULAR TELESCOPE
FRENCH c.1900

The more exotic instruments such as astrolabes, astrolabe-quadrants, quadrants and various dials can sell for huge sums in the London, European and American salerooms. However, if taken into the context of their value when new, prices are still remarkably low. We are perhaps living in a period where scientific instruments represent one of the finest long term bargains to be had within the world of Fine Art.

If one considers the low survival rate of such objects and the lack of space which they take up in the modern home, delicate, small and unobtrusive instruments of the 16th and 18th centuries can be collected, with relative ease by the enthusiast with even a very modest pocket.

To encourage collectors worldwide, the Scientific Instrument Society was formed in the early 1980s. It holds up to six international meetings a year, and has held meetings with visits to great collections in the USA, Spain, France, Italy, Germany, Austria and Czechoslovakia. Among many of its members there are museum curators, academics, members of the trade and collectors.

Of interest to the Society is the growing number of forgeries that are appearing on the market, as the result of the successful sale of original objects at auction. The amateur collector should be wary of such objects, purely by making note of originals that appear in public and private collections and the sudden mysterious arrival of similar pieces on market stalls and in antique shops.

Top
SELECTION OF SCIENTIFIC INSTRUMENTS
GERMAN 18th C.

Left
SELECTION OF SCIENTIFIC INSTRUMENTS
ENGLISH 18th C.

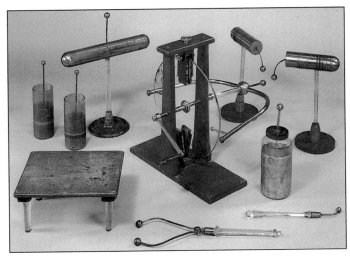

BOOKS AND MANUSCRIPTS

SARAH SOAMES

Above
ABRAHAM ORTELIUS
THEATRUM ORBIS TERRARUM
FLEMISH 1573

Before Johann Guttenberg discovered the art of printing from movable type over 500 years ago, books were written by hand, mostly in Latin. These medieval manuscripts, produced in monasteries for wealthy patrons, would sometimes take years to complete. Generally speaking, only ephemeral texts were written in the vernacular and are of great rarity. Such is our appreciation today of the work of these masters that many of these early manuscripts have been cut up and the individual miniatures and leaves of calligraphy sold separately.

Guttenberg's first book, his Bible of 1455, of which only 45 copies are known to exist, is the most valuable printed book in the world today. Since then, the Bible has been printed more often than any other book.

Books from the press of England's first printer, William Caxton, are naturally some of our greatest treasures. A single leaf from Caxton's first edition of *Canterbury Tales* by Geoffrey Caucer is valued at £1000.

The spread of printing

IN THE SECOND half of the 15th century, following Guttenberg's invention, printing presses sprang up with surprising speed all over Europe. The books they printed are termed 'incunabula' from the Greek word meaning cradle. In effect they are the cradle of printing and as such have ever since been collectors' items. The goal of some past collectors was to obtain an example from each press established before 1500, but this would be almost impossible to achieve today.

Left
**INITIAL P FROM
ILLUMINATED MANUSCRIPT**
ITALIAN c.1490

Below
HARTMANN SCHEDEL
LIBER CHRONICARUM
GERMAN 1493

The invention of printing transformed the world. Books were produced in large quantities, to the great benefit of schools; public libraries became larger and more numerous, and the standard of literacy rose dramatically.

Today, in spite of their age, much of this material of the 16th and 17th centuries is in little demand. The exception is the work of the new authors and thinkers of the Renaissance. The scarcity and importance of a first edition of Sir Thomas More's *Utopia*, 1516, is reflected in the price of £100,000 that it commands today.

William Shakespeare's *First Folio*, the first collected edition of his *Comedies, Histories and Tragedies*, published in 1623 by his friends and admirers after his death; is as near as we can get to a Shakespeare 'first', nearly all the original copies of many of the individual plays

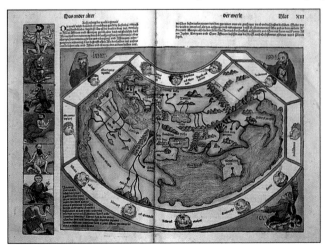

having been lost or worn out by the original actors. However, a *First Folio* is beyond the reach of most of us. The most important book ever printed in English, it contains 20 plays that had never been printed before. The general guideline for collectors of English literature is to go for the first editions of the classic authors, the household names Alexander Pope, Jonathan Swift, Jane Austen, Charles Dickens, Charlotte Brontë, and so on. The 'Collected Works' of most authors, are not what are sought by the bibliophile.

Illustrated books

THE OBVIOUS APPEAL and delight of illustrated books of all periods ensures them a permanent place on collectors' shelves. From block-books and the earliest medicinal herbals, psalters, histories, technological books, right through to children's books of recent times, Edmund Dulac, Arthur Rackham, and

Above
RUDOLPH ACKERMANN
VIEW OF THE HIGH STREET, OXFORD
ENGLISH 1814

Below
BEATRIX POTTER
FROM THE TALE OF PIGLING WOOD
ENGLISH 1904

Beatrix Potter, there are enthusiasts for all categories. French illustrated books of the 18th century deserve a special mention with their exquisite engravings after the greatest artists of the day: Boucher, Fragonard, Watteau, Oudrey, and others. They attained a peak of excellence recognized by all, and many were also bound in the highest quality gilt-tooled bindings of the period.

In the early 19th century came the great period of the English book with coloured plates. Watercolour painting, one of England's major contributions to the visual arts, reached its height at the time when the technique of aquatint engraving was perfected. The Napoleonic wars provided exciting scenes of battle, picturesque uniforms and never-ending inspiration for caricature. Artist's watercolours were reproduced by means of handcoloured aquatint in an enormous range of publications: landscape gardening, costume, travel, guide books and, above all, remarkable topographical productions. Outstanding was the publisher Rudolph Ackermann, famous for his sporting books and prints, whose massive output included three fine works on

families. In an auction of botanical books in London in the mid 1980s, no less than ten individual books were sold, including two by and Redoute two English books of the same period, Robert John Thornton's *Temple of Flora* with its massive coloured plates, and John Sibthorp's *Flora Graeca* in ten volumes with almost 1,000 coloured plates of the flora of Greece.

John James Audubon's famous four elephant folio volumes of *The Birds of America*, published in 1827–38, are already legendary, and so is the price – millions in any currency. Britain's Audubon is Prideaux John Selby, one of Audubon's own pupils. He, too, produced fine folios of life-sized ornithology. Perhaps Britain's most loved and most prolific ornithological artist was John Gould.

Regency England, the *Microcosm of London*, histories of the universities of Oxford and Cambridge, and a history of the Public Schools. All have numerous aquatint illustrations after various artists including Pugin, Westall and Nash.

This was also the heyday of natural history, in particular botany and ornithology. Pierre Joseph Redoute's mastery of flower painting has seldom been equalled, nor the sheer quantity of superb books he illustrated, especially his masterpieces on the rose and lily

Above
ROBERT JOHN THORNTON
FROM THE TEMPLE OF FLORA
ENGLISH 1800

Below
PRIDEAUX JOHN SELBY
BRITISH ORNITHOLOGY
ENGLISH 1833–4

A mention too must be made of atlases. The Dutch were the pre-eminent cartographers, and the 16th and 17th century engraving of maps and charts of the old and new world, often artistically embellished and coloured by hand, then bound into splendid folio atlases, assured that no literate person was without a knowledge of geography. The fact that every home today has an atlas of some sort is probably due to their industry. The *Theatrum Orbis Terrarum* of Abraham Ortelius, published in Antwerp in 1570, was the world's first regularly produced atlas. Such was its popularity that no less than 42 folio editions, in seven different languages, were printed between 1570 and 1612. Today they are rare, many were broken up and the maps framed and sold individually.

Gould's coloured plates were reproduced by means of lithography, a method of engraving on stone which was used with great success during most of the 19th century. David Roberts' *The Holy Land, Syria, Idumea, Arabia, Egypt and Nubia* in six volumes was another *magnum opus* to employ this method. It has been described as 'one of the most important and elaborate ventures of 19th century publishing, and the apotheosis of the tinted lithograph'. The technique ideally suited Roberts' romantic landscapes of the Middle East.

Architecture is a very important, and extensive, branch of the illustrated book and has become an increasingly popular one. From early editions of Palladio to architects of this century such as Frank Lloyd Wright, all are collected. This applies also to voyages and travel books. Accounts of Christopher Columbus' discovery of America and subsequent early voyages are valuable, as are first accounts of Australian discoveries. The price of a set of Captain James Cook's three famous voyages (1773-84), illustrated with charts and plates, can fetch £10,000 (US$16,500).

Amongst the many other areas of antiquarian books, perhaps the first printed accounts of all man's greatest intellectual achievements, whether in science, mathematics, economics, politics, philosophy, art, history, poetry or fiction, are specially important to the bibliophile. So too are many dictionaries, encyclopedias and reference books of all kinds including bibliographies.

Modern first editions and fine bindings

MODERN FIRST EDITIONS are nearer the financial reach of many of us. It is important to concentrate on authors of high standing and the condition and rarity are paramount. To take Ian Fleming's James Bond novels as an example, it is the first, *Casino Royale*, published in a far smaller quantity than the later ones, which, complete with dustjacket, can fetch £1,000 ($1,650) today, the others nearer £100.

To be a fine and desirable copy, a book of any period must be complete. Once it is defective, lacking any part of the text or illustrations, down to a word or even a letter, the value is immediately impaired.

Leather bindings have been created for books since long before the invention of printing and these can be some of the greatest treasures to be found, sometimes regardless of the book they encase.

Above
LUIGI ROSSINI
RACCOLTA DI PROSPETTIVE DELLE PIU BELLE FABRICHE DI ROMA
ITALIAN 1822

Left
DAVID ROBERTS
PLATE FROM THE HOLY LAND, SYRIA, IDUMEA, ARABIA, EGYPT AND NUBIA
ENGLISH 1842–9

DOLLS AND TOYS

Above
HEYDE
ARMY SUPPLY COLUMN
GERMAN c.1920

DOLLS AND DOLLS HOUSES

BY JEREMY COLLINS

The collecting of dolls is not a recent phenomenon, collections were forming in the 1930s and 1940s. Christie's have been holding specialist sales since March 1969.

Most dolls that appear on the market date from the 18th century or later. The 1st century roman doll in the Museo Capitolini with her gold jewellery appears to have been made originally as a doll, and survived because it was buried with its young owner.

This doll also makes another point about their survival. An expensive professionally made doll was a household article of value, and more likely to be passed on to future generations. The condition of some dolls still surviving in original condition, point to their being a status symbol that children were made to treasure most carefully.

Surviving dolls

WOOD WAS THE most common material used in the 17th and 18th centuries. Most English dolls of this period had the head and torso turned on a lathe, the back sliced off, nose and ears carved and enamel eyes inserted before being covered with gesso and brightly painted. They had simply jointed legs, roughly painted, white, stick-like arms with crudely carved fingers and hoof-like

Top
TURNED AND CARVED WOODEN DOLL
ENGLISH 1760

Above
GESSO COVERED WOODEN DOLLS
ENGLISH Early 19th C.

feet. They seem to have been dressed before sale, judging by the professionalism and fit of many of the surviving clothes. By the l9th century this type of doll appears to have declined in popularity. Cheap peg wooden dolls with carved heads, some with yellow painted combs were being imported from the Grodner Tal.

Wax and papier maché dolls

THERE WERE ALSO English wax doll-makers who made beautiful poured bees-wax heads. A cheaper form of English doll, made from the late 18th century to the 1860s, was crude with a papier maché head, dipped in a thin layer of wax to give a more subtle flesh-like effect. The arms are generally of coloured kid or of the same construction as the heads, and the wigs were of mohair, sometimes inserted in a slit from forehead to nape.

The papier maché dolls from Germany were highly sophisticated, with elaborate hairstyles, painted eyes and slim kid bodies with wooden arms and legs. Usually the attachment to the body was concealed by a coloured paper band. Sometimes these survive in their original sewn-on clothes; others have home-made clothes, as the contemporary toy catalogues show that they were usually sold undressed.

By the middle of the century porcelain heads from Germany and bisque heads from France were in production. The German heads from the 1840s were often of exceptional quality, with well modelled coiffures, bands, necklaces, earrings and even bodices. The early French bisque heads have a translucent quality; those made for Mesdames Rohmer and Huret often have plump cheeks and an almost child-like appearance, although dressed in rich fashionable clothes.

Above right
JUMEAU BÉBÉ
FRENCH

Right
KESTNER GOOGLI-EYED DOLLS
GERMAN

Below
SCMITT BÉBÉ DOLL
FRENCH

French luxury dolls

FROM THE MIDDLE of the century French dolls began to surpass their German rivals in quality and invention. While the Germans continued to have the mass market, the French produced superb dolls for the luxury trade. There were fashionably dressed dolls, modelled as women, and they also introduced *bébé* dolls. Jules Nicholas Steiner was the most inventive of the Paris makers. Dolls that walked, cried, moved their arms, kicked their legs and closed their eyes, were all patented by him. The *bébé* first appeared in the 1870s. The main makers were Leon Casimir Bru, Jules Nicholas Steiner and Emile Jumeau.

Each firm had its own distinctive facial type. Bru's was typified by his small pouting mouths. Steiner had several facial types, the open mouth dolls usually had a speaking mechanism. Jumeau dolls are remarkable for their large and jewel-like eyes, heavy brows, and on the early models for their shaded eyelids. During the 1890s the Germans were also producing bisque-headed dolls, usually with sweet faces, sleeping eyes, open mouths, blonde or brown mohair wigs and jointed wood and composition bodies. They were often sold in chemise, shoes and socks. The most prolific firms were Armand Marseille, J. D. Kestner and Simon and Halbig.

Above
STEIFF FELT SOLDIER
GERMAN Early 20th C.

The early 20th century

IN 1909 THERE seems to have been an explosion in the doll world. It was not only the birth of the so-called character doll, modelled as a real child, but the firm of Steiff also produced marvellous ranges of cloth child dolls, and Marion Kaulitz made the Munich Art dolls.

These dolls are very sought after by collectors. Prices depend on the rarity of the mould, its quality and size. The originality and type of body are also important, as are the clothes. It is possible to have every expression. Bisque char-acter children are also made as figures for use as ornaments or as tiny solid standing dolls with only the arms jointed at the shoulder.

In recent years not only Steiff and Lenci cloth dolls have become popular but also English firms, such as Dean's Rag Book Co., Chad Valley, Farnell's, Merrythought and Norah Wellings. The prices of these cloth dolls depend pri-marily on their condition and the survival of their original clothes. Dean's dolls were at first simply printed on cotton. Later felt and cotton was used with only the faces printed on a moulded mask. In the late 1930s rubber heads were made.

Collecting dolls

WHEN COLLECTING OLD dolls it is better to go for a doll in mint condition from a cheaper cate-gory than to spend a lot on a poor-quality specimen from a rarer form, such as a French bisque bébé, badly repainted, re-wigged and with new clothes.

To acquire knowledge of dif-ferent types of doll and their market value, attend specialist sales to examine dolls freely and note prices reached in the cata-logue for future reference. Celluloid, tiny dolls of the 1920s and 30s can still be bought for a few pounds or pence. More expensive are the North American composition and mama dolls from the 1920s to 1940s.

Dolls' houses

THE COLLECTING, OR perhaps the furnishing of dolls' houses, has been a hobby since the 16th century, the most fabulous being the Dutch cabinet houses of the 17th and 18th centuries.

Houses that appear on the market now date mainly from the 19th and 20th centuries. They normally fall into three main types, the first being early large strongly made baby houses of the late 18th and early 19th centuries. Each is unique, and it is probable that they were made by estate carpenters, for a well-to-do local child or children.

The second type are the toy-man houses dating from the last quarter of the 19th century. These are generally rather crude in construction. Because of the general simplicity of design, home-made houses may be in this group as well.

The third type, and highly sought after, are the smaller manufactured houses, many from firms such as Christian Hacker, Moher of Bavaria, Muller, Gottschalk, Lines Bros., Bliss, Amersham, Tri-ang, Silber and Fleming and Swan. Prices depend on architectural detail, much of it supplied, by colour lithography. Furnishing, is a long term project, particu-larly if one is determined to have items of the correct scale and period for the house. Finding one already furnished will reflect this in the price.

ANTIQUE TOYS

BY JAMES OPIE

The history of toymaking

It could be said that many of the toys keenly collected today are not old enough to qualify as antiques. This results from the strong nostalgic tug exerted by the memories of childhood playthings, an attraction that seems to be strongest at the age of about 35 onwards. As each generation of children grows up, the enthusiasm for the toys they played with causes a boom in new collecting subjects; for instance, in the 1980s, the most popular collectable by far was the die-cast model, reflecting the most popular toy of the 1950s.

Collecting more recent toys is made easier by the much wider availability, and therefore lesser expense. Earlier toys are much more directly related to the normal criteria by which antiques are judged, their decorative attraction and intellectual interest. It is unlikely that an antique toy would be bought for practical use by a modern child in the same way as antique furniture.

Below

COLLECTABLE TOYS
EUROPEAN AND AMERICAN
19th/20th C.

THE HISTORY OF toymaking closely parallels that of industrial development, since toys are an item for which there was a huge demand once they were able to be manufactured cheaply. In the 18th century, toymaking was a cottage industry turning out wooden trinkets for pedlars and fairs, or a sideline for jewellers, clockmakers and metalworkers. Turning out a toy would utilize the handmade dexterity available, and occasionally someone would become sufficiently well-known at making a particular type of toy that he could earn a large part of his living at it.

The main categories of toys are as follows: automata, board games, cast iron toys, character toys, construction toys, die-cast toys, dolls, doll houses and furniture, jig-saws, lead figures, mechanical toys, money banks, optical toys, paper toys, penny toys, plastic toys, robots and space toys, teddy bears, tin toys, toy guns and soldiers, train sets and toy theatres.

Toys can date from the Renaissance (automata) to the present day (robots) and prices can reach thousands of pounds.

Toys can be divided into categories by purpose, i.e. baby play objects, companions such as dolls or teddy bears, models of the real world and its activities, entertainments by way of games, sports or spectacles, puzzles providing various challenges of intellectual or physical prowess, or constructive activities where something is built. Many toys cover more than one category, and the specializations within sub-divisions are equally diverse, including a choice of manufacturer, manufacturing process or subject matter.

Character toys, include the toys showing characters from Disney cartoons, sometimes known as Disneyana. Toys possessing the added attraction of fitting into other collections can fetch prices out of all proportion to non-character items.

Many toys, are so damaged, home-made, or plainly unattractive that they are worth very little. There are no hard and fast rules, but the more intricate and attractive the toy, the more expensive it is likely to be.

Above
WOODEN NOAH'S ARK
GERMAN 19th C.

Below
BING
TINPLATE LINER
GERMAN c. 1920

High quality toys

COSTLY TOYS HAVE always been fashion objects, and such toys are very often still desirable today. It is in this context, where toy collecting meets the art world, that the highest prices are to be found. The cunning mechanisms of the automata, where prices are always in the thousands, the frigate made in bone by a Napoleonic prisoner-of-war, or the lithographic fantasies of the tinplate circus performers.

Consider the humble glass marble, a toy sold in millions every day, yet with an almost infinite variety of shape and swirl held within the rattling spheres. They are much collected by children, but not much by adults. Early hand-made marbles

Above
TINPLATE TOYS
GERMAN Early 20th C.

Below
TOY TRAINS
BRITISH, FRENCH AND
GERMAN 20th C.

can be spectacularly interesting compared to most modern machine moulded specimens. Judging by the number of toy collector's fairs held each weekend, it is possible to estimate that there are some hundreds of thousands of people collecting toys in Britain alone.

As the industrial age gathered momentum, the toymakers became major companies and thrived as businesses. Often it is by manufacturer that toys are collected. For instance, among the best-known for tin toys are Arnold Gunthermann and Lehmann of Germany, Bandai in Japan, Bergmann in America, Mettoy in Britain and Jep in France. Hornby is of course the best-known manufacturer of toy trains, but Bassett-Lowke (another British company) predates them and both Bing of Germany and Ives of America made trains, as did Rossignol of France. Specialist books give details of the enormous range.

MUSICAL INSTRUMENTS

Above
LYRAFLUGEL
GERMAN c.1820–30

COLLECTING INSTRUMENTS

BY FREDERICK W. OSTER AND SARAH McQUAID

The history of musical instruments is bound together with the social and technical history of music. As new forms of musical language came into being, musical instruments evolved. Some instruments were rendered obsolete, others changed in size and appearance.

Musical instruments have served many social purposes. They have been used to entertain, to frighten enemies, to inspire religious devotion, to facilitate dancing, to rally troops. During the American Civil War, it was common for a band to march in front of the troops. This created a need for the 'over-the-shoulder' horn, the bell of which pointed back toward those marching behind.

The effect of technical developments

INNOVATIONS HAVE ALSO been dictated by the technical aspects of music. By the beginning of the 19th century, the violin had acquired a longer neck and fingerboard, a larger bass bar, a thicker soundpost, and a more highly pitched neck angle While these changes occurred, they were directly related to developments in the music of the time. Composers were writing pieces that required musicians to use the 7th fingering positions.

Before the late 18th century, nearly all instruments were hand-made in small workshops. Most were made for the use of peasants or townspeople; only a few makers catered to the nobility. With the evolution of mass-production, came the distinction between hand-made and commercially produced instruments. Joseph Guarneri del Gesù, was in his day thought to be a maker of 'rough' instruments; today, his instruments command prices often equal to those of Antonio Stradivari, whose refined productions were made for the aristocracy.

The 19th century saw new manufacturing methods that made instruments affordable to the public at large, and it became fashionable to take up music as a hobby. By the 1880s, nearly every household had a piano. Minstrel bands popularized the five-string banjo in both England and America. The musical fervor of the 19th century generated a profusion of musicians, music instructors, instrument-makers, and music publishers. Makers continued to produce hand-crafted instruments, but their creations were outnumbered by millions of commercially manufactured instruments.

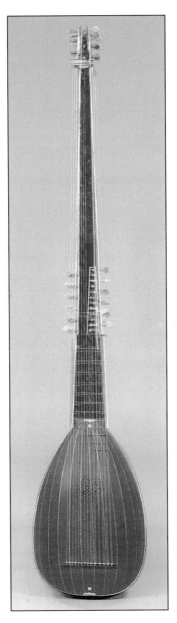

Left
DAVID TECCHLER
CHITARRONE
GERMAN 1725

Many of the commercially made instruments were altered to make them appear older, and it was common to insert into factory-made violins of this period facsimile labels of such famous makers as Stradivari, Guarneri, Guadagnini, Amati, Maggini, and Stainer. These instruments were seldom produced as intentional forgeries; rather, the label indicated that the violin was inspired by or styled after one of these makers. They were commonly sold through music shops and catalogues and today constitute the bulk of available old violins. However, deliberate forgeries do exist. Leopoldo Franciolini (1844–1920), perhaps the most infamous instrument forger, produced a great many fake early stringed instruments and altered others to make them appear older or more ornate.

Factors that Determine Price

IN GENERAL, THE highest prices for musical instruments are commanded by violins, followed by historical keyboards and early stringed and wind instruments. In November 1990, at an auction sale at Christie's of London the Mendelssohn Stradivari violin of 1720 was sold for for £902,000 (about US$1.5 million). A number of criteria work together to determine the value of a musical instrument. These include the maker, model, provenance, date, condition and availability.

The most important of these factors is the maker. Violins by Antonio Stradivari (1644–1737) and Joseph Guarneri del Gesù (1686–1744) have been the choice of great virtuosi, as have bows by Francois Tourte of Paris (1747-1835). Consequently, they are universally acknowledged to represent the apex of violin and bow making, and will always occupy the top tier of the market. Below that level, it is largely a question of trends; makers may come in and out of favour as musical styles change. Outside the violin family, there are no makers that have achieved a status equivalent to that of Stradivari, Guarneri del Gesù and Tourte; however, instruments by great innovators within an instrument classification are highly sought after. These include pianos by Bartolomeo Cristofori (1655–1731), who is credited with the earliest pianos, and more refined fortepianos by Johann Andreas Stein (1728–92). Other revolutionary instruments that fetch high prices include: harps by Sebastian Erard (1752–1831), inventor of the modern double

Left
GIOVANNI PAOLO MAGGINI
VIOLA
ITALIAN c. 1600

Left
JACOB KIRKMAN
HARPSICHORD
ENGLISH c. 1761

Below
ANTONIO STRADIVARI
COLOSSUS VIOLIN
ITALIAN c. 1716

action pedal harp; flutes by Theobald Boehm (1794–1881), creator of the modern key system for the flute; early flutes and woodwinds by Johann Christoph Denner (1655–1707) and by members of the Hotteterre family (late 17th to early 18th century); bassoons by Johann Heckel (1812–77); saxophones and brasswinds by Adolphe Sax (1814–94); and brasswinds by Francois Perinet (active 1829–55), inventor of the piston valve, and by Johann Moritz (1777–1840), inventor of the tuba and the 'Berliner' valve.

As the needs of musicians change with prevailing musical forms, certain physical characteristics become more or less desirable. In violins, for example, a preference has arisen for instruments with a flatter arch to the back as such instruments are more likely to produce the louder and more powerful sound currently in favour among orchestra players.

Left

DEVELOPMENTAL INSTRUMENTS

FRENCH, ENGLISH, AMERICAN

From left to right:
Serpent-Foreville c. 1831.
English keyed bugle c 1830
Mid 19th century drum.

Boxwood clarinet, c 1825.
Boxwood flute c. 1850.
Stained maple bassoon 1820.
An early bass viol, 1806

Highly arched violins by Florentine and Roman makers are still popular with chamber musicians. Flat-backed mandolins after the designs of Orville Gibson replaced Neapolitan-style round-backed mandolins; larger 'dreadnought' model guitars like those developed by the C. E Martin Company have replaced the smaller parlour guitars popular before the 1930s.

The history of a musical instrument, is also a significant consideration in determining market value. An instrument that has been used by a famous musician is often worth a great deal more than one with a less distinguished history. In 1986, Christie's New York auctioned a platinum flute made in 1939 by Verne Q. Powell of Boston. This flute, had belonged to William Kincaid, who was considered to be the greatest flautist and most influential teacher in the United

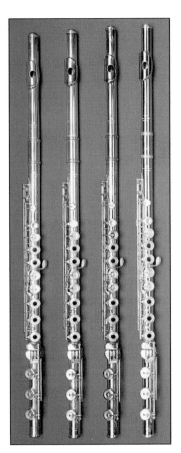

Above right
POWELL
FLUTES
AMERICAN
19th C.

....

Left
VON SCHRATT
ALTO
RECORDER
GERMAN
Mid 16th C.

States. A collector purchased it for US$187,000 (£115,000). Similarly, Jimi Hendrix's 1968 white Fender Stratocaster guitar played at the Woodstock festival sold at auction in 1990 for £198,000 (US$325,000). Also in 1990, Buddy Holly's 1945 Gibson J-45 guitar sold at auction in New York for US$242,000 (£145,000).

The value of some instruments may be affected by their date and 'period of making'. Giovanni Battista Guadagnini,

worked in five different cities, each inspiring a different style; violins from his Turin period are worth more than his earlier work. Violins made by Antonio Stradivari before 1700 are far less valuable than his later instruments.

An instrument's condition is also an important criterion. This is especially true for violins. While no one expects a 250-year-old violin to look exactly the way it did the day it was made, it must meet certain standards. Investment grade instruments should be free of 'post cracks' to the back, be free of poorly executed or unsightly repairs, retain a large amount of original varnish, and be original in all their essential parts (back, table, ribs, and scroll). For other instruments, condition is not quite as crucial, although those in an overall original state and playable are more desirable.

The final factor that determines the value of a particular musical instrument is availability. Some instruments such as those of the Renaissance, are valuable simply because so few have survived. In March of 1988, a rare mid 16th century columnar alto recorder (see photograph left) by Hans Rauch von Schratt sold at auction at Christie's for £44,000 (US$73,000), a record price for an early wind instrument. In a few cases, however, such as when the maker's output was so small they never achieved wide renown, lack of availability can lead to a lower valuation being assigned to instruments.

THE VIOLIN FAMILY

BY FRANCES GILLHAM

The most popular type of antique musical instrument is the violin family – violins, violas, violoncelli and bows. This is the field that commands the highest prices and captures the imagination of the world at large.

Unlike other antiques, the violin family should not be viewed primarily as works of art. The violin was conceived and produced to function – the majority of purchasers will earn their living by using them. Those attending auctions of musical instruments will be: professional players, teachers and students, dealers, makers, restorers, and amateur musicians.

The violin market has developed substantially in the last ten years. One of the main reasons for this growth has been the entry into the field of the Japanese, and more recently, the Koreans and the Chinese. Western classical music has gained enormous appreciation in the Far East and performance standards attained there are now of top international quality. Demand as a result spans the whole instrument range, from Stradivaris to childrens' violins.

The most sought-after instruments are Italian, then French, with English and German makers in general less popular. During the 16th century, the design of the violin as

we know it now had more or less taken shape. During the 17th century, the violin increased in popularity. Louis XIV had a court orchestra of violins. By the early 18th century, composers such as Bach, Handel and Vivaldi were all writing prolifically for violin.

Stradivari and the Cremona workshops

THE MOST FAMOUS Italian violin-making centre was Cremona, and it was here that Antonio Stradivari was apprenticed to Nicolo Amati before setting up his own workshop. Cremona was already considered to be at the forefront of this craft. Violins are generally made of maple, with pine fronts facilitating resonance. These raw materials grew in abundance along the Po River valley. Since the end of the 18th century Stradivari has been considered to be at the zenith of violin-making, and his instruments have never been surpassed either tonally or visually.

Other celebrated names are also attached to Cremona: the Guarneri family, Carlo Bergonzi, Francesco Rugeri and Lorenzo Storioni.

Left
CARLO BERGONZI
BERGONZI VIOLIN
Front and back views
ITALIAN 1739

Above and right
CAPPA VIOLONCELLO
ITALIAN 1697

However, there were other thriving centres as well, Venice and Naples especially could boast several generations of the well-established violin-makers. During the 19th century, Turin makers are considered worthy successors. Instruments by Giovanni Francesco Pressenda and Joseph Rocca have become particularly desirable in recent years. All these makers also made violas and violoncelli of comparable quality.

Assessing the quality

WHAT DO PEOPLE seek in a violin? Condition and tonal qualities are most important as well as proportion and appearance. Tone is without doubt a personal and subjective matter. Even in the world of Stradivaris, one soloist may be enraptured, another disappointed and a third may find a specific example difficult to play. Much can be done to alter the way a violin responds. An instrument may need structural work, such as changing the angle of the neck. Old internal repairs might need to be redone and some instruments have been fitted inside with so-called tonal improvement patches which could have the opposite effect. Restoration of instruments is highly skilled work which should only be carried out by well-respected repairers.

Assessing string instruments

ASSESSING VIOLINS REMAINS the preserve of the dedicated specialist. Throughout the history of violin-making there have been copies, fakes and mislabelling. It is very simple to place a label inside any violin in order to improve its saleability. Generations of makers have copied and followed the models of earlier great makers. In Germany and France during the last century huge numbers of violins carried a copy of the maker's label on whose model these commercial instruments were based. Hundreds of thousands of violins bearing reproduction Stradivari labels have survived. These instruments cost about 25 shillings in 1900, complete with case, strings and bow and were not meant as fakes. However, with a further 90 years of ageing, these instruments are constantly retrieved from attics, sheds and even skips by hopeful, but ultimately disappointed, owners from all over the world. Their value is rarely more than a few hundred pounds.

WINE

DUNCAN McEUAN

Above
VINTAGE COGNAC

It is a common complaint that there is never enough time to spend on the serious laying down of a cellar. The fact that the space in which to lay it down does not exist is neither here nor there. Time is the critical factor; the availability of a fairly modest amount of money, and the interest in collecting, are the corner stones on which to build.

Why wine?

COLLECTING AND LAYING down wine can be a rewarding and fascinating pastime, as well as an efficient investment. Income from the investment should be seen as the money saved by buying early and consuming later, when the price of the wine will have risen, due to scarcity, and strong demand in the market for a ready-to-drink product. Capital appreciation has been self-evident over the past 20 years, although performances like that of Chateau Latour

1961 – opening offer in 1962 around £25 (US$40) per case, recent price at auction £5,000 (US$8,250) per case are going to be hard to match, medium term. However, as long as patience is exercised and the rules followed, profits can be made and perhaps used to purchase new vintages and help contribute towards free drinking.

Why buy at auction?

BUYING AT AUCTION is the simplest method because of the vast range offered and encapsulated in one well laid out catalogue. For instance, Christie's Wine Sales take place twice a month, one sale devoted entirely to Bordeaux wines – classed growth reds and sauternes, vintages 1955 to 1986; the second to more mature wines, from rare old Bordeaux, through fine red and white burgundy, German wines and champagne to vintage port and cognac.

Catalogues can be obtained from the auctioneers by subscription and the wines, which lie in various locations, can be delivered for a charge, depending on distance. Considerable care is taken to check on condition and provenance before cataloguing takes place and when possible wines and cellars are inspected. Many of the wines offered at auction lie in bonded warehouses where ideal conditions prevail and often private collectors who have had their stocks stored in wine merchants' cellars, decide to sell and are steered by their merchant to an auctioneer. These stocks of impeccable provenance have the advantage of being offered generally in small quantities and are of undoubted quality.

The catalogue arrives well in advance of the sale date and so gives ample time for study and decision making. With advance

Left
SELECTION OF VINTAGE BORDEAUX AND BURGUNDY
FRENCH Mid 20th C.

notice, advice can be sought from the auctioneer, and here the advantage of time at the buyer's disposal can be best used to make unhurried choices and a study of prevailing market conditions.

What to buy

THE CRITICAL FACTOR is what to buy. At a time of recession, a buyer's market prevails. Prices, which for several years have moved upwards, have now settled. The opening prices demanded by the producers for each new vintage, resulted in strong price resistance, and while stocks were taken up, more remained in growers' and negociants' cellars in France. The wine market is international, and when the dollar is weak,

demand from the United States is muted. The result is that good recent vintages can be bought elsewhere cheaply, providing there is a good quantity. In 1990 some of the abundant vintages of the 1980s could be bought for less, in real terms, than was being asked when they were first available, providing that you weren't buying in dollars.

In the space available it is only possible to give broad outlines of what should be purchased. Red Bordeaux and vintage port are the safest bets. Red Bordeaux is produced in a ratio to vintage port of 90:10. The best Bordeaux vintages to go for with a view to medium term investment, are: 1982, 1983, 1985 and 1986. You can buy these for as little as £60 (US$100) a case. For vintage port 1977, 1983 and

1985 are the years to look for, at upwards of £96 (US$160) a case.

There is no doubt that buying the best produces the best results. Avoid dubious vintages such as 1984 and 1987. These will provide attractive drinking wines, but definitely not good investments. Which châteaux to buy? Safe bets are Lafite, Mouton-Rothschild and Latour, or 'super-seconds', such as Palmer, Pichon-Lalande, Ducru-Beaucaillou, Canon, Lynch-Bages or Léoville- Las-Cases. For reasonable prices, good drinking and a perfectly safe investment, châteaux such as Beychevelle, Gruaud-Larose, Gloria, Grand-Puy-Lacoste, Giscours, Cissac, d'Angludet and Chasse-Spleen, to name but a few, fit the bill.

For vintage port, the choice

is much easier. The top shippers, in commercial terms, are Taylor, Graham and Fonseca, closely followed by Cockburn, Dow, Warre, Croft and Sandeman.

Burgundy has become very expensive in recent years, and even new vintages fetch high prices. With a smaller output than Bordeaux, many of Burgundy's better labels fetch as much as first growth clarets, and there is little of quality at the cheaper end of the range. Many good Californian wines are as highly valued as high-quality French ones. Labels to look for include Robert Mondavi, Diamond Creek and Joseph Phelps, and the best of recent years (for reds) are 1976, 1984 and 1985.

Storage

ONCE YOU HAVE bought your wine, how you store it is important. A cellar or basement is preferable. You can use a cool cupboard, on a north-facing wall in a bedroom or under the stairs, even a secure garage. A steady temperature, ideally 13–16°C (55–60°F), darkness and stillness are advisable. If it is any warmer, the wine matures a trifle faster. Storage in a public warehouse is easily available, providing ideal conditions and at a fairly reasonable cost.

Finally, the above information provides a mere skeleton of a complex and fascinating subject. With time at your disposal and with plenty of wine books and specialist magazines bursting with knowledgeable articles, further study is strongly recommended.

Below
VINTAGE PORT AND MADEIRA
PORTUGESE AND SPANISH

COLLECTOR'S
SECTION

Above
A SELECTION OF LADIES' SHOES
EUROPEAN 17th–19th C.

Buying and Selling

ANYONE ENTERING THE field of antiques as a potential purchaser has essentially three options to choose from: they can attempt building a collection by themselves on the basis of trial and error, word-of-mouth, and information derived from magazine articles and books such as this; they can purchase primarily at auction, taking their chances and competing with experts and professionals, but at least being assured that the auction house is, to a degree, acting in their interest as well as that of the seller; or they can form a relationship with a dealer in their chosen category, who can become, if the dealer is a good one, not only a supplier, but also a guide and mentor.

Of the three, the first can be the most fun and it is a route to be highly recommended. There is nothing more exciting to the collector-acquirer than browsing at street-markets, trade fairs, second-hand shops or front-yard sales in order to find that vital finishing piece for their collection, or that mythical item such as a Ming vase that has been used as a door-stop for the last twenty years. Recently in England an Italian Renaissance bronze discovered at the back of a garden shed fetched over £650,000 at auction – so such things do happen.

However, buying without expert guidance, especially where significant sums of money are involved, can be hazardous and purchasing on a regular basis by trial and error is obviously out of the question for most people. A book such as this is able to furnish the background information and factual data, but when it comes to an important, high-value decision, on the spot, an on-the-spot assessment should be made by someone whose professional life has been devoted to buying and selling items in very specific disciplines. Even some of the experts who have contributed to this volume, will have made mistakes themselves while they were learning their trade. It is these hard knocks, and the sometimes costly lessons they teach, that fashion authority and expertise. There is no need for the average collector to 'learn by experience' when such professional help is at hand.

By buying at a reputable auction house, or by buying through a trustworthy dealer, the collector can be assured of certain things. Firstly, the item for sale will have been thoroughly appraised by someone who knows what they are doing; secondly, that it will be accurately described; and thirdly, that the auctioneer or dealer will be considering their own reputation as well as the possibility of making a profit. After that, it is a question of 'Caveat Emptor' (Buyer Beware). After all, the buying and selling of antiques these days is big business, and people are in it to make money. The majority of traders in antiques maintain high professional standards and deal with honour, but that does not stop them from attempting to make the profits that their training deserves. The best traders, and the best collectors, are those who never lose their appetite for excitement, and who never let excitement affect their judgement.

The Advantages of Buying at Auction

● The leading auction houses are household names, and would not continue as such unless they maintained the highest standards of integrity. This serves as a guarantee to the buyer as well as to the seller, of fair play within reasonable commercial parameters. An auctioneer's catalogue, like any sales brochure, is not going to dwell on the bad points of the product it is advertising, so although what is mentioned in the description will be scrupulously accurate, the buyer has to retain a sensible level of cynicism. Items purchased at auction are bought 'as seen'.

● For many potential sellers, the major auction houses are the obvious first point of contact. The best houses offer free appraisal services without commitment, allowing the sellers to discover the value of their objects, and on the basis of the valuation, whether they wish to put them up for auction or not. The benefit to the auctioneers it provides them with a regular source of items to handle. The benefit to the buyer is the potential these sources offer for bargains, and also the regular influx they provide of fresh material into the market place.

Auction houses always provide the opportunity for the items at any forthcoming sale to be viewed several days in advance. At these viewings the sale pieces are on display, usually with experts on hand. Under supervision, virtually all the objects can be examined in detail and handled. This is absolutely invaluable for the collector as there is no substitute for close examination. Unless you know a piece and its condition, it is inadvisable to bid at auction without having viewed it thoroughly.

Left
JAPANNED BRACKET CLOCK
ENGLISH c.1760

● Auction houses are fine 'documenters' for the antiques business. For their own purposes, they keep thorough and accurate records of items and transactions, thus building up excellent libraries and databases. Their photographic libraries are particularly good, most of which were provided by the individual experts. The particular benefit this sound practice of recording affords the buyer is in the provision of exceptionally well-produced sale catalogues, which are circulated some way ahead of the main auctions. It is very easy to get on the mailing lists for these catalogues, though, depending on the auction house, and sometimes on the particular sale, there may be a charge. The catalogues are useful to the serious collector for two reasons: first, to let them know what will be available for sale on a specific date; but also, as they tend to be lavishly illustrated, to contain detailed descriptions, they form an excellent record of activity and current price-points in particular categories. A library of these catalogues can quickly build into an invaluable professional reference source.

● Perhaps the most important advantage to most buyers is that, given that most auction houses take a commission of around 10–12.5%, and that a private dealer could be attempting to mark up an item by anything from 50% to 200% or more, it can obviously be very much cheaper to buy at auction.

The Advantages of Buying from Dealers

● The main advantage of buying from a dealer is the benefit of personal contact. This benefit is substantially diluted if items are purchased piecemeal from a variety of sources, most collectors who favour this route will prefer to work closely with a small circle of dealers. It is still a good idea to build a relationship with more than one dealer: that will keep them on their toes and keep prices competitive. Good dealers will take the time and trouble to get to know their clients, even if no immediate purchases arise, both because they have a personal love of their subject, and wish to share their interest with others, and for the very sound commercial reason that, in the long term, if their advice, service, and contacts are good, business will be done.

● One of the main advantages good dealers offer is that they will often prevent their clients from purchasing. All collectors make mistakes early in their careers. Commonly the sympathetic dealer, may have a better idea of the shape that the overall collection is taking, and can nurture and focus attention in the right direction.

● The best dealers offer a much broader service than merely having their goods on display and 'selling from stock'. Once they know the needs of a particular collector they can actively seek specific items to fill gaps in the collection. Because it is their business, to which they devote themselves full-time, they will inevitably have a much wider network than any non-professional collector can ever develop. As a matter of course they can enquire about the availability of pieces from dealers in other cities and, most vitally in some categories, from overseas. They will be routinely circulated with news of all auctions and important private sales, and should be well-enough connected to hear occasionally, of items which are not yet quite on sale but might be available for a certain price. In turn, they can circulate their own contacts with 'want-lists' of desired items or subjects, multiplying their client collectors' chances of expanding their collections.

● Purchases from dealers, depending on individual arrangements, can be less risky than those from auctions. The 'as seen' element need not apply, as most reputable dealers are happy to issue receipts and guarantees that a piece is in a certain condition, backed up by a full professional description. Once a relationship has been formed, many dealers are even prepared to offer a piece on a trial basis – allowing the client to keep it for a while to see how it sits with the rest of the collection, and to see how they feel about it before a final decision is made and money changes hands (or the piece is returned). Purchases from dealers are very often made on the understanding that if ever the client changes their mind the piece will be repurchased by the dealer at the original price paid though this should be clarified at the time that the deal is made. It is not in the long-term interest of the dealer to force goods on their clients, or to persuade them to take items which are not suitable – though there are many less scrupulous traders around who do not view business in quite these terms.

Restoration, Care and Display

THE BEST ADVICE commonly given about repairing and restoring antiques is – don't! If you are weighing up this option, then your piece is already imperfect, and the damage is done. In virtually every antique category there is very little or no difference in price between a damaged item and a repaired or restored item, so there is unlikely to be any financial benefit.

Right
BLACKFOOT PIPE BAG
NATIVE AMERICAN c.1880

Prevention is better than cure. Think very hard before you purchase a piece knowing that it is imperfect; and transport, store and display your antiques in the most careful manner possible, however much it costs.

If you have some personal or aesthetic reason for wishing to restore or repair a piece, do not attempt to carry out the work yourself. Use the highly talented professionals who specialize in all categories. Their involvement will ensure that the damage will not be made worse. Specialist craftspeople can use techniques and materials current at the time the piece was originally made.

Cleaning antiques is a highly controversial subject, and advice will vary from expert to expert. As usual, the best practical guidance is that if you have any doubts, leave it alone. Certainly never ever attempt to touch any antique with any

form of proprietary cleaner, especially anything abrasive or corrosive. Cleaning is still a task best left to a paid professional. Even the final decision about whether an item needs cleaning or not is a decision to be taken by an expert.

Caring for and maintaining your antiques is something quite different. It is difficult to cover the subject of care and maintenance in a comprehensive volume such as this, as each category of antique has its own rules and guidelines. The right conditions for storing wine, for example, are obviously totally unsuitable for a quilt or etching. Many specialist articles and books have been published on the care of items within the individual antique disciplines, and anyone collecting in a specific category must thoroughly familiarize themselves with this information. Particular attention should be paid to the three

essential variables of temperature, humidity and light, all of which can be great allies or very dangerous foes.

If you have purchased an item from a dealer he will almost certainly give you instructions on how to care for it – whether you want them or not! Listen carefully and you will not regret it. If you are buying for the love of a piece, then you will want to keep it in the best possible condition: and if you are buying with an eye to financial gain, then, if anything, care is even more vital to safeguard your investment.

Displaying antiques is one of the most enjoyable aspects of collecting. There is no point, after all, in investing a large amount of time, money and effort in assembling a fine group of items if you do not then take an enormous amount of pride in displaying it to the best effect. Nothing is sadder than to hear of fine pieces locked away, stored in bankers' vaults, or hidden in basements because of lack of display space. Sometimes the best light for viewing can be the worst possible light for conservation, and where this is the case it is unfortunately necessary to err on the side of caution.

Some collectors prefer to stick to traditional methods – plan chests and glass-fronted cupboards – while others commission simple shelving systems and invest more heavily in various forms of indirect or spotlighting. The main thing is to choose a style that you feel comfortable with and that attractively complements the nature and feel of the antiques you are collecting. On a grander scale a whole house interior or room can be designed around the theme of your collection.

Good display adds an extra intangible dimension to a collection. In addition, if you have any intention of dealing in antiques, even at the most basic level, and you are ever likely to invite a fellow collector to view an item and make an offer on it, it is undoubtedly the case that good display can add value to the piece on offer. One constantly hears the complaint from buyers that the piece that looked so charming, striking, dignified, or colourful in the shop, and for which they therefore paid such an exorbitant sum of money, became charmless, inconsequential, vulgar, or subdued as soon as they got it

home. This is because the merchant, has thought carefully about the character of the item and designed a setting in his shop to accentuate its finest virtues.

Care and display are fundamental elements of the collector's art, but are too often neglected, as they are relatively expensive. A rough estimate might be that 10% of the value of a collection should be set aside for its care and display. Items such as sophisticated temperature and light controls, and burglar alarms or other security measures are costly, but worth every penny. It is good advice to budget for these 'hidden' costs of collecting when planning purchases. If all of your financial allocation goes on the pieces themsleves, you might very well quickly assemble fine items, but be forced to keep them at your bank for fear of robbery!

Recording and Cataloguing

METICULOUS RECORDS SHOULD be kept from the first day a collection is started. Most collectors enjoy this aspect, as the urge to collect normally reflects a wellorganized and retentive personality, but evenfor those who find this an unexciting prospect, it is nevertheless vital that scrupulous documentation should be maintained, for the following reasons:

● In order to develop as a collector, it is important to be able to look back at previous buying and selling activity. At a minimum, notes on the date of purchase, the piece, the seller's

Below
SELECTION OF TOYS
VARIOUS COUNTRIES 20th C.

address, and the price are obviously crucial, and you can add details on how you located it, the way the negotiation or bidding was handled. It is only by constantly reviewing your motivation, successes and mistakes that you will improve as a collector. That improvement will be reflected in higher quality pieces at lower prices.

● As well as your personal records, you will need to keep the basic details of any transaction, including a sales receipt and any other documentation provided, for both tax and insurance purposes. These should be kept together in a safe place, probably outside your home.

● Recording prices and keeping documentation is also essential in order to allow a piece to be sold. Whether you set off to be a trader or not, as a collector you will inevitably end up by being a dealer. You cannot continue to

acquire endlessly. A stage will be reached when you will need to sell some pieces in order to buy others. Just as the tendency is to upgrade the type of house we live in or the car we drive, so a collection will go through several distinct phases, dependent on variables such as the collector's disposable income, personal style and experience. Items which seemed strange and exciting early in a collector's development may turn out to be commonplace, and these pieces will be traded in for finer or more expensive antiques. Obviously when an item has to be sold, the new buyer will want some details and some proof that you own what you are selling. This will be provided by the original receipt you have kept. In order to get the maximum benefit, you need to be sure that you are selling an article for more than you paid – allowing for inflation – and this, again, is where good record-keeping is absolutely vital.

Starting a Collection

THERE ARE TWO basic elements which link all collector-acquirers, whatever their speciality: these are a love of their subject, and, principally, a love of collecting. As the urge to collect generally precedes the selection of the item to be acquired, it is worth examining a few basic rules to be followed when planning a collection and choosing a subject:

● Most collections are started by accident rather than deliberately. Perhaps the latent collector inherits one or two items and decides to build on this nucleus. This is particularly common in the fields of coin, stamp, model soldier, comic book, cigarette card, doll, and train collecting. The collection exists almost before the collector knows or acknowledges it. It may well be, having experimented with a juvenile collection that those

Below
CEREMONIAL HALBERDS
GERMAN Early 17th C.

pieces cease to be of interest, but the collecting bug remains, in which case a new field will need to be researched.

● Whether you have previously experimented with a collection of one sort, or are starting completely from nothing, the most important thing is to combine your urge to collect with your personal taste. One well-known collector started with a practical interest in needleworking, and acquired all sorts of accessories to use and experiment with before specializing in thimbles and eventually forming one of the best collections in the world.

● If you are genuinely unsure about a category to collect, then visit some general antique fairs, to look at a wide range of objects. Only by looking at items close up and handling them will you know if you have an empathy with the subject. Talk to as many people as you can and read about the history of the categories you are considering.

● Think hard about the practical aspects before committing yourself to a subject. If you live in a small flat, there is little point, even if you are wealthy, in setting out to build a collection of large-scale stone sculpture or Tudor oak furniture, as you won't have the space to display it. Similarly if you have a limited amount of time, the main dealers you need to attend and see regularly should be situated locally.

● Principally, think about the amount of money you have to spend in relation to the prices you will have to pay. If you are starting from nothing you will want very quickly to form a nucleus of four or five items which can legitimately be described as 'a collection'. After that you will want to add to it regularly, and how regularly will depend on how much the pieces cost in proportion to your resources. You will probably become very frustrated if you cannot splash out on a new piece at least once every six months, and if that is the case, then the calculations and decisions become straightforward. If the items in your chosen subject category cost (in round figures) about £50 (U$100), then you will need an initial input of around £250/US$500 and a minimum of £100/US$200 per year to keep the collection growing and developing.

● Think hard about the budget and your own collecting urges and style. Too often what should be a great pleasure is spoiled either because collectors have chosen to operate in an area which is too expensive. Buy less frequently in order to devote your budget to purchasing the best quality you can. If this simply does not suit your personality, then try to choose a category in which the best items are inexpensive enough to allow you to buy relatively frequently within your resources.

Above
NICHOLAS HILLIARD
A GENTLEMAN
ENGLISH Late 16th C.

INTERNATIONAL DIRECTORY

MUSEUMS, AUCTIONEERS AND SPECIALIST DEALERS

Australia

ASA STAMPS CO PTY
138–140 Rundle Mail, Adelaide, SA 5001
Tel: 223 2951
auctioneer

ASSOCIATED AUCTIONEERS PTY
800–810 Parramatta Rd, Lewisham,
NSW 2049
Tel: 560 5899
auctioneer

BRIGHT SLATER PTY
Brisbane Club Building, Isles Lane, Brisbane,
Queensland 4000 Tel: 312415
auctioneer

CHRISTIE, MANSON & WOODS
298 New South Head Road, Double Bay,
Sydney, NSW 2028
Tel: 326 1422
auctioneer

JOHNSON BROTHERS
328 Main Road, Glenorchy, Tasmania 7011
auctioneer

SOTHEBY PARKE BERNET
115 Collins Street, Melbourne, Victoria 3000
Tel: 633900
auctioneer

H E WELLS & SONS
326 Rokeby Road, Subiaco, WA
Tel: 381 9040
auctioneer

Austria

CHRISTIE'S
A-1030 Wien, Ziehrerplatz 4–22
Tel: Vienna 732644
auctioneer

KUNSTHISTORISCHES MUSEUM
Vienna
museum: general collection

Belgium

CHRISTIE, MANSON & WOODS
33 Boulevard de Waterloo, Bruxelles
B-1000 Tel: Brussels 512 8830
auctioneer

MUSÉE HORTA
Brussels
museum

SOTHEBY PARKE BERNET
32 Rue de l'Abbaye, Bruxelles 1050
Tel: Brussels 343 5007
auctioneer

Canada

CHRISTIE'S INTERNATIONAL
1055 West Georgia Street, Vancouver,
BC V6E 3P3 Tel: 685 2126
auctioneer

MUSEUM OF FINE ARTS
1379 Sherbrooke Street, Montreal, Quebec
Tel: 514 285 1600
museum: general collection, Native art

ROYAL ONTARIO MUSEUM
100 Queen's Park, Toronto, Ontario
Tel: 416 586 5736
museum: general collection, arts of the East

SOTHEBY PARKE BERNET
156 Front Street, Toronto, Ontario
M5J 2L6 Tel: 416 596 0300
auctioneer

WINNIPEG ART GALLERY
300 Memorial Boulevard, Winnipeg,
Manitoba Tel: 204 786 6641
gallery: general collection, Native and Canadian folk art

France

DE CAGNY
4 rue Drouot, Paris 75009
Tel: 246 0007
auctioneer

CHRISTIE'S
17 rue de Lille, Paris 75007
Tel: 261 1247
auctioneer

MUSÉE DE LOUVRE
Paris
museum: general collection

SOTHEBY'S
3 rue de Miromesnil, Paris 75008
Tel: 266 4060
auctioneer

Germany

ANTIQUITÄTEN LOTHAR HEUBEL
371 Odenthaler Strasse, Köln 1
auctioneer

AUKTIONSHAUS TIEJEN
30 Spitaler Strasse,
D-2000 Hamburg 1
auctioneer

BAYERISCHES NATIONALMUSEUM
Munich
museum: general collection

AUGUST BODIGER
4 Oxfordstrasse, Bonn
auctioneer

CHRISTIE'S
Maximilianstrasse 20,
D-8000 Munich 22
auctioneer

GERMANISCHES NATIONALMUSEUM
Berlin
museum: general collection

GERMANISCHES NATIONALMUSEUM
Nuremberg
museum: general collection

GERNET DORAU
2 Johann-Georg Strasse,
D-1000 Berlin 31
auctioneer

HISTORISCHES MUSEUM
Dresden
museum: general collection

SOTHEBY PARKE BERNET
Odeonsplatz 16,
D-8000 Munich 22
auctioneer

Holland

CENTRAAL MUSEUM
Utrecht
museum: general collection

CHRISTIE, MANSON & WOODS
Rokin 91, Amsterdam 1012 KL
Tel: 231505
auctioneer

RIJKSMUSEUM
Amsterdam
museum: general collection

SOTHEBY'S
Rokin 102, Amsterdam 1012 KZ
Tel: 246215
auctioneer

Hong Kong

SOTHEBY PARKE BERNET
64 Queen's Road Central, Hong Kong
Tel: Hong Kong 225454
auctioneer

Italy

CHRISTIE'S
114 Piazza Navona, Roma 00186
Tel: Rome 6541217
auctioneer

FINARTE
Piazzetta Bossi 4, Milano 20121
Tel: Milan 877041
auctioneer

GALLERIA DEGLI UFFIZI
Florence
gallery/museum: mainly paintings

SOTHEBY PARKE BERNET
Via Gino Capponi 26, Firenze 50121
Tel: Florence 571410
auctioneer

VATICAN MUSEUM
Rome
museum: general collection

New Zealand

ALEX HARRIS LTD
377 Princess Street, Dunedin
Tel: 740703
auctioneer

DUNBAR SLOANE LTD
32 Waring Taylor Street, Wellington
Tel: 721 367
auctioneer

THORNTON AUCTIONS
89 Albert Street, Auckland
1 Tel: 30888
auctioneer

D J VISSER
90 Worcester Street, Christchurch
Tel: 67297
auctioneer

South Africa

SOTHEBY PARKE BERNET
Total House, Rissik Street, Braamfontein
3017 Tel: 393726
auctioneer

Spain

CHRISTIE'S
5 Casado del Alisal, Madrid
Tel: 228 9300
auctioneer

United Kingdom

ADAM & SONS
26 St Stephen's Green, Dublin
Tel: Dublin 760261
auctioneer

ALDRIDGES
130 Walcot Street, Bath, Avon
Tel: 01225 462830
auctioneer

ALFIES ANTIQUE MARKET
13–25 Church Street, London NW8
Tel: 0171 723 6066
market; over 350 stands including: desks and bureaus; clocks and watches; paperweights; samplers; sporting items and ephemera; ceramics; silver; jewellery; marine items; lighting; radios; Art Deco furniture and artefacts; bohemian glass; fireplaces; French mirrors; Art Deco ceramics; scientific instruments; postcards; handbags; paintings of all types; rare books; mechanical items; Victoriana; carpets and textiles; corkscrews; etc

THE AMERICAN MUSEUM IN BATH
Claverton Manor, Claverton, Bath, Avon
Tel: 01225 463538
Americana and American folk and decorative arts

AMERSHAM AUCTION ROOMS
125 Station Road, Amersham, Bucks
Tel: 01494 729292
auctioneer

ART DECO CERAMICS
The Oakbury, 10 Mill Street, Warwick
CV34 4HB
Tel: 01926 498068
dealer; specializes in Art Deco ceramics

THE ASHMOLEAN MUSEUM
Beaumont Street, Oxford
Tel: 01865 278000
museum; fine and decorative arts

AVON ANTIQUES
25–27 Market Street, Bradford-on-Avon,
Wilts
Tel: 01225 862052
dealer, eight showrooms; specializes in 17th, 18th and 19th century furniture; also clocks and barometers; etc

GILBERT BAITSON
The Edwardian Auction Galleries,
194 Anlaby Road, Hull
Tel: 01482 865831
auctioneer

BATE COLLECTION OF HISTORICAL INSTRUMENTS
Faculty of Music, Oxford University,
St Aldate's, Oxford Tel: 01865 276139
museum: musical instruments

BAYLES
Childs Farm, Cottered Buntingford, Herts
Tel: 01763 81206
auctioneer

BETHNAL GREEN MUSEUM OF CHILDHOOD
Cambridge Heath Road, London E2
Tel: 0181 980 3204
museum: dolls, dolls houses, toys, costume, ephemera, juvenilia

BIGWOOD AUCTIONEERS
The Old School, Tiddington, Stratford-on-
Avon, Warwicks Tel: 01789 69415
auctioneer

BIRMINGHAM MUSEUM AND ART GALLERY
Chamberlain Square, Birmingham B3
Tel: 0121 235 2834
museum; comprehensive general collection

BONHAMS
Montpelier Street, Knightsbridge,
London SW7
Tel: 0171 584 9161
auctioneer

BONHAMS (WEST COUNTRY)
Devon Fine Art Auction House, Dowell
Street, Honiton
Tel: 01404 41872
auctioneer

BRIGHTON MUSEUM AND ART GALLERY
Church Street, Brighton, East Sussex
Tel: 01273 503005
museum; decorative arts, decorative arts movements, general collection

BRITISH ANTIQUE DEALERS' ASSOCIATION
20 Rutland Gate, London SW7 1BD
Tel: 0171 589 4128
trade association; will provide lists of accredited members, lists of antiques fairs, and various other consumer services to collectors on request

BRISTOL MUSEUM AND ART GALLERY
Queen's Road, Bristol, Avon BS8 1RL
Tel: 0117 922 3571
general collection

BRITISH MUSEUM
Great Russell Street, London WC1
Tel: 0171 636 1555
museum; general collection, antiquities

WILLIAM BROWN
11–14 East Hill, Colchester, Essex
Tel: 01206 868070
auctioneer

BRUTON, KNOWLES & CO
111 Eastgate Street, Gloucester, Glos
Tel: 01452 21267
auctioneer

BURREL COLLECTION
Pollok Country Park, Glasgow
Tel: 0141 649 7151
museum; general collection, silver, applied arts, decorative arts, fine arts

CARLESS & CO
58 Lowesmoor, Worcester, Worcs
Tel: 01905 612449
auctioneer

CHANCELLORS
32 High Street, Ascot, Berks
Tel: 01990 872588
auctioneer

CHEFFINS, GRAIN & COMINS
2 Clifton Road, Cambridge, Cambs
Tel: 01223 358721
auctioneer

CHELTENHAM ART GALLERY AND MUSEUM
Clarence Street, Cheltenham, Glos
Tel: 01242 237431
museum; Eastern ceramics, textiles, arts and crafts movement, general collection

CHRISTIE'S
8 King Street, St James's, London SW1
Tel: 0171 839 9060
auctioneer

CHRISTIE'S SOUTH KENSINGTON
85 Old Brompton Road, London SW7
Tel: 0171 581 7611
auctioneer

CHURCHGATE AUCTIONS
66 Churchgate, Leicester, Leics
Tel: 0116 262 1416
auctioneer

CLARE'S AUCTION ROOMS
70 Park Street, Birmingham
Tel: 0121 643 09226
auctioneer

CLEVELAND CRAFTS CENTRE
57 Gilkes Street, Middlesbrough,
Cleveland TS1 5EL
Tel: 01642 226351
permanent display of ceramics and jewellery

COOPER HIRST
Granary Saleroom, Victoria Road,
Chelmsford, Essex Tel: 01245 25814
auctioneer

THOS COULBORN & SONS
Vesey Manor, Sutton Coldfield,
West Midlands B72 1QP
Tel: 0121 354 3974
dealer; general antiques, fine arts, clocks, silver and works of art

COURTAULD INSTITUTE GALLERY
Somerset House, Strand, London WC2
Tel: 0171 873 2526
gallery; the arts collection of the University of London

THE CUMBERLAND TOY AND MODEL MUSEUM
Bank's Court, Market Place, Cockermouth,
Cumbria
Tel: 01900 827606
20th century British toys

DARLINGTON RAILWAY CENTRE AND MUSEUM
North Road Station, Darlington,
Co Durham Tel: 01325 460532
museum; railway equipment and ephemera

DERBY MUSEUM AND ART GALLERY
The Strand, Derby, Derbys
Tel: 01332 293111
museum/gallery; general collection

ENTWISTLE GREEN
The Galleries, Kingsway, Lytham St Anne's,
Lancs Tel: 01253 735442
auctioneer

G H EVANS
The Market Place, Kilgetty, Dyfed
Tel: 01834 811151
auctioneer

FAIRFAX HOUSE
Castlegate, York, N Yorks YO1
Tel: 01904 655543
private collection open to the public; general collection, furniture, clocks

THE FAN MUSEUM
10 Crooms Hill, London SE10 8ER
Tel: 0181 858 7879
museum; fans

FITZWILLIAM MUSEUM
Trumpington Street, Cambridge,
Cambs
Tel:
museum; antiquities, coins, tribal art, books and manuscripts, etc

FRASERS
28 Church Street, Inverness
Tel: 01463 232395
auctioneer

GALLERY OF ENGLISH COSTUME
Platt Hall, Platt Fields, Rusholme,
Manchester
Tel: 0161 224 5217
exceptional collection of costume and textiles

G A AUCTION GALLERIES
40 Station Road West, Canterbury, Kent
Tel: 01227 763337
auctioneer

G A FINE ARTS
Royal Auction Rooms, Queen Street,
Scarborough, Yorks
Tel: 01723 3553581
auctioneer

GEFFRYE MUSEUM
Kingsland Road, London E2
Tel: 0181 739 8363
museum; antiquities, period decor, decorative arts, books and manuscripts, furniture, Art Deco

STANLEY GIBBONS AUCTIONS
399 Strand, London WC2
Tel: 0171 836 8444
auctioneers; stamps; coins

THE GINNEL ANTIQUE CENTRE, HARROGATE
Corn Exchange Building, Parliament Street,
Harrogate, Yorks HG1 2RB
*40 shops, including jewellery, linen and lace,
longcase clocks, prints, arms and armour,
porcelain and glassware*

GLASGOW ART GALLERY AND MUSEUM
Kelvingrove, Glasgow Tel: 0141 357 3929
gallery/museum; fine and decorative arts, arts and crafts movements

GLOUCESTER CITY MUSEUM AND ART GALLERY
Brunswick Road, Gloucester, Glos
Tel: 01452 24131
museum; general collection

GRAYS ANTIQUE MARKET
58 Davies Street, London W1
Tel: 0171 629 7034
*nearly 80 stalls, including the following
specialities: lace (Diana Harby, 629 5130); glass
and drink-associated antiques (Ronald Falloon,
499 0158; and Vintage, 483 9457); cameras,
lighters and watches (Cozy World, 409 0269);
netsuke and oriental objects (David Bowden,
495 1773); antique weapons, arms and armour
(Amanda Antiques, 499 1087; and Armoury
Antiques, 408 0176); jewellery (J M Davies,
493 0624; Abacus, 629 9681; Renate, 408 1059;
R&R Jewellery, 629 6467; Westminster Group,
493 8672; Trianon, 491 2764; Ventura-Pauly,
408 1057; Sandra Ventura, 495 6147; RBR
Group, 529 4769; and A&H Antiques,
493 7497); tools and instruments (David Hogg,
493 0208); smoking antiques (Kunio Kikuchi,
529 6808); quilts and textiles (Sue Maddon,
493 1307); thimbles (The Thimble Society,
493 0560); scientific instruments (Steven
O'Donnell, 491 8852); and toys (Pierre Patau,
4990 0539)*

GRAYS MEWS
1–7 Davies Mews, London W1
Tel: 0171 629 7034
*c 80 stalls, including golf collectibles; oriental
objects; silver; boxes, jewellery; toys; mechanical
toys; needlework; Art Deco; watches; Victoriana;
dolls; arms and armour; pictures and paintings;
bronzes; tribal antiquities; fine books; Art
Nouveau glass; Islamic objects; netsuke; chinese
textiles; and chess books and ephemera*

GREENSLADE
13 Hamlet Street, Taunton, Somerset
Tel: 01823 277121
auctioneer

HALL AND LLOYD
South Street Auction Rooms, Stafford, Staffs
Tel: 01785 58176
auctioneer

HALL, WATERBRIDGE & OWEN
Welsh Bridge Saleroom, Shrewsbury
Tel: 01743 50212
auctioneer

HAMPSHIRE AND BERKSHIRE AUCTIONS
82 Sarum Hill, Basingstoke, Hants
Tel: 01256 840707
auctioneer

HAMPTONS
71 Church Street, Malvern, Worcs
Tel: 01684 892314
auctioneer

HEATHCOTE, BALL & CO
albion Auction Rooms, Commercial Street,
Northampton
Tel: 01604 22735
auctioneer

CECIL HUGHES ART GALLERY AND MUSEUM
Castle Close, Bedford
Tel: 01234 211222
museum; general collection, decorate arts, lace

HOBBS AND CHAMBERS
15 Royal Crescent, Cheltenham, Glos
Tel: 01242 513722
auctioneer

HORNIMAN MUSEUM
100 London Road, London SE23
Tel: 0181 699 2339
*museum; tribal art, musical instruments, crafts,
design*

ILFRACOMBE MUSEUM
Wilder Road, Ilfracombe, Devon
museum; general collection

IMPERIAL WAR MUSEUM
Lambeth Road, London SE1
Tel: 0171 735 8922
museum; arms and armour, militaria, uniform

RAYMOND INMAN AUCTION GALLERIES
35 Temple Street, Brighton, East Sussex
Tel: 01273 774777
auctioneer

JOHN JEFFREY & SON
The Livestock Market, Christ's Lane,
Shaftesbury, Dorset
Tel: 01747 52720
auctioneer

A JOHNSON & SONS
Nottingham Auction Rooms, Meadow Lane,
Nottingham
Tel: 01602 869128
auctioneer

LACY SCOTT
10 Risbygate Street, Bury St Edmunds,
Suffolk
Tel: 01284 763531
auctioneer

**THE LEICESTERSHIRE MUSEUM AND
ART GALLERY**
New Walk, Leicester
Tel: 01162 554100
museum

**LEIGHTON HOUSE ART GALLERY
AND MUSEUM**
12 Holland Park, London W14
Tel: 0171 602 3316
*museum/gallery; decorative arts, arts and crafts
movements*

LEWES AUCTION ROOMS
56 High Street, Lewes, East Sussex
Tel: 01273 478221
auctioneer

LITHGOW SONS & PARTNERS
The Auction House, Station Road, Stokesley,
Middlesborough Tel: 01642 710158
auctioneer

LIVERPOOL MUSEUM
William Brown Street, Liverpool L3
museum; general collection

LUTON MUSEUM AND ART GALLERY
Wardown Park, Luton, Beds LU2 7HA
Tel: 01582 36941
museum; general collection

MAGGS BROS
50 Berkeley Square, London W1
Tel: 0171 493 7160
dealer; rare and antiquarian books

MAIDSTONE MUSEUM AND ART GALLERY
St Faith's Street, Maidstone, Kent
Tel: 01622 54497
museum

MANCHESTER CITY ART GALLERY
Moseley Street (0161 236 5244) and Princess
Street (0161 236 9422), Manchester
galleries; one of the best collections in the UK

MILLER
Lemon Quay Auction Rooms, Truro,
Cornwall
Tel: 01872 74211
auctioneer

THOMAS MILLER
18 Gallowgate, Newcastle, Tyne and Wear
Tel: 0191 232 5617
auctioneer

J MILNE
9 North Silver Street, Aberdeen
Tel: 01224 639336
auctioneer

PAUL MITCHELL
99 New Bond Street, London W1Y 9LF
Tel: 0171 493 8732
dealer; picture frames

MORGANS AUCTIONS
Dunroe Crescent, Dunroe Road, Belfast
Tel: 01232 771552
auctioneer

WILLIAM MORRIS GALLERY
Water House, Lloyd Park, Forest Road,
Walthamstow, London E17
Tel: 0181 527 3782
*museum; based at Morris' childhood home, arts
and crafts movement*

MUSEUM OF CHILDHOOD
38 High Street, Edinburgh
Tel: 0131 225 2424
museum; costume, toys, ephemera, dolls

MUSEUM OF COSTUME
Assembly Rooms, Bennett Street, Bath, Avon
Tel: 01225 461111
Costume from the 1500s to the present day

MUSEUM OF COSTUME AND TEXTILES
51 Castlegate, Nottingham
Tel: 01602 483504
museum; lace, textiles, costume

MUSICAL MUSEUM
368 High Street, Brentford, Middx
Tel: 0181 560 8108
museum; musical instruments of all periods

NATIONAL ARMY MUSEUM
Royal Hospital Road, London SW3
Tel: 0171 730 0717
museum; uniform, militaria, weaponry

NATIONAL GALLERY
Trafalgar Square, London WC2
Tel: 0171 839 3321
gallery

NATIONAL GALLERY OF SCOTLAND
The Mound, Edinburgh
gallery

NATIONAL MOTOR MUSEUM
Beaulieu, Hants Tel: 01590 612345
museum; over 250 motor cars and vehicles

NATIONAL MUSEUM OF IRELAND
Kildare Street and Merrion Street,
Dublin
Tel: 00 353 618811
museum; fine and decorative arts

NATIONAL MUSEUM OF WALES
Main Building, Cathays Park, Cardiff
Tel: 01222 397951
museum; general collection, paintings

NATIONAL POSTAL MUSEUM
King Edward Street, London EC1
Tel: 0171 432 3851
museum; stamps and associated items

JAMES' NORWICH AUCTIONS
33 Timberhill, Norwick, Norfolk
Tel: 01603 624817
auctioneer

OUTHWAITE & LITHERLAND
Kingsway Galleries, Fontenoy Street,
Liverpool
Tel: 0151 236 6563
auctioneer

P A OXLEY
The Old Rectory, Cherhill, Nr Calne, Wilts
Tel: 01249 816227
dealer; clocks and barometers

PEACOCK
26 Newnham Street, Bedford, Beds
Tel: 01234 66366
auctioneer

**PERCIVAL DAVID FOUNDATION OF
CHINESE ART**
53 Gordon Square, London WC1
Tel: 0171 387 3909
*private collection open to the public; arts of the
East*

PHILLIPS
17 East Parade, Leeds, Yorks
Tel: 01532 448011
auctioneer

PHILLIPS
101 New Bond Street, London W1
Tel: 0171 629 6602
auctioneer

PHILLIPS
Armada Street, North Hill, Plymouth,
Devon
Tel: 01752 673504
auctioneer

PHILLIPS, BROOKS
39 Park End Street, Oxford, Oxon
Tel: 01865 723524
auctioneer

PHILLIPS IN CHESTER
150 Christleton Road, Chester, Cheshire
Tel: 01244 313936
auctioneer

PHILLIPS FINE ART
56 Machen Place, Cardiff
Tel: 01222 374320
auctioneer

PHILLIPS FINE ART
Baffins Hall, Baffins Lane, Chichester, Sussex
Tel: 01243 787548
auctioneer

PHILLIPS FINE ART
71 Oakfield Road, Clifton, Bristol
Tel: 01272 734052
auctioneer

PHILLIPS FINE ART
Millmead, Guildford, Surrey
Tel: 01483 504030
auctioneer

PHILLIPS FINE ART
114 Northenden Road, Sale, Manchester
Tel: 0161 962 9237
auctioneer

PHILLIPS FINE ART
Cinque Ports Street, Rye, East Sussex
Tel: 01797 222124
auctioneer

PHILLIPS FINE ART
49 London Road, Sevenoaks, Kent
Tel: 01732 740310
auctioneer

PHILLIPS FINE ART
The Red House, Hyde Street, Winchester,
Hants
Tel: 01962 62515
auctioneer

PHILLIPS IN SCOTLAND
65 George Street, Edinburgh
Tel: 0131 225 2266
auctioneer

PHILLIPS IN SCOTLAND
207 Bath Street, Glasgow
Tel: 0141 221 8377
auctioneer

PITT RIVERS MUSEUM
South Parks Road, Oxford
Tel: 01865 270927
museum; tribal art, antiquities

PLYMOUTH CITY MUSEUM AND ART GALLERY
Drake Circus, Plymouth, Devon
Tel: 01752 264878
museum; general

POOLEY & ROGERS
9 Alverton Street, Penzance, Cornwall
Tel: 01736 63816
auctioneer

JAMES REEVE
9 Church Street, Warwick
Tel: 01926 498113
*dealer; specializes in 17th, 18th and early 19th
century English furniture*

RIDDETTS
26 Richmond Hill, Bournemouth, Dorset
Tel: 01202 25686
auctioneer

RIPLEY ANTIQUES
67 High Street, Ripley, Surrey
Tel: 01483 224981
*dealer; specializes in 18th and 19th century
furniture*

ROYAL COLLEGE OF MUSIC
Prince Consort Road, London SW7
Tel: 0171 589 3643
*museum; over 450 musical instruments of all types
and periods*

ROYAL MUSEUM OF SCOTLAND
Chambers Street, Edinburgh
Tel: 0131 225 7534
*museum; general collection, scientific instruments,
decorative arts*

THE ROYAL PAVILION
Brighton, East Sussex
Tel: 01273 6033005
*historic pleasure pavilion, regency furniture and
decor, chinoiserie*

RUSSELL-COATES ART GALLERY AND MUSEUM
East Cliff, Bournemouth, Dorset
museum; general collection

THE SCIENCE MUSEUM
Exhibition Road, London SW7
Tel: 0171 589 3456
*museum; scientific and medical instruments from
all periods, motor cars, aircraft*

ALLAN SMITH CLOCKS
162 Beechcroft Road, Upper Statton,
Swindon, Wilts
Tel: 01793 822977
*dealer in and restorer of clocks, some furniture;
call for appointment*

SNEDDON'S SUNDERLAND AUCTION ROOMS
30 Villiers Street, Sunderland, Tyne and Wear
Tel: 0191 514 5931
auctioneer

SOTHEBY'S
28 Watergate Street, Chester, Cheshire
Tel: 01244 315531
auctioneer

SOTHEBY'S
34–35 New Bond Street, London W1
Tel: 0171 493 8080
auctioneer

SOTHEBY'S SUSSEX
Summers Place, Billingshurst, East Sussex
Tel: 01403 783933
auctioneer

HENRY SOTHERAN
2–5 Sackville St, London W1
Tel: 0171 734 1150
*dealer; rare and antiquarian books, maps and
prints*

HENRY SPENCER & SONS
1 St James Road, Sheffield, Yorks
Tel: 0114 272 8728
auctioneer

STEPHENSON & SON
Livestock Centre, Murtom, York, Yorks
Tel: 01904 489731
auctioneer

SWORDERS
Northgate End Salerooms, Bishop Stortford,
Herts Tel: 01279 651388
auctioneer

TATE GALLERY
Millbank, London SW1 Tel: 0171 821 1313
gallery

TATE GALLERY LIVERPOOL
Albert Docks, Liverpool L3 Tel: 0151 709 3223
*gallery; houses overflow and special exhibitions
from Tate in London*

TENNANTS AUCTIONEERS
27 Market Place, Leyburn, N Yorks
Tel: 01969 23780
auctioneer

THEATRE MUSEUM
Russell Street, London WC2
Tel: 0171 831 1227
museum; costume, masks, manuscripts, ephemera

TIFFIN KING & NICHOLSON
12 Lowther Street, Carlisle, Cumbria
Tel: 01228 25259
auctioneer

TOWER OF LONDON
Tower Hill, London EC3
Tel: 0171 709 0765
*one of the finest collection of arms, armour and
weaponry; also costume, textiles, furniture,
jewellery and decorative arts*

UNIVERSITY OF HULL ART COLLECTION
The Middletone Hall, Cottingham Road,
Hull
Tel: 01482 465192
gallery

**VICTORIA AND ALBERT
MUSEUM**
Cromwell Road, London SW7
Tel: 0171 589 6371
*museum; decorative arts from all parts of the
world, lace, textiles, costume, furniture, decorate
arts movements*

THE WALLACE COLLECTION
Hertford House, Manchester Square,
London W1
Tel: 0171 935 0687
*private collection open to the public; paintings,
decorative arts*

JOHN WALTER
1 Mint Lane, Lincoln, Lincs
Tel: 01552 525454
auctioneer

**WARRINGTON MUSEUM AND
ART GALLERY**
Bold Street, Warrington WA1 1JG,
Cheshire
Tel: 01925 444400
museum; general collection

WEDGWOOD MUSEUM
Josiah Wedgwood and Sons, Barlaston,
Staffs ST12 9ES
Tel: 01782 204218
*museum of Wedgwood pieces and manufacturing
equipment*

WHEATCROFT & SON
39 Dale Road, Matlock, Derbys
Tel: 01629 584591
auctioneer

**WHIPPLE MUSEUM OF THE HISTORY
OF SCIENCE**
Free School Lane, Cambridge,
Cambs
Tel: 01223 334540
museum; scientific instruments 1500s–1800s

WHITTON AND LAING
32 Okehampton Street, Exeter, Devon
Tel: 01392 52621
auctioneer

WHITWORTH ART GALLERY
Oxford Road, Manchester
Tel: 0161 273 4865
gallery

ARNOLD WIGGINS & SONS
4 Bury Street, London SW1
Tel: 0171 925 0195
dealer; picture frames

WOOLEY & WALLIS
Castle Street, Salisbury, Wilts
Tel: 01722 411422
auctioneer

United States of America

ABERDEEN ORDNANCE MUSEUM
Aberdeen, MA
*museum; specializing in firearms and weapons of
the world*

ALABAMA AUCTION ROOM
2112 5th Ave Nth, Birmingham,
AL 35203
Tel: 205 252 4073
auctioneer

ALLEN ART MUSEUM
Oberlin College, Oberlin, OH
museum; general, glass

AMERICAN CARNIVAL GLASS ASSOCIATION
PO Box 273, Gnadenhutten, OH 46629
information service

THE AMERICAN CLOCK AND WATCH MUSEUM
Bristol, MA
museum; clocks and timepieces

W GRAHAM ARADER III
1000 Boxwood Court, King of Prussia, PA
auctioneer

ART DECO SOCIETIES OF AMERICA
3447 Sheridan Ave, Miami Beach, FL
Tel: 305 538 8352
information service

ART INSTITUTE OF CHICAGO
Michigan Ave at Adams, Chicago, IL
Tel: 312 4453 3500
*gallery/museum; primarily paintings and
decorative arts*

BARRIDOFF GALLERIES
242 Middle Street, Portland, ME 04101
Tel: 207 772 5011
gallery; auctioneer

BALTIMORE MUSEUM OF ART
Charles between 31st and 32nd Streets,
Baltimore MD
Tel: 301 396 7100/7101
museum; paintings, sculpture, general

J N BARTFIELD GALLERIES
30 W 57th Street, New York,
NY 10019
dealer specializing in art of the American West

**BEINECKE RARE BOOK AND MANUSCRIPT
LIBRARY**
121 Wall Street, New Haven, CT
Tel: 203 432 2977
at Yale University; books and manuscripts

BENNINGTON MUSEUM
West Main Street, Bennington, VT
Tel: 802 447 1571
museum; Americana, folk art

BERSTROM ART CENTER AND MUSEUM
Neenah, WI 54956
museum; specializes in glass and paperweights

BOSTON MUSEUM OF FINE ARTS
465 Hungtingdon Ave, Boston, MS
Tel: 617 267 9300
*museum; Americana, arts of East, impressionists,
general*

R W BRONSTEIN
3666 Main Street, Buffalo, NY 14226
Tel: 716 835 7666
auctioneer

BROOKLYN MUSEUM
200 Eastern Parkway at Washington Ave,
Brooklyn, NY
Tel: 718 638 5000
museum; general and Americana

BUCKINGHAM GALLERIES
4350 Dawson Street, San Diego,
CA 92115
Tel: 714 283 7286
gallery; auctioneer

BUSHELL'S AUCTION
2006 2nd Ave, Seattle, WA 98121
auctioneer

BUTTERFIELD & BUTTERFIELD
1244 Sutter Street, San Francisco,
CA 94109
auctioneer

CARNEGIE INSTITUTE: MUSEUM OF ART
4400 Forbes Ave, Oakland, Pittsburgh, PA
Tel: 412 622 3131
*museum; general collection of international
renown*

CHAPEL HILL RARE BOOKS
143 W Franklin Street, Chapel Hill,
NC 27514
Tel: 919 929 8351
dealer; books

C B CHARLES GALLERY
825 Woodward Ave, Pontiac,
MI 48053
Tel: 313 338 9023
gallery; auctioneer

CHRISTIE'S EAST
219 East 67th Street, New York,
NY 10021 Tel: 212 570 4141
auctioneer

CINCINNATI ART MUSEUM
Eden Park Drive, Cincinnati, OH
Tel: 513 7212 5204
*museum; general collection, Islamic, musical
instruments*

MARVIN COHEN AUCTIONS
Box 425, Route 20 & 22, New Lebanon,
NY 12125
auctioneer

COLONIAL WILLIAMSBURG
Williamsburg, VA
*authentically recreated and preserved historical
site, featuring Americana, decorative arts,
costume and early American furniture*

COOPER-HEWITT MUSEUM
2 East 91st Street, New York, NY
Tel: 212 860 6894
museum; arts, crafts, design

CORNING MUSEUM OF GLASS
1 Museum Way, Corning, NY
Tel: 607 937 5371
museum

DEGENHART PAPERWEIGHT AND GLASS MUSEUM
Cambridge, OH 43725
museum

DENVER ART MUSEUM
100 W 14th Ave, Denver, CO
Tel: 303 575 2793
museum; fine collection of Native American artefacts

DETROIT MUSEUM OF ART
5200 Woodward Ave, Detroit, MI
Tel: 313 833 7900
museum; general collection

DUMOCHELLE ART GALLERIES
409 East Jefferson, Detroit, MI 48226
Tel: 313 963 6255
gallery; auctioneer

THE FINE ARTS COMPANY
2317 Chestnut Street, Philadelphia,
PA 19103 Tel: 215 564 3644
auctioneer

HENRY FORD/GREENFIELD VILLAGE MUSEUMS
Interstate-94, Dearborn, MI
Tel: 313 271 1620
12 acre site, mainly featuring Americana, American folk art and American decorative arts, American ephemera, scientific instruments, machinery, motor cars, aircraft, carriages, etc

FORDEM GALLERIES
3829 Lorain Ave, Cleveland,
OH 44113
Tel: 216 281 3563
gallery; auctioneer

JACK FRANCIS AUCTIONS
200 Market Street, Lowell,
MA 01852
Tel: 508 441 9708
auctioneer

THE FRICK COLLECTION
1 East 70th Street, New York, NY
Tel: 212 288 0700
private collection open to public; mainly paintings; some sculpture and furniture

GARTH'S AUCTIONS
2690 Stratford Road, Delaware,
OH 43015 Tel: 614 362 4771
auctioneer

M M GOLDBERG
215 Nth Rampart Street, New Orleans,
LA 70112 Tel: 504 522 8364
auctioneer

GRAMERCY AUCTION GALLERIES
52 East 13th Street, New York, NY 10003
Tel: 212 477 5656
gallery; auctioneer

GREENFIELD VILLAGE MUSEUM
(see Henry Ford)

CHARLTON HALL GALLERY
930 Gervais Street, Columbia, SC 29201
Tel: 803 252 7927
gallery; auctioneer

HANZEL
1120 South Michigan Ave, Chicago,
IL 60605
Tel: 312 922 6234
auctioneer

HARRIS AUCTION GALLERY
873 Nth Howard Street, Baltimore,
MD 21201
Tel: 301 728 7040
gallery; auctioneer

HART
2311 Westheimer, Houston, TX 77098
Tel: 713 524 2979
auctioneer

G R HAWKINS
7224 Melrose Ave, Los Angeles, CA 90046
Tel: 213 550 1504
auctioneer

THE HEART MUSEUM
22 E Monte Vista, Phoenix, Arizona
Tel: 602 252 8848
museum; Native American arts and crafts, general

HIGH MUSEUM OF ART
1280 Peachtree Street, Atlanta, GA
Tel: 404 892 4444
museum

WILLIAM HILL AUCTIONS
Route 16, East Hardwick, VT 05834
Tel: 802 472 6308
auctioneer

HOUSTON MUSEUM OF FINE ARTS
1001 Bissonet, Houston, TX
Tel: 713 526 1361/713 639 7300
museum; general collection

F B HUBLEY
364 Broadway, Cambridge, MA 02100
Tel: 617 876 2030
auctioneer

HERBERT JOHNSON MUSEUM OF ART
University Ave at Central Ithaca, NY
Tel: Ithaca 255 6464
museum; Islamic, painting, general

KENNEDY ANTIQUE AUCTION GALLERIES
1088 Huff Road, Atlanta, GA 30318
Tel: 404 351 1464
auctioneer

KENNEDY GALLERIES INC
40 W 57th Street, New York,
NY 10019
dealer; art of the American West

LIBRARY OF CONGRESS
Independence and 1st Street, Washington,
DC
Tel: 202 707 5000
books and manuscripts

LIPTON
1108 Fort Street, Honolulu, HI 96813
Tel: 808 533 4329
auctioneer

LOS ANGELES COUNTY MUSEUM OF ART
5905 Wilshire Boulevard, Los Angeles, CA
Tel: 213 857 6000/6111
museum; arts of the East, painting, largest general collection in any individual museum in North America

MAIN AUCTION GALLERY
137 W 4th Street, Cincinnatti, OH 45202
Tel: 513 621 1280
gallery; auctioneer

METROPOLITAN MUSEUM OF ART
5th Ave at 82nd Street, New York, NY
Tel: 212 879 5500
museum; general collection

MILWAUKEE ART MUSEUM
750 N Lincoln Memorial Drive,
Milwaukee, WI
Tel: 414 271 9508
museum

MILWAUKEE AUCTION GALLERIES
4747 West Bradley Road, Milwaukee,
WI 53223
Tel: 414 355 5054
gallery; auctioneer

MONGERSON-WUNDERLICH
704 North Wells, Chicago,
IL 60610
dealer; art of the American West

MUSEUM OF THE AMERICAN INDIAN
Broadway at 155th Street,
New York, NY
Tel: 212 283 2420
specialist collection; Native American art

NATIONAL ASSOCIATION OF DEALERS IN ANTIQUES
PO Box 421, Barrington, IL 6011
Tel: 312 381 7096
professional trade association; its listings and code of behaviour are available on written request

NATIONAL ASSOCIATION OF WATCH AND CLOCK COLLECTORS
Columbia, PA
information service and collectors club

NEDRA MATTEUCCI'S FENN GALLERY
1075 Paseo de Peralta, Santa Fe, NM 87501
dealer; art of the American West

NELSON-ATKINS GALLERY OF ART
4th Terrace at Rockhill,
Kansas City, MO
Tel: 816 751 1278/816 561 4000
gallery/museum; arts of the East, general collection

NEW BEDFORD GLASS MUSEUM
New Bedford, MA 12742
museum; glass

NEW ENGLAND RARE COIN AUCTIONS
89 Devonshire Street, Boston,
MA 02109
Tel: 617 227 8800
auctioneer; coins

NORTHGATE GALLERY
5520 Highway 153, Chattanooga,
TN 37443
Tel: 615 842 4177
auctioneer

NORTON SIMON
(see Simon)

O'GALLERIE
537 SE Ash Street, Portland, OR 97214
Tel: 503 238 0202
gallery; auctioneer

PEABODY MUSEUM OF ARCHAEOLOGY
11 Divinity Street, Cambridge, MS
Tel: Cambridge 495 1310
at Harvard University; early Native American art

GERALD PETERS GALLERY
439 Camino Del Monte Sol, PO Box 908,
Santa Fe, NM87504
dealer; art of the American West

PHILADELPHIA MUSEUM OF ART
Fairmount Park, Philadelphia, PA
Tel: 215 763 8100
museum; comprehensive and highly-regarded general collection

PHILLIPS
525 E 72nd Street, New York,
NY 10021
Tel: 212 570 4852
auctioneer

PHOENIX ART MUSEUM
1625 N Central, Phoenix, AZ
Tel: 602 257 1222
museum; general collection

POLLACK
2780 NE 183rd Street, Miami, FL 33160
Tel: 305 931 4476
auctioneer

PORTLAND MUSEUM OF ART
7 Congress at Free Street, Portland, ME
Tel: 207 775 6148
museum; mainly painting

LLOYD RALSTON TOYS
447 Stratfield Road, Fairfield, CT 06432
auctioneer; specializing in toys

**RHODE ISLAND SCHOOL OF DESIGN
MUSEUM OF ART**
224 Benefit Street, Providence, RI
Tel: 403 331 3511
museum; arts of the East, general

ROSVALL AUCTION CO
1238 South Broadway, Denver, CO 80210
Tel: 303 777 2032
auctioneer

ST LOUIS ART MUSEUM
Forest Park, St Louis, MO
Tel: 314 721 0067
museum; general collection

SEATTLE ART MUSEUM
14th Street E and Prospect, Volunteer Park,
Seattle, WA
Tel: 206 625 8900/1
museum; general collection, arts of the East

B J SELKIRK & SONS
4166 Olive Street, St Louis, MO 63108
Tel: 314 533 1700
auctioneer

NORTON SIMON MUSEUM OF ART
North Orange Blvd at Colorado, Pasadena, CA
Tel: 818 681 2484/818 449 3730
museum; mainly paintings and sculpture

ROBERT W SKINNER
585 Boylston Street, Boston, MA 02116
Tel: 617 236 1700
auctioneer

SMITHSONIAN INSTITUTION
The Mall, near the Capitol,
Washington, DC
Tel: 202 357 2700 for general information
a group of 14 museums and galleries, including American history; African art; natural history; national gallery of art; national portrait gallery; air and space museum; arts and industries building (a recreation of the World's Fair of 1876); and the Freer Gallery (arts of the East)

SOTHEBY PARKE BERNET
980 Madison Ave, New York, NY 10021
Tel: 212 472 3400
auctioneer

J B SPEED ART MUSEUM
2035 3rd Street, Louisville, KY
Tel: 502 636 2893
museum

SPRINGFIELD ARMORY MUSEUM
Springfield, MA
museum; very comprehensive coverage of American small arms and other firearms

THE TIME MUSEUM
Rockford, IL
museum; clocks and timepieces

TUSCON MUSEUM OF ART
140 N Main, Tuscon, AZ Tel: 602 624 2333
museum; general collection, excellent pre-Columbian art and artefacts

VIRGINIA MUSEUM OF FINE ARTS
Grove and N Boulevard, Richmond, VA
Tel: 804 367 0844
museum; general collection, jewellery, Art Nouveau, decorative arts

WADSWORTH ATHENEUM
600 Main Street, Hartford, CT
Tel: 203 247 9111
museum; fine painting collection

WALTERS ART GALLERY
Charles at Center Street, Baltimore, MD
Tel: 301 547 9000
gallery/museum; general, arms and armour

WHITE PLAINS AUCTION ROOMS
572 North Broadway, White Plains,
NY 10603 Tel: 914 428 2255
auctioneer

THE WILLARD CLOCK MUSEUM
Grafton, MA
museum; clocks and timepieces

THE WILSON GALLERY
PO Box 102, Fort Defiance, VA 24437
Tel: 703 885 4292
gallery; auctioneer

WINTERTHUR MUSEUM
Winterthur, Route 52, Nr Wilmington, DE
Tel: 302 888 4600
museum; American decorative arts and general

JOHN WOODMAN HIGGINS ARMORY
Worcester, MA
European and Far Eastern arms and weaponry from the middle ages

YALE UNIVERSITY ART GALLERY
1111 Chapel Street, New Haven, CT
Tel: 203 432 0600
gallery

GLOSSARY

AIRTWIST STEMS stems of drinking glasses containing hollow spirals created out of bubbles in the glass

ANNEALING process by which a metal or glass is repeatedly heated and cooled to prevent its becoming brittle

AQUATINT method of engraving, or print made by this method, that enables the engraver to produce tonal as well as linear variety

ARMOIRE a cupboard, usually grand in appearance with architectural details on the front

ASTROLABE disc-shaped instrument made for ascertaining the altitudes of stars and planets

BALUSTER a short pillar with a curving outline and a round section: commonly part of banisters, but also a furniture leg or glass stem of this shape

BISQUE unglazed white fired clay, especially of dolls

BRACKET CLOCK a sprung-driven clock, small enough to sit on a piece of furniture or to be hung from the wall

BRISÉ FAN a fan that has no leaf but consists of sticks pivoting at the base and then held together by ribbons

CABOCHON a smooth, uncut, oval gemstone

CABRIOLE LEG a furniture leg that curves outwards at the middle and then tapers inwards, finishing in a decorate foot

CHAMPLEVÉ (1) referring to a process in enamelling where grooves are cut into the object to be decorated, the enamel is poured in, and then rubbed down to the same level as the metal; (2) the technique of removing areas of coloured slip from ceramics to make a pattern through exposing the colour of the clay

CHASING process in metalworking whereby the metal is worked with a hammer to remove blemishes or to create raised patterns

CHINOISERIE style of decoration intended to imitate motifs and forms found in Chinese art

CLOISONNÉ referring to a process of enamelling whereby the surface is separated by metal bands and the coloured enamels poured into them. The bands make the clear boundaries between the colours

CHEVRON a v-shaped pattern

CLARET any red wine from Bordeaux

CRISTALLO the name given by 15th century Venetian glass makers to soda glass, the earliest known form of glass, which uses sodium carbonate as a flux

CROSSHATCHING method of depicting shade and depth by intercrossing lines

DIPTYCH a painting consisting of two equal-sized panel which are joined – usually with hinges – to each other

ENTRELAC two ribbons of stone or other material carved into strips so as to appear interwoven

FAÇON DE VENISE type of glass-making practised by the Venetians in the 16th and 17th centuries using soda glass. It was very light and brittle

FAMILLE VERTE a form of chinese porcelain in which the decoration is dominated by a bright green enamel

FAVRILE GLASS iridescent glassware made by the American Art Nouveau designer Louis Comfort Tiffany

FORM WATCH a watch made in the shape of an animal, plant or other feature from the natural world

GADROONS a continuous pattern of short repetitive reeding set vertically, diagonally or twisted

GUARDSTICKS the outer sticks of a fan

GUILLOCHE a continuous pattern of overlying strips in a plait

GUILLOCHÉ formed into a guilloche

GUM ARABIC a fine gum taken from the acacia tree, used to bind together pigments for watercolour paints

INCUNABLE (plural incunabula) a printed book from the early years after the invention of printing

JACQUARD LOOM loom invented in the early 19th century by Joseph-Marie Jacquard, needing only one person to work it but capable of producing elaborate designs

JAPANNING imitation Oriental lacquer, most commonly applied to wood, though sometimes also to metal objects

KNOP a component, usually spherical or

oblate, of the stem of a drinking glass: it can be made in many styles, hollow or solid

LEAD CRYSTAL colourless clear glass made by mixing a silica with an alkali and lead

LIMNER a painter: in medieval times a manuscript illuminator, then in the Elizabethan and Jacobean periods a painter of miniatures

LONGCASE CLOCK pendulum-driven clock with weight that stands on the floor

LOST-WAX TECHNIQUE method of casting in which a model is made of wax and set in clay which is then baked: the wax is then run off and the clay forms a mould for the material of which the object is to be made

LUSTRE (1) a shiny decoration used on ceramics that is derived from metals; (2) a chandalier; (3) a Victorian vase with cut-glass drops hanging from the rim

MAINSPRING the coiled driving spring of a clock or watch

MAIOLICA tin-glazed earthenware, especially from Italy

MAMLUK from the period of the Mamluk rule in Egypt – 1250–1517

MARQUETRY a veneer applied to wooden furniture consisting of small pieces of wood assembled into a design

MENUISIER French furniture maker who would construct the frame of a piece: the menuisier's role was listed by the guild system to that of a joiner, also making small plain objects, while an ébéniste was a cabinet-maker, dealing with veneered furniture

MILLEFLEUR tapestries tapestries in which finely dressed figures appear against backgrounds of large numbers of brilliant flowers, small animals and birds

MOUNT material a picture is fixed on before framing: it is often deliberately exposed in framing to provide a border to the picture

ORMOLU decorative cast bronze, chased and fire-gilt

PARURE a set of jewels designed to be worn together

PEARLWARE a form of creamware but with a less creamy hue, developed by Josiah Wedgwood

POUNCING the application of a decorative surface by hammering, giving rise to a powdered appearance

PRUNT a decorative, shaped blob made of molten glass, on a glass object

PRUNTED bearing a prunt or prunts

RÉGENCE the style dominant in France during the early part of the reign of Louis XV, about 1710–30. It is a somewhat formal and extravagant form of Rococo

REPOUSSÉ referring to metal embossed from within or underneath, by hammering the inner surface

SAMPLER a piece of embroidery in which the embroidress uses several stitches in order to manifest her skill: samplers were generally executed by children and often incorporate biblical quotations or religious exhortations

SLIP a mixture of clay and water applied to ceramic objects: it was originally used to make porous surfaces less porous, but then came to serve as a form of decoration, especially when coloured

SFUMATO technique in painting of merging colours so finely that there is no clear division between them: the word means 'smoked', in reference to the delicate blending

STRETCHER the wooden frame on which a canvas is stretched and then fixed prior to painting

SWAG material suspended from each end and falling into a loop, or wood cared to resemble this shape

TABLE of a violin, the flat front of the body over which the strings are suspended

tempera technique of making artists' colours in which the pigment is mixed with egg – sometimes just the egg-white

TIN-GLAZING a glazing technique in which fired pottery is dipped in a mixture of tine and lead to give it a white surface

TOPOGRAPHIC PAINTING paintings intended to give an accurate record of a place

TRIFID divided into three lobes, as sometimes with furniture feet

TROMP L'OEIL the depiction of scenes or objects in a highly realistic way, designed to trick the observer into thinking that they are real

UNDERGLAZE COLOURS colours that are applied to ceramic objects before they are fired: not all colours are made from materials that can withstand the temperatures used in firing ceramics, so the development of a range of underglaze colours has involved a long history of discovery

VEDUTISTI painters of vedute, highly realistic depictions of urban scenes or landscapes

VELLUM a material for writing or drawing on, predating paper, and made from the skin of a calf

VERNIS MARTIN a gilt imitation lacquer decorated with sprays of flowers

WASH an area of single colour in watercolour painting

B I B L I O G R A P H Y

Furniture

English and Continental Furniture

HAYWARD, HELENA (ed.); World Furniture, Hamlyn, London, 1965

KREISEL, HEINRICH; Die Kunste des Deutschen Mobels, Vols. 1, 2, 3, Munich 1968, 1970, 1973.

MACQUOID, PERCY AND EDWARDS, RALPH; The Dictionary of English Furniture, 2nd ed. 3 vols. London, 1960.

PAYNE, CHRISTOPER; 19th Century European Furniture, Woodford, 1981.

PRADORO, ALEXANDRO; French Furniture Makers of the Eighteenth Century, London, 1989.

American Chippendale Furniture

BATES, ELIZABETH BIDWELL AND FAIRBANKS, JONATHAN L.; American Furniture – 1620 to the Present, Richard Marek, New York, 1981.

COOPER, WENDY A.; In Praise of America – American Decorative Arts, 1620–1830/Fifty Years of Discovery Since the 1929 Girl Scouts Loan Exhibition, Alfred A. Knopf, New York, 1980.

HECKSCHER, MORRISON H.; American Furniture in The Metropolitan Museum of Art – Late Colonial Period: The Queen Anne and Chippendale Styles, The Metropolitan Museum of Art and Random House, New York, 1985.

KIRK, JOHN T.; American Chairs – Queen Anne and Chippendale, Alfred A. Knopf, New York, 1972.

Shaker Furniture

ANDREWS, E. D. AND F.; Shaker Furniture, Dover, NY and Constable, London, 1950.

China and Ceramics

CHARLESTON, R. (ed.); World Ceramics, Paul Hamlyn.

CUSHION, J. P.; Handbook of Pottery and Porcelain Marks, Faber and Faber.

VALENSTEIN, SUZANNE G.; A Handbook of Chinese Ceramics, Metropolitan Museum of Art.

Glass

BATTIE, DAVID AND COTTLE, SIMON (ed.); Sotheby's Concise Encyclopedia of Glass, Conran Octopus, London, 1991.

KLEIN, DAN; Glass, A Contemporary Art, Collins, London, 1989.

KLEIN, DAN AND LLOYD, WARD (ed.); The History of Glass, Orbis, London, 1989.

MARSHALL, JO; The Glass Source Book, Quarto, London, 1990.

ROSSI, SARA; A Collector's Guide to Paperweights, Letts (London), 1990.

Silver

BLAIR, CLAUDE (ed.); The History of Silver, McDonald Orbis.

CLAYTON, MICHAEL; A Collector's Dictionary of Gold and Silver of the British Isles and North America, Antique Collectors Club.

TARDY (ed.); Les poincons de garantie internationaux pour l'argent, Tardy, 1985.

Jewellery and Fans

Jewellery

BURY, SHIRLEY; Jewellery, 1789–1910: The International Era, Vols I and II, Antique Collectors Club, 1991.

NERET, GILES; Boucheron, Four generations of a world renowned jewellery, Rizzoli International Publications, 1988.

Fans

ALEXANDER, H.; Fans, 1984.

ARMSTRONG, N.; A Collector's History of Fans, 1974.

CUST, LIONEL; Catalogue of the Collection of Fans and Fanleaves presented to the Trustees of the British Museum by Lady Charlotte Schreiber, 1893.

L'EVENTAIL; Miroir de la Belle Epoque, Exhibition, Palais Galliera, Paris, 1985.

MAYOR, S.; Letts Guide to Collecting Fans, 1991.

RHEAD, C. W.; Wolliscroft, The History of the Fan, 1910.

FANS FROM THE EAST; Victoria and Albert Museum, 1978.

VOLET, MARYSE; L'imagination au service de l'Eventail, Vezenaz, Switzerland, 1986.

Textiles

BREDIF, JOSETTE; Toiles De Jou, 1989.

COLBY, AVERIL; Patchwork, 1958.

JOHNSTONE, PAULINE; Three Hundred Years of Embroidery, 1986.

KING, DONALD; Samplers, 1960.

KING, DONALD AND MONIQUE; European Textiles in the Kier Collection, 1990.

PARRY, LINDA; Textiles of the Arts and Crafts Movement, 1988.

ROTHSTEIN, NATALIE; Silk Designs of the 18th Century, 1990.

SAFFORD, CARLETON, L. AND BISHOP, ROBERT; America's Quilts and Coverlets, 1974.

SYNGE, LANTO; Antique Needlework, 1989.

THOMSON, W. G.; A History of Tapestry, 1930.

THORNTON, PETER; Baroque and Rococo Silks, 1965.

Lace

EARNSHAW, PAT; Identifying Lace, Shire Publications, 1980.

JOURDAIN, M.; Old Lace, B. T. Batsford Ltd, London 1988, republished from original 1908 edition.

LAPRADE, MME LAUCRENCE DE; Le Poinct de France et les Centres Dentellieres au XVII et XCIII siecles, Paris, 1908.

LEVEY, SANTINA M.; Lace, A History, Victoria and Albert Museum, W. S. Maney and Son Ltd, 1983.

MRS. PALLISER; History of Lace, 1st Edition 1865, revised and enlarged by Margaret Jourdain and Alice Dryden (1902).

Shawls

AMES, FRANK; The Kashmire Shawl, Antique Collectors' Club.

IRWIN, J.; The Kashmir Shawl, V&A Publications.

LEVY-STRAUSS, MONIQUE; The Cashmire Shawl, Dryden Press, 1988.

Costume

MANSFIELD, A. AND CUNNINGTON, P.; A Handbook of English Costume, 5 vols, Medieval, 16th, 17th, 18th, 19th and 20th century, Faber and Faber.

MCDOWELLS DICTIONARY OF 20TH CENTURY COSTUME – Muller.

Paintings

Painting

GOMBRICH, E. H.; The Story of Art, Phaidon, Oxford 1989.

CLARK, KENNETH; Looking at Pictures, John Murray, London, 1960.

CONSTABLE, W. G.; The Painter's Workshop, Dover Publications, New York, 1979.

STOUT, GETTENS; Painting Materials, Dover Publications, New York, 1966.

LEVEY, MICHAEL; Giotto to Cezanne, Thames and Hudson, London, 1989.

REWARD, JOHN; A History of Impressionism, Weidenfeld and Nicholson, London, 1973.

ARNASON, H. H.; A History of Modern Art, Thames and Hudson, London 1989.

Watercolours

HARDIE, MARTIN; Watercolour Painting in Britain, 3 volumes, published B. T. Batsford, London, 1966.

WILLIAMS, IOLO; Early English Water-Colours, published The Connoisseur, London, 1952.

WILTON, ANDREW; British Watercolours 1750–1850, published Phaidon, Oxford, and E. P. Dutton, New York, 1977.

MALLALIEU, HUON; The Dictionary of British Watercolours up to 1920, published Antique Collectors Club, Woodbridge, 1976.

MALLALIEU, HUON; Understanding Watercolours, Antique Collectors Club, Woodbridge 1985.

Drawings

MEDER, JOSEPH; The Mastery of Drawing, translated by Winslow Ames, published Abaris Books, New York, 1978.

OLSZEWSKI, EDWARD J.; The Draughtsman's Eye, published Cleveland Museum of Art, 1981.

SHOOLMAN, REGINA AND SLATKIN, CHARLES E.; Six Centuries of French Master Drawings in America, Oxford University Press, New York, 1950.

HAVERKAMP-BEGEMANN, EGBERT AND LOGAN, CAROLYN; Creative Copies, Interpretative Drawings from Michelangelo to Picasso, published Drawings Center, New York, in association with Sotheby's, New York, 1988.

AMES-LEWIS, FRANCIS; Drawing in the Italian Renaissance Workshop. Victoria and Albert Museum, London, 1983.

LUGT, FRITS; Les Marques de Collectione de dessins et l'estampes, Amsterdam, 1921.

US Impressionists

BOYLE, RICHARD J.; American Impressionism, Boston, New York Graphic Society Ltd, 1974.

GERDTS, WILLIAM H.; American Impressionism, Seattle: The Henry Gallery Association, 1980.

GERDTS, WILLIAM H.; American Impressionism, New York, Abbeville Press, 1984.

HOOPES, DONELSON F.; The American Impressionists, New York, Watson-Guptill Publications, 1972.

PIERCE, PATRICIA JOBE; The Ten, Concord, Rumfold Press, 1976.

American 19th Century Landscapes

BAUR, JOHN I. H.; Trends in American Painting 1815–1865 in M. and M. Karolik Collection of American Paintings, 1815–1865, Harvard University Press, Cambridge, Mass., 1949.

CZESTOCHOWSKI, JOSEPH S.; The American Landscape Tradition, E. P. Dutton Inc, New York, 1982.

HOWAT, JOHN K.; American Paradise; The World of the Hudson river School, The Metropolitan Museum of Art, Harry N. Abrams, Inc., New York, 1987.

NOVAK, BARBARA; Nature and Culture, Oxford University Press, New York, 1980.

WILMERDING, JOHN; American Light: The Luminist Movement 1850–1875. Harper and Row, National Gallery of Art, Washington, DC, 1980.

Art of the American West

AXELROD, ALAN; Art of the Golden West, Abbeville Press, New York, 1990.

BRODER, PATRICIA JANIS; The American West; the modern Vision: Little, Brown and Co, Boston, 1984.

BRUCE, CHRIS, ET AL; Myth of the West, Rizzoli/The Henry Art Gallery/University of Washington, Seattle.

GOETZMANN, WILLIAM H. AND WILLIAM N.; The West of the Imagination, Norton and Company, New York, 1986.

HASSICK, PETER H.; Artists of the American Frontier, Promontory Press, New York, 1988.

ROSSI, PAUL A. AND DAVID C. HUNT; The Art of the Old West, Promontory Press, New York, 1981.

TYLER, RON; Visions of America; Pioneer Artists in a New Land, Thames and Hudson, New York, 1983.

TYLER, RON ET AL; American Frontier Life, Early Western Paintings and Prints, Abbeville Press, New York, 1987.

Portrait Miniatures

FOSKETT, DAPHNE; British Portrait Miniatures, London, 1963.

FOSKETT, DAPHNE; John Smart, the Man and his Miniatures, London, 1964.

FOSKETT, DAPHNE; Samual Cooper, 1974, London.

FOSKETT, DAPHNE; Miniatures Dictionary and Guide, London, 1987.

FOSTER, J.J.; British Miniature Painters and their Works, London, 1898.

FOSTER, J. J.; Samual Cooper and the English Miniature Painters of the XVIIth Century, 2 vols, London, 1914–1916.

LEMBERGER, ERNST; Portrait Miniatures of Five Centuries, London, New York and Toronto.

LONG, BASIL, S.; British Miniaturists, London, 1929.

O'BRIEN, THE HON. D.; Miniatures in the 18th and 19th Centuries, London, 1951.

REYNOLDS, GRAHAM; English Portrait Miniatures, Cambridge, 1988.

SCHIDLOF, LEO R.; The Miniature in Europe, 4 vols, Austria, 1964.

STRONG, DR. ROY; Nicholas Hilliard, London, 1975.

STRONG, DR. ROY; The English Renaissance Miniature, London, 1983.

WALLACE COLLECTION; Miniatures and Illuminations Catalogue, W. P. Gibson, London, 1935.

WILLIAMSON, DR. GEORGE C.; Richard Cosway, R.A., London, 1905.

WILLIAMSON, DR. GEORGE C.; George Engleheart, privately printed, 1902.

WILLIAMSON, DR. GEORGE C.; Andrew and Nathanial Plimer, London, 1903.

WILLIAMSON, DR. GEORGE C.; The History of Portrait Miniatures, 2 vols, London, 1904.

WILLIAMSON, DR. GEORGE C.; Catalogue of the Collection, the property of J. Pierpont Morgan, 4 vols, privately printed, 1906–07.

WILLIAMSON, DR. GEORGE C.; Ozias Humphry, R.A., London and New York, 1918.

Sculpture

AVERY, CHARLES; Studies in European Sculpture, Vols I and II, Christie's, London, 1981 and 1988.

BAXANDALL, MICHAEL; The Limewood Sculptors of South Germany, Yale University Press, New Haven and London, 1980.

KEUTNER, HERBERT; Sculpture: Renaissance to Rococo, Michael Joseph, London, 1969.

LICHT, FRED; Sculpture 19th and 20th Centuries, Michael Joseph, London, 1969.

RANDALL, RICHARD H. JR.; Masterpieces of Ivory from the Walters Art Gallery, Sotheby's Publications, London, 1985.

SALVINI, ROBERTO; Medieval Sculpture, Michael Joseph, London, 1969.

SOUCHAL, FRANCOIS; French Sculptures of the 17th and 18th Centuries, 3 vols, London, 1977.

Decorative Arts Movements

The Arts and Crafts Movement

KLEIN, DAN AND BISHOP, MARGARET; Decorative Art 1880–1980, Phaidon, Christie's, 1986.

GARNER, PHILIPPE; Encyclopedia of Decorative Arts 1890–1940, Phaidon, Oxford, 1978.

Art Deco

ARWAS, VICTOR; Art Deco, Academy Editions, London, 1980.

BRUNHAMMER, YVONNE; Le Style 1925, Paris.

DUNCAN, ALISTAIR; Art Deco Furniture, Thames and Hudson, London, 1984.

KLEIN, DAN, HASLAM, MALCOLM AND MCCLELLAND, NANCY; In the Deco Style, Thames and Hudson, 1989.

Art Nouveau

AMAYA, MARIO; Art Nouveau, London and New York, 1966.

BATTERSBY, MARTIN; The World of Art Nouveau, London, 1968.

BOUILLON, JEAN-PAUL; Art Nouveau, 1870–1914, Geneva, 1985.

BUFFET-CHALLIE, LAURENCE; The Art Nouveau Style, London, 1982.

RHEIMS, M.; The Age of Art Nouveau, London, 1966; L'Art 1900, Pairs, 1945.

SCHMUTZLER, ROBERT; Art Nouveau, London, 1964.

TSCHUDI MADSEN, S.; Art Nouveau, translated by R. I. Christopherson, London, 1970.

WARREN, G.; Art Nouveau, London, 1972.

WEISBERG, GABRIEL P.; Art Nouveau Bing, Paris Style 1900, New York, 1986.

North American Art and Artefacts

BATKIN, JONATHAN; Pottery of the Pueblos of New Mexico, Colorado Springs Fine Arts Center, 1987.

CONN, RICHARD; Circles of the World, Denver Art Museum, 1982.

EWERS, JOHN; Plains Indian Sculpture, Smithsonian Institution Press, 1986.

FURST, PETER AND JILL; North American Indian Arts, Rizzoli International Publications Inc, 1982.

HALL, BARBARA; Hau Kola, Haffenreffer Museum of Athropology, 1980.

HARLOW, FRANCIS; Two Hundred Years of Historic Pueblo Pottery: The Gallegos Collection, Morning Star Gallery Publishers, 1990.

KENT, KATE; Navajo Weaving, School of American Research Press, 1985.

MCCOY, RONALD; Kiowa Memories, Morning Star Gallery, 1987.

PETERSEN, KAREN; American Pictographic Images, Alexander Gallery and Morning Star Gallery, 1988.

WHITEFORD, ANDREW; Southwestern Indian Baskets, School of American Research Press, 1988.

The Arts of the East

Chinese Works of Art

DE BOULAY, A.; Christie's Pictorial History of Chinese Ceramics, Phaidon Christie's, Oxford, 1984.

FONG, WEN (ed.); The Great Bronze Age of China, The Metropolitan Museum of Art, New York, 1980.

HOWARD, D. AND AYERS, J.; China for the West, Sotheby Parke Bernet, London and New York, 1978.

MEDLEY, M.; The Chinese Potter, Phaidon, Oxford, 1976.

CHINESE JADE CARVING, CATALOGUE; Ip Yee, Hong Kong, 1983.

Islamic Works of Art

ALLAN, JAMES; Islamic Metalwork, the Nuhad Es-Said Collection, London 1982.

ATIL, ESIN; The Age of Suleyman the Magnificent, Washington DC, 1987.

CRESWELL, K. A. C.; A Bibliography of the Arts and Crafts of Islam, Vaduz, 1978 (with two later supplements).

ETTINGHAUSEN, RICHARD; Arab Painting, Skira/Rizzoli, 1977.

GRAY, BASIL; Persian Painting, Skira/Rizzoli, 1971.

HALL; London (leading journal for carpets and textiles).

LANE, ARTHUR; Early Islamic Pottery, Faber, London 1947. Later Islamic Pottery, Faber, London, 2nd edn, 1971.

LENTZ, T. AND LOWRY, G.; Timur and the Princely Vision, Persian Art and Culture in the Fifteenth Century, Washington DC, 1989.

ROBINSON, B. W. ET AL; Islamic Art in the Keir Collection, London, 1988.

Japanese Works of Art

BUSCH, NOEL F.; A Concise History of Japan, Cassell, London.

COLLCUTT, JANSEN AND KUMAKURA; Central Atlas of Japan, Phaidon, Oxford.

EARLE, JOE (ed.); Japanese Art and Design, Victoria and Albert Museum.

Arms and Armour

Swords

NORMAN, A. V.; The Rapier and Small-Sword 1460–1820, Arms and Armour Press, London, 1980.

RAWSON, P.; The Indian Sword, Herbert Jenkins, London, 1978.

ROBSON, B.; Swords of the British Army, Arms and Armour Press, London, 1971.

SOUTHWICK, L.; The Price Guide to Antique Edged Weapons, The Antique Collectors Club, Woodbridge, 1982.

TARRASUK, L. AND BLAIR, C.; The Complete Encyclopedia of Arms and Weapons, B. T. Batsford, London, 1979.

SWORDS AND HILT WEAPONS; Weidenfeld and Nicholson, London, 1989 (various authors).

WILKINSON, F.; Edged Weapons, Guiness, London, 1970.

Militaria

KIPLING, A. AND KING, H.; Head-Dress Badges of the British Army, Frederick Muller (2 vols), London, 1972 and 1978.

ROSIGINOLI, G.; The Illustrated Encyclopedia of Military Insignia, Quarto, London, 1987.

WILKINSON, F.; Badges of the British Army, Arms and Armour Press, London, 1987.

WILKINSON, F.; Battle Dress, Guiness, London, 1970.

WILKINSON, F.; Collecting Military Antiques, Ward Lock, London, 1978.

Firearms

BAILEY, D. W.; British Military Longarms 1715–1865, Arms and Armour Press, 1986.

BLACKMORE, H. L.; British Military Firearms, Herbert Jenkins, 1969.

FLAYDERMAN, N.; Flayderman's Guide to Antique American Firearms, Northfield, 1978.

WILKINSON, F.; The World's Great Guns, Hamlyn, London, 1972.

Armour

BLAIR, C.; European Armour, Batsford, London, 1972.

Coins, Medals and Stamps

Coins

GRIERSON; Coins and Medals: a select bibliography, Historical Association, London, 1954.

CARSON, R. A. G.; Coins, Ancient, Medieval and Modern, London, 1962.

CRIBB, J., COOK, J. AND CARRADIC, I.; The Coin Atlas, London, 1990.

HOBERMAN, G.; The Art of Coins and their Photography, London, 1981.

JONES, M.; The Art of the Medal, London, 1979.

PORTEOUS, J.; Coins in History, London, 1969.

PRICE, M. J. (gen. ed.); Coins, an Illustrated Survey, 650 BC to the Present Day, London, 1980.

SUTHERLAND, C. H. V.; Art in Coinage, London, 1955.

Stamps

STANLEY GIBBONS STAMP CATALOGUE PART 1; British Commonwealth.

LOWE, ROBSON (ed.); Encyclopedia of British Empire Postage Stamps, Vols 1–5, Christie's, Robson Lowe.

MUIR, DOUGLAS; Postal Reform and the Penny Black, National Postal Museum.

WATSON, JAMES; Stanley Gibbons Book of Stamps and Stamp Collecting, revised by John Holman.

Clocks, Watches and Scientific Instruments

BRITTEN, F. J.; Old Clocks and Watches and Their Makers, Antique Collectors Club, Woodbridge, 6th Edition, 1932, and then subsequent revised editions by Bailey, Clutton and Kent.

CAMERE CUSS, T. P.; Antique Watches, Antique Collectors Club, 1976.

CARDINAL, CATHERINE; The Watch, Wellfleet Press, Secaucus, NJ, USA.

DAWSON, DROVER AND PARKES; Early English Clocks, Antique Collectors Club, Woodbridge, revised edition, 1985.

ROSE, R. E.; English Dial Clocks, Antique Collectors Club, 1988.

TARDY; French Clocks the World Over, Tardy, Paris, 1985.

WHITE, GEORGE; English Lantern Clocks, Antique Collectors Club, Woodbridge.

Dolls and Toys

Dolls

KING, C. E.; The Price Guide to Dolls Antique and Modern, Antique Collectors Club, Woodbridge, updated 1982.

Toys

ANTIQUE TOY WORLD MAGAZINE; PO Box 34509, Chicago, Illinois 60634, USA.

HILLER, MARY; Automata and Mechanical Toys, Jupeter, 1976.

FRASER, ANTONIA; A History of Toys, 1966.

LEVY, ALLEN; A Century of Model Trains, New Cavendish, 1986.

O'BRIEN, RICHARD; The Story of American Toys, New Cavendish, 1990.

OPIE, JAMES; Britain's Toy Soldiers 1893–1932, Gollancz, 1985.

OPIE, JAMES (ed.); Collector's Guide to 20th Century Toys, Letts, 1991.

PRESSLAND, DAVID; The Art of the Tin Toy, New Cavendish, 1976.

PRESSLAND, DAVID; The Book of Penny Toys, New Cavendish, 1991.

RICHARDSON, MIKE AND SUE; Dinky Toys and Modelled Miniatures, New Cavendish, 1989.

Musical Instruments

BAINES, ANTHONY; European and American Musical Instruments, New York, 1966.

HENLEY, WILLIAM; Universal Dictionary of Violin and Bow Makers, Brighton, 1973.

MARCUSE, SIBYL; Musical Instruments: A Comprehensive Dictionary, New York, 1964.

MONTAGU, JEREMY; The World of Medieval and Renaissance Musical Instruments, London, 1976.

MONTAGU, JEREMY; The World of Baroque and Classical Musical Instruments, London.

SACHS, CURT; The History of Musical Instruments, New York, 1940.

THE NEW GROVE DICTIONARY OF MUSICAL INSTRUMENTS; London, 1984.

THE NEW GROVE MUSICAL INSTRUMENT SERIES; London, 1989.

Wine

CHRISTIE'S WINE COMPANION; Christie's Wine Publications in association with Webb and Bower.

BRADFORD, SARAH; The Story of Port, Christie's Wine Publications.

MICHAEL BROADBENT'S POCKET GUIDE TO WINE TASTING; Christie's Wine Publications in association with Mitchell Beazley.

JOHNSON, HUGH; The World Atlas of Wine, Mitchell Beazley, 1971 and reprints.

SPURRIER, STEPHEN AND DUVAZ, MICHEL; Académie du Vin Wine Course, Christie's Wine Publications in association with Mitchell Beazley.

ABOUT THE CONTRIBUTORS TO THIS VOLUME

These short biographies appear in the order of the contributions in the book:

DAVID BATTIE (Introduction) left Art School and became a Graphic Designer before starting a new career as a porter at Sotheby's in 1967. He worked in several departments including heading the Ceramics and Oriental Works of Art Department at Sotheby's Belgravia (now closed) since its inception in 1971. He became a Director in 1976.

He has written Price Guides to both *19th Century British Pottery and Porcelain*, is the Editor of *Sotheby's Encyclopedia of Porcelain*, and has contributed articles and chapters to various other publications.

He has appeared on the *Antiques Roadshow* since the first series in 1979 as well as making numerous other radio and television programmes. He lectures on a wide range of topics in this country and abroad to the National Association of the Decorative and Fine Arts Societies, other antiques societies, to business executives, and other groups.

JOHN TAYLOR (English Furniture; Continental Furniture) studied History of Art at Cambridge University, England, and worked in the Furniture Department at Sotheby's, London, for three years. He is now an independent consultant. He has contributed to *The Sotheby's Encyclopedia of Furniture* (Conran Octopus, UK; Harper Collins, USA, 1990), and to *The Antique Collector's Club Magazine*.

LEIGH R. KENO (American Chippendale Furniture), who holds a BA in the History of Art from Hamilton College (1979), has been active in the field of American antiques since childhood. In 1979 he became the Director of The American Furniture Department at the William Doyle Galleries in New York City, and between 1984 and 1986 he held the positions of Vice President of Appraisals and specialist in American Furniture at Christie's, new York. He left this position in 1986 to open his own gallery – Leigh Keno, 19 East 74th Street, New York 10021 (tel: 212 734 2381) – specializing in 18th and early 19th century American furniture and decorative arts. He lectures extensively throughout the United States and has written articles for *Art and Antiques Magazine* and *The Magazine Antiques*.

JOHN CUSHION (China and Ceramics) is a Fellow of the Royal Society of Arts. He has been a lecturer with the National Association of the Decorative and Fine Arts Societies since its founding over twenty years ago. He spent many years on the staff at the Victoria and Albert Museum, mostly in the Department of Ceramics, where he was the Senior Research Officer. From 1960–1980 he conducted courses in the History of Porcelain and Pottery for the University of London Extra-Mural Department. He has since lectured on behalf of the National Trust, Sotheby's and Christie's Art Courses, and the Society of Fine Art Auctioneers. He has lectured in many parts of the world, including the USA.

SIMON COTTLE (Glass) worked in Museums for ten years – at London, Newcastle and Glasgow – before joining Sotheby's, London, in 1990 as a specialist in Glass and Ceramics. He has published several books and many articles on glass.

CHARLES TRUMAN (Silver) began his career at the Victoria and Albert Museum, London, where he spent nine years in the Department of Metalwork before becoming Assistant Keeper of the Department of Ceramics in 1980. Having been recruited to run the London silver department of Christie's in 1984, he was appointed a Director in the following year. In 1990 he left Christie's to set up his own business as an independent consultant. He has published extensively on the subjects of silver and gold boxes.

DAVID WARREN (Jewellery) is a Director of Christie's, London.

SUSAN MAYOR (Fans) is Head of the Textiles Department and a Director of Christie's, South Kensington, London. She was educated at London's Lycée Français and joined Christie's in 1964. Since then she has made her Department an international venue for the sale of fans, textiles, lace, embroidery and costume. She is married to the architectural historian Professor J. Mordaunt Crook, F.B.A.

DIANA FOWLE (Textiles) received a BA (Hons) in History from Oxford University, England. She has been with Christie's, South Kensington, London, for four years, where she is a Specialist in Textiles. She has contributed to *Samplers* (Studio Editions, 1990) and *The History of Textiles* (Studio Editions, 1991, Ed. Madeleine Ginsburg).

PATRICIA FROST (Lace, Shawls and Costume) received a BA (Hons) in English at Cambridge University, England. She has been at Christie's, South Kensington, London, for four years, where she is Cataloguer of Costume, Lace, Shawls and Islamic Textiles. She has contributed a section on Tapestry to *The History of Textiles* (Studio Editions, 1991, Ed. Madeleine Ginsburg).

JEREMY HOWARD (Oil Paintings, Drawings and Watercolours) worked at the Clarendon Gallery for eight years before joining Colnaghi, the old master gallery of Bond Street, London, nearly four years ago. He has published numerous articles and contributed to many books on the subject of paintings.

LAUREN RABB (American Impressionists) graduated with honours from Rutgers University in 1981, and began working at the Princeton Gallery of Fine Art, Princeton, New Jersey, as a gallery assistant. She moved to Washington, DC, in 1983, and after a brief stint at the National Gallery of Art was hired by Taggart and Jorgensen Gallery, of P Street, Washington, as the gallery manager, where she has remained since. She has written numerous essays on American art for the gallery, including catalogues for two major exhibitions: *In The Open Air*, a comparison of French and American Impressionism published in 1988, and *The Pennsylvania Impressionists, Painters of the New Hope School*, an exhibition which travelled to the James A. Michener Art Center in Pennsylvania in 1990.

HOWARD REHS (19th Century American Landscapes) is Managing Director of Schillay and Rehs Gallery in New York City. Mr Rehs is a recognised expert in the field of 19th century painting and has a personal love for the art and artists of the Hudson River School. Mr Rehs received a BA in art history from New York University and has been with Schillay and Rehs Gallery since 1981, first as a Director of European Operations, and then as Managing Director.

ROBYN G. PETERSON (Art of the American West) is Curator of Collections at The Rockwell Museum in Corning, New York. Raised in the American West, Ms Peterson received a PhD in art history and archaeology from the University of Wisconsin, Madison, in 1987, and has published articles on various cultural topics.

CLAUDIA HILL (English Portrait Miniatures) studied the History of Art at Reading University. Between 1984 and 1990 she was an expert in Portrait Miniatures at Christie's London, and she is now an independent.

JAMES BRUCE GARDYNE (Picture Frames) is at Christie's, King Street, London, where he is a Specialist in Old Master Paintings and Picture Frames.

LYDIA CRESSWELL-JONES (The Arts and Crafts Movement) is Cataloguer for the Applied Arts Department at Sotheby's, London.

OLIVIER BROMMET (Art Deco) is an Associate Director of the 20th Century Decorative Arts Department at Christie's. He is responsible for organizing the auctions in this field in the company's continental salesrooms, and has contributed to the *Ceramics and Glass International Auction Records*.

JANE HAY (Art Nouveau) graduated from Manchester University in 1982 with an honours degree in Modern History and Economics, going on to complete an MA at the School of Oriental and African Studies in London. She has worked for three years at Christie's, South Kensington, London, where she is a Specialist in the Decorative Arts Department.

JOE RIVERA (Native American Artefacts) was born, raised and educated in New York City. He served as an ethnographer and Research Curator for the Museum of the American Indian, after which he moved to the Sioux Reservation at Rosebud, South Dakota, where he spent ten years engaged in fieldwork.

He is currently the Director of the largest American Indian Artifact gallery in the United States – the Morning Star Gallery, 513 Canyon Road, Santa Fe, New Mexico (tel: 505 982 8187).

DAVID A. SCHORSCH (American Folk Art) was born in Philadelphia, and established himself at a remarkably early age (he started dealing aged fourteen) as one of the best-known antique dealers in America.

In the field of folk art he is a market leader, having set numerous records at sales and auction in categories such as folk painting, folk sculpture, Shaker furniture, weather vanes and needlework. He is frequently interviewed for both TV and magazines, including *The New York Times, Barrons, Antiques Monthly, Art and Auction Magazine, Americana Magazine* and *The New Yorker*.

He has published articles on American folk art and its associated categories in a wide variety of prestigious specialist magazines and journals, and he regularly organizes specialist exhibition at his own gallery – David A. Schorsch, Inc, New York – which he catalogues himself.

RODDY ROPNER (co-author: Chinese Works of Art) is a Specialist in the Chinese Department at Christie's, King Street, London.

PETER TUNSTALL-BEHRENS (co-author: Chinese Works of Art) is Specialist in the Chinese Department at Christie's, King Street, London.

PROF. JOHN CARSWELL (Islamic Works of Art) is a Director of Sotheby's, London, and Head of the Islamic Art, Rugs and Textiles Department.

WILLIAM TILLEY (Japanese Works of Art) studies at the Royal College of Art and at the Sorbonne and L'Ecole des Beaux Arts in Paris. He acquired his first Japanese sword in 1947, and began a lifelong commitment to the serious study of Japanese art, developing an exceptionally fine personal collection. Since joining Christie's, London, where he has worked for twenty-two years, he has supervised some of the largest sales of Japanese artefacts ever held, including the record-breaking sale of the Nagasone Kotetsu blade and the Ichimonji Nobufusa blade at Christie's, New York. More recently he has overseen the gift of 600 pieces from the Raymond and Frances Bushell Netsuke Collection to the Los Angeles County Museum, supervising the auctioning of further 1080 lots from the collection in London, New York and Los Angeles. He is currently the senior technical specialist in the Japanese Department of Christie's, London, of which he is a former Head. His published works include the editing of Sasano Masayuki's *Sukashi tsuba* – the standard reference work on this type of sword fitting.

FRED WILKINSON (Arms and Armour) is the President of the Arms and Armour Society, and a consultant to the Arms and Armour Department at Sotheby's. He is also Vice President of the Historical Breech Loading Small Arms Association, an Associated of the Royal Historical Society, a Fellow of the Royal Society of Arts, and the author of many well-known books.

RICHARD BISHOP (Coins and Medals) is an Associate Director of Christie's. He has been with the company for eleven years, four of which were spent in the New York branch. He is currently in charge of the Coins and Medals Department at Christie's, King Street, London.

TIMOTHY HIRSCH (Stamps) joined Stanley Gibbons Ltd in London in 1979 as a Junior Dealer, and was appointed Managing Director in 1986. In 1990 he joined Christie's in London as the Director responsible for stamp auctions worldwide (London, New York and Zurich).

RICHARD GARNIER (Clocks and Watches) has a BA in history. He is on the Livery of the Clockmaker's Company, and was the Director of the Clocks and Watches Department at Christie's Auctioneers, London, between 1975–1990. He is currently Head of the Antique Clock Department at Garrads Crown Jewellers of Regent Street, London. He is a regular contributor to *Antique Collector's Club Magazine* and *Country Life*, and a lecturer to Christie's Fine Arts Courses, to local branches of the Antiquarian Horological Society, and to the National Trust.

JEREMY COLLINS F.S.V.A. (Scientific Instruments) is a Director of Christie's, London, and heads the Scientific Instruments Department.

SARAH SOAMES (Books and Manuscripts) is an Associated Director of Christie's, London, and has been with the company for fifteen years.

OLIVIA BRISTOL contributed the section on Dolls and Dolls Houses.

JAMES OPIE (Antique Toys) is commonly recognized as one of the world's leading authorities on the subject of model soldiers and figures, and his expertise and experience also embrace the other types of toy discussed in his contribution. He has written a number of books about toys, including *British Toy Soldiers, 1893 to the Present* (Arms and Armour Press, 1985), *Britain's Toy Soldiers 1893–1932* (Gollancz, 1985), *Collecting Toy Soldiers* (Wm Collins, 1987), and, as Consultant Editor, *The Letts Guide to Collecting 20th Century Toys* (Charles Letts, 1991).

FREDERICK W. OSTER and **SARAH MCQUAID** (Collecting Musical Instruments). Mr Oster resides in Philadelphia, where he has been dealing in and appraising musical instruments for over twenty years. He has for ten years been Consultant to the Musical Instruments Department of Christie's, Manson and Woods, and specializes in the violin family, early wind and American fretted instruments. Sarah McQuaid works as Mr Oster's assistant.

FRANCES GILLHAM (The Violin Family) is the daughter of two professional musicians. She was educated at St Paul's Girls School, going on to read music at St Catherine's College, Oxford. She joined Christie's in 1979, and was appointed a Director in 1990. She heads the Musical Instruments Department of Christie's in London.

DUNCAN MCEUAN (Wine) is a Director of Christie's, London.

INDEX

ACKNOWLEDGEMENTS

THE PUBLISHERS and authors would like to thank the following for their kind permission to reproduce photographs in this book:
Agnew's, London: 98, 109 top. America Hurrah, NY: 156; 162 below, 163 Uoel and Kate Kopp collection). Asprey's London: 49, 51, 52, 54, 55 below right, 56, 58, 59, 60 top. Christie's: 65-97, 101 below, 103 below, 105 right, 106 top, 107, 114 below (Taggart & Jorgensen Gallery), 116 (Berry-Hill Galleries, NY), 121-4, 126-35, 142-4, 145 top, 149-55, 167-77, 184-91, 192 right (Major General Sir Leonard Atkinson Collection of Great Britain Stamps and Covers), 192 top left, 193–213, 218-29. Clandon Park (National Trust): 45 top. Colnaghi, London: 97 top, 99, 100, 102 below, 104, 105 left, 106 below, 108, 112 top. Richard Green, London: 101 top, 103 top. Leger Galleries, London: 111, 113. Leigh Keno:

19-23. Maas Gallery, London: 112 below. Morning Star Gallery, Santa Fe: 157, 158. Phillips Fine Art Auctioneers, London: 214-16. Private Collection: 42 below, 43 top, 109 below, 159 top. Rockwell Museum, Corning, NY: 119, 120. Schillay&Rehs, Inc., NY: 117 top. David Schorsch, Inc., NY: 24, 25; 159 below, 160, 161, 162 top, 164, 165 (G. William Samaha Collection). Sotheby's: 8-18, 23 top, 48, 50, 53, 55 left and top, 57, 60 below, 61-3, 136-41, 178-83, 125. Taggart & Jorgensen Gallery, Washington, D.C.: 114 top, 118 Victoria & Albert Museum: 26, 27, 29-34, 36 below, 37-41, 42 top, 43 below, 44-47. Richard York Gallery, NY: 117 below

Claudia Hill writes: My obligations go to all the authors referred to in the bibliography of the miniature portrait section. I am however, particularly

grateful to Mrs. Daphne Foskett, whose book *British Portrait Miniatures* supplied me with a general survey of the subject and descriptions of the various forms that it takes. The idiosyncracies of individual artists and the subject of collecting including the delicate matter of fakes is recorded in her scholarly book *Miniatures Dictionary and Guide*. This book is a valuable source of reference and any serious collector would be well advised to read it. I am also indebted to Graham Reynolds whose revised edition of *English Portrait Miniatures* has taken account of recent research.

The publishers particularly wish to thank Claudia Brigg, of the Christie's Colour Library, in London, for her expert advice and assistance.